TACTICS OF PERSUASION

William H. Stiles, Ph.D., C.HT.

Cover Illustration By
William S. F. Stiles

KENDALL/HUNT PUBLISHING COMPANY
4050 Westmark Drive Dubuque, Iowa 52002

ISBN 0-8403-9313-X

Printed in the United States of America
10 9 8 7 6 5 4 3 2 1

CONTENTS

Section III : Features, Benefits, Proof, and Value Presentations 143

Section IV : Getting Ready to Sell—Planning 187

SECTION I
You Must Close To Sell

If you can't close, you can't sell. Closing is what selling is all about. It is the end result of your professional activity. For that reason, this book begins at the end . . . with **tactics** that will help you close more sales, resulting in the exchange of your customer's money for your products and services.

Also, that's how this book is written . . . **in a tactical format**, a "how to" presentation that will allow you to put the tactics to work immediately, beginning on this page with the very first tactic that requires you to have a **closing consciousness**.

Tactic # 1
Develop a Closing Consciousness

It is absolutely necessary to **believe** that you will close sales in order to do so. This is a matter of developing an attitude of expectancy. As you do this, your prospect will also begin to feel that a successful outcome is to have an agreement. That prospect will expect to **buy**.

The closing consciousness becomes one of the most useful sales tools you could ever develop. It is simply a matter of **imagining a desired outcome**. Most professionals know that this is not difficult to do when the successful outcome is one that will greatly benefit the customer after he accepts the proposal.

This attitude of expectancy is displayed through your manner and your actions. It is always there . . . in your expressions, your responses, the way in which you handle the order form; in the ways in which you demonstrate and explain your product or service. **You expect the prospect to buy now**. By doing this, you project **the closing consciousness** into your customer's mind.

— Tactic # 2 —

You Must Have a Closing Method

Along with a closing consciousness, it is absolutely necessary that you develop a **closing method**. You must learn to create your own closing opportunity. Most of the sales you will make will not close themselves. In fact, studies show that 20% of the time, salespeople initiate closes; 20% of the time, the customer actually asks for the product, and the remaining 60% of the time, **no one** initiates a closing conversation.

You must guide and direct your prospect's behavior. By developing a closing method, you will play the part of an **assistant buyer**, helping your customer make decisions.

Customers and prospects will buy when it's **their idea**. How does it become their idea? Only when they are methodically guided to make such a decision.

Suppose you have a prospect that has been very attentive but has indicated no strong interest to move ahead. He has not indicated that he wants the product and he has not asked any revealing questions that would show he has a specific area of doubt or interest. This is where you must create a situation in which interest can reveal itself. In other words, do and say things that would cause your customer/prospect to react.

Here is a simple four-step method that will help you do exactly that:

1. Summarize your selling conservation.
2. Ask for your prospect's questions
3. Ask your questions.
4. Stimulate some action.

Let's look at each of these steps:

First you will **summarize** the buyer benefits. All of the benefits are blended together in such a manner that your summation accomplishes the purpose of refreshing your prospect's memory. In this step, you **assure** by affirmation and **create** understanding.

Next, ask for your **prospect's questions**. You are, now probing for any major objections. You won't ask for objections outright. Instead, you ask for questions. The end result is the same . . . it smokes out any final objection your prospect might have.

Now, you must ask **your questions**. Take the prospect's mind off the big decision and put it on the little decisions. Obviously, the big decision in every sale is "will you buy now?"

Develop a series of little questions you can ask that gain agreement on minor points. If your prospect is not quite ready to buy, your questions will merely seem a part of their normal routine. If the prospect is ready to buy, he or she will cooperate by answering your questions easily and naturally.

Stimulate action. This final step in developing a closing method is one shared by all selling professionals who close a large percentage of their planned presentations. You must start to do something that requires your prospect to stop you if he wants to avoid agreement.

In other words, you could summarize benefits for your product and then simply say, "Fine. I'll go ahead and arrange for its delivery and installation."

So, the second tactic of persuasion is to have a **closing method**.

— Tactic # 3 —

Stay in Control

Every selling situation ends in someone selling someone. It isn't always the salesman selling the prospect. Too often, the salesman has been sold on the idea that the customer should not or is not going to buy. As a salesperson, you will either **control** or be **controlled**. Realizing this, you also know you have a choice.

The only way to lead the customer to a decision that is good for him is to maintain control. That means you must dominate. Understand that domination is not a negative, crass, aggressive, obnoxious force. It is a power that is used by professional, well-practiced salespeople who know how to employ the tactics of persuasion in such a way that it benefits both the customer and the salesman.

The salesman who has a closing consciousness and a closing method already developed, will have a fire in his belly that will allow him to dominate the situation without intimidating the customer.

As long as your customer needs the products and the services you are offering, he is going to eventually win when he agrees to accept your proposal.

Customers want and need your expertise. And, they appreciate the pleasantly forceful presentation of benefits that will contribute to their own success showing them how to make more money or otherwise gain from your proposal. Too often, customers become indecisive because salespeople appear to be undecided about the value of their products as relates to that customer. The fact of the matter is that only dominant salespeople become highly successful. So, if you want to be highly successful, you must use the tactics of persuasion contained in this book to achieve control.

— Tactic # 4 —

Dominate Customers to Achieve Involvement

Highly successful salespeople will involve customers as soon as they can in the selling presentation. By doing this, the salesperson becomes an assistant buyer, simply helping the customer investigate ways that he can benefit from the salesman's product and service.

If you have a customer who is hesitant to take part in the presentation, don't just ask him. To dominate means to use power . . . to actually "force" him into participating. If you have a sample product or a demonstrator, even backup supplementary material such as specification sheets, put it in the customer's hand. Let him experience these sales tools that you have brought along. If it's a product, he has to see the product, feel the product and, of course, hear what you have to say about it. **This is control**. You are focusing your customer's attention **where you want it**. You are helping him to experience some of the exclusive properties that you offer so that he will miss it when he is exposed to your competitor. You are getting him **mentally past the point of purchase**. When he is mentally past the point of purchase, he is thinking about application, about using the product. In effect, you have controlled his mind to the extent that you have projected it into the future. He is thinking about activities involving that product and, therefore, he has mentally purchased it. You are helping the customer close the sale for you.

— Tactic # 5 —

Be the Authority

Don't expect to close a high percentage of sales if you're not an expert. Before you make a presentation to any customer, you must be thoroughly schooled by having done your homework. You must know what you can do for the customer and what you cannot do for him. You must know all of the policies and procedures required by your company. You must know all features and benefits of the product as it relates to your customer. You must know your competitor's products and how to compare. You must have even anticipated the objections and questions your customer would have and be thoroughly prepared to handle them in conversation. You must be an expert . . . you must be the total authority. When you say something, it must be above doubt. When your customer questions a fact that you present, you must be able to give him supporting evidence. Once again, it's the salesperson who consistently exhibits authority, who is able to dominate and to close more sales.

— Tactic # 6 —

Be Prepared to Kill the Competitor's Deal

Don't believe all the garbage you hear about your competitors. As a result of a quarter of a century in dealing with salespeople, I've noticed that too many believe the competitor has some kind of extraordinary offering that borders on the mystical, magical formula akin to the universal elixir of life. I know that's overstated, but a lot of salespeople act that way. Don't believe it. Your competitors don't have any secret mystical powers. And a lot of their deals aren't even as good as your own.

Have you ever thought of this? . . . to the competitor, you are that mystical, magical person. Since that's the case, let them believe it, but employ your own tactics to shoot down the competitor's supposed better deal. Don't accept every rumor you hear about competition. That's the worst thing you can do, because it simply helps the competitor. In fact, you're probably giving him an edge that he does not legitimately deserve.

If a customer says that your competitor has a better deal, simply ask him what it is. When you understand the situation, you will be in a much stronger position to overcome the offering and close the sale.

It's at this point that you have the opportunity to make comments similar to the following:

"I appreciate that you feel that way, but what are you specifically referring to? Is it the quality, service, the features of the product after five years of use . . . or is it the price?"

"Well, then, obviously you've had a chance to look at their product and their entire service offering. What impressed you most?"

"I'm absolutely astonished that you could say that. We have always had the reputation for having the best of this type of product in the industry. Would you please tell me exactly what you think is better?"

Oftentimes your customer will simply be using what we call "negative leverage." This kind of a head-on approach not only shows gentle dominance, but exposes your confidence, implies a back up of expertise (knowledge) and allows your customer to respond in such a way that can work himself out of the comment and allow you to simply close the sale.

Yes, once this situation has been established and you have gotten response from the customer, it is important that you attempt the close. Closing is simply asking for the order . . . is the **attempt** to get it. If you don't succeed, use some of the other tactics.

—— Tactic # 7 ——

Compare with the Competition, Point-By-Point

Any competitor is going to have some weak spots. This is why it's important that you know all about your competitor's products. Make sure, however, you do not deal in generalities when you're working the point-by-point method to close the sale. You must be convincing. Explain **exactly** why your product is superior to your competitor's. Show your customer **exactly** how the product will benefit him over and above your competitor's. Tie in extra benefits and greater value to be realized by the customer when he deals with you over your competitor salespeople. Keep pointing out to the customer the old W.I.I.F.M. . . . "What's in it for me" . . . because that's what he wants to hear.

When a customer knows what's in it for him, he will be anxious to help you close the sale. Using this point-by-point method will give him the solid facts that will stimulate action.

While you are using this tactic, bring out your pen and tablet. As you go from point-to-point, write them down. Get the customer involved as he follows each point. Actually write down the competitor's points, along side yours. Then, make the comparison, showing where you are superior.

Remember, where I insisted that you know the competitor's products? Well, this is why. At some point during this tactic, however, you must stop listing the competitor's points and continue listing your own features and benefits. In this way, when you look at your tablet paper, your product far and above the competitor is the logical choice. There it is in black and white! How could anybody make any other decision? That's right, you don't have to list every feature that you know about the competitor's product, you "tactically" run out. If the customer wants to remind you of a few, add them, but again, make a favorable comparison with your own points. I suppose, in a sense, that is "damning the competitor with faint praise."

—— Tactic # 8 ——

Be "Johnny-on-the-Spot"

There's not much to say here because it is self-evident. When you've got stiff competition, it is absolutely necessary that you be there first with the most. Anytime you can close the sale before your competitor gets to the customer, you have left those competitor salespeople in the dust. It is **always** easier to close the sale when you've gotten there first and done a superb job of presenting the facts.

Even if a customer brings up your competitor, you can head him off by saying something like this, "Most of my best customers are people who have used that company's product. They know what I'm telling you is the absolute truth. Here, let me give you their names and telephone numbers. Call them up. Every one of them will tell you why our product is so much better."

—— Tactic # 9 ——

Try to Get the Customer to Object to Price

Wow! Most of the salespeople I talk with say that this is exactly what they don't want to have happen. Why not? When a customer is talking about price, he **is** mentally past the point of purchase. In other words, the quality of the product is okay, you service is okay, and he is thinking about using the product. He just has to find a way to justify making the **investment.** When you think of it that way, your job is to simply show him how he is going to get a sufficient and adequate **return**. That's right. He is not going to simply pay a price . . . he will **enjoy** an **investment**.

So, how do you use price? First of all, don't be terrified. I have observed that a high percentage of sales are closed as a result of a customer objecting strongly to price. Since he's already made up his mind to buy, he's just trying to see what he can do to increase the value of the proposition. I would be willing to bet you do the same thing when you're buying an automobile or any other product that involves a substantial investment. I'm sure you already decided to buy the car, you're just trying to get the best deal.

Price objections are blatant buying signals!

I don't care how rough and tough the buyer may appear, When is he discussing price, he is vulnerable. Every buyer of a product knows when a price goes down, it can only happen when the value of the offering decreases. It is your job as a professional salesperson to make sure that he understands the total value of the offering . . . even more, it is your job to keep building that value.

First you have to learn to hold your ground. You know that a lot of buyers feel the only way to get the price down is to try to intimidate the salesperson. Well, we have already made up your mind that you are the expert and you know why your product is fairly priced based on the points you are prepared to discuss.

Never panic. Buyers who are trying to use intimidation are using a very old and quite crude tactic on you.

Always fall back on **value**. Price is never the only consideration in buying a product. When you are equipped to present the total value of your offering, you are not only able to overcome the price objection, but you are in an ideal position to ask for the order . . . close the sale.

When you **stimulate** the customer to bring up price, be prepared to comment in the following ways:

"I'm really happy you brought up the matter of price. I was just going to get to it myself. That's really the most wonderful part of the entire offering. Our quality is the highest you can find anywhere and that means you're going to pay less over the lifetime of the product than you would with any of our competitors. I know you realize that paying any price for poor quality is one of the worst things you could ever do. By the way, have you ever actually sat down and figured the price of not having good quality products? Have you ever thought about the cost of repair bills, breakdowns of equipment . . . all of your wasted time involved in trying to get your problems solved? The higher quality we build into our product is actually going to save you a lot of money in the long term."

Or, you could simply get him talking so that you can call his bluff. You do that this way.

"I'm really surprised to hear you say that our price is high. What are you comparing it to?"

"What do you mean by that? What did you expect to pay? If it was a lot cheaper, would you want it? (Let the customer respond and say "yes".) Well, I'm happy to hear that, too, because it says that you do want it. Now, let's look at the reason this is the very best investment."

Again, when he is trying to make a price comparison with one of you competitors, you could use this approach:

"I wonder if you have ever tried to figure out why our competitor is cheaper? I looked into this situation and had to ask myself these questions . . . I wonder where they cut corners? . . . I suppose they cut back on quality control . . . What about the materials, are they cheaper? . . . What did they cut out and lower the value so that they could also lower the price?"

And then you could finish up with this type of a question:

"There's something else I've been wondering about . . . does your company pay you only to buy the very cheapest products on the market? I suppose that you and your company are interested in getting the best value for the money that you spend . . . isn't that right?"

And, once again, you have gained control, you are dominating and you have a wonderful opportunity to present the features and benefits of your product compared point-by-point to your competitors.

Once you've gone through all of this, though, remember to simply ask for the order . . . that is giving the customer an opportunity to "go ahead" concluding the conversation.

When you have finally done this, sit back, relax, and shut up. In this case, the first person to speak is the one that is going to be **sold**.

— Tactic # 10 —

Close with Every Objection

As long as we're talking about price and handling it as if it was an objection, then turning it into a closing opportunity, you should consider this approach with **every objection**. Most good closers use this tactic consistently to gain more sales and, of course, that's what this book is all about . . . that has to be extremely important to you.

Let's suppose your customer has objected to a point of your sales message. Perhaps he has even said "no" for some reason. Normally, salespeople would not expect the customer to buy. Starting right now, take the opposite approach. Expect him to buy! **Rush** your closing comment. Answer the objection and then simply say something of this nature, "Well, I guess that's that . . . why don't we go ahead?"

This is a very logical communicative process that will work for you at least half the time. Let's suppose you try to close on strong objections and you fail. What do you lose? Fifty percent is a great potential close rate.

— Tactic # 11 —

Use the Power of Persistence

This tactic will help you close prospects and existing customers you formerly considered near impossible. **Keep trying**. That's all there is to it. No matter how many times your customer has said, "no", give him a new reason to buy.

Suppose you try to close an objection and fail. Start covering more points, keep on selling and try to close again. Try every closing tactic you can think of until he says, "yes" . . . or until he asks you to leave. As long as the customer lets you go on with your presentation, persistently close.

— Tactic # 12 —

Use Assumptive Projection

If you expect to get orders, you will. It's a matter of projecting this assumptive attitude to your customers so that your customers **expect to give you orders**. Assuming means taking something for granted. You must take for granted the fact that the customer will buy. Perhaps your customer has not given you a direct comment saying that he will buy, but top notch professionals always assume the customer has no other thought in mind. Be definite about everything you present. If you show doubt or uncertainty about any part of your presentation, your customer is going to pick up on that doubt and also be uncertain. If you waiver or question, he will waiver and question. When you are firm, positive, dogmatic, absolute and totally confident your customer will pick up these qualities in his mind, and begin to close.

Let's suppose that you have presented a product and your customer has listened to your entire sales message. During the presentation, you have indicated that you would like to ship him six units within the next week. Using the tactic of assumptive projection, stand up and say, "I will have them delivered next week. Now, let me explain how you can use the product." Simply do a product demonstration and have the customer initial the order. It's all a process of getting up in preparation to walk out.

At all times, assume that you are going to get an order. Never think **if** you get the order. Always think **when** you get the order. Talk about service, delivery or follow-up. Always assume the order has been placed as you converse with the customer.

Remember my earlier comment about the fact that the customer's ready to close when he is mentally past the point of purchase? You can place your customer's mind mentally past the point of purchase by talking about those areas that generally occur after your product is delivered. Keep uppermost in your mind the fact that your customer **needs** what you are selling. Just work on **when** he needs it and get him to center on the specific time. In this way, you will force a close without either of you feeling pressure.

Here's an example of how to use the "**when**" part of the tactic of assumptive projection:

Let's suppose you have demonstrated an item and you can see that your customer wants it, but he is hesitating. Close by saying, "Look, you will want to start using this soon. This is Friday, and we do not deliver to this area on Saturday. We can arrange to have it to you by Monday afternoon." You see, you do not have to ask . . . just assume he is buying and establishing the **when**. Through the tactic of assumptive projection, you have closed. In fact, at this point, you have made it easier for your customer to buy than not to buy.

Remember this tactic will only work when it is firmly in your mind. It is a tactic that depends upon your opinion of yourself, your belief in yourself as a closer and your total belief in your product and service as being the very best for the customer. You will project your state of mind to your customer. You will lead him with self-assurance and forcefulness.

Do and say nothing that is not based on the belief that the sale is already made. Once you have practiced this key for a couple of months, it will become such a part of your personality, that it will work automatically.

A variation on the assumptive projection tactic is to try for a bigger order than you really expect to get. Teenagers often use this on their parents . . . The boy wants $5.00, asks for $10.00, and is satisfied when his parents compromise at $5.00. Using this tactic means assuming your customer needs and will buy a certain quantity of product. Go for it! The customer will probably compromise with you for the quantity that you previously wanted to sell. Throughout this process, you will be using the power of suggestion. Psychologists tell us that seven out of ten people mentally respond to suggestion. You are direct, you infer, you suggest . . . seven out of ten of your customers will act according to your suggestions. Here are further examples of the type of thing that you can say that will help you employ the tactic of assumptive projection:

"I'm glad you see the same value in our product that I do. It looks like we agree on most of the points. When would you like us to ship?"

"Looks like we've talked about everything you were concerned about. We ought to go ahead and put this down on paper so we get it right. How do you spell your last name?"

"I think you've made a great decision. Would you just go ahead and okay this agreement?"

Tactic # 13

Use Sudden Action

One time I was in the middle of a selling presentation an... stopped, picked up the phone and called the factory. While waitin... the customer service department, I told the prospect, "I just want to mak... sure they can ship right away, if we give them the order now. I would hate to disappoint you after we've come so far. That prospect did nothing to stop me. I got the order and, thereafter, used the key of **sudden action** at every opportunity.

The crux of sudden action is to do something that requires your customer to stop you in order to avoid agreeing to buy. This is the type of tactic that most salespeople have been grasping for all of their selling careers. It's one that you should be using often. It helps the customer make a decision. Use sudden action to close by detecting the right moment in your presentation to reach into your briefcase and bring out your order pad. Then start writing, **all the time looking down at the pad**. Do not look up. Force the customer to get your attention and stop you. While writing and looking at your pad, ask him safe questions concerning the order. This is a reinforcer. Remember, always treat signing an order as an expected consequence of your actions, and you will close more sales. Make it easier for the customer to buy than to stop you.

Tactic # 14

Try "This or That"

Don't give customers an opportunity to buy your product . . . give them a choice. Never ask "if" the customer will buy. Ask, "which" he will buy.

What you are actually doing is having the customer choose between two positives. No matter what the customer says, you close the sale.

It has been my experience that in more than 60% of the cases, this close works. In some cases, you might want to give the customer many choices on which he can make a "yes" decision. For example, when talking about payment, you could say something like this, "If you're looking for extended billing, would you prefer to be invoiced at the end of the month which will give you an extra 30 days, did you want to break this into three payment segments, or would you like to go ahead and pay cash and get the back up literature and sales aids free?"

Other examples of this type of close are:

"We could have this product delivered to you tomorrow, but if you can wait, we can ship it on our normal delivery schedule and save you the delivery charges. How would you like us to handle that?"

"We could send this out UPS or regular parcel post. How would you like to have it sent?"

"There are really three ways to go on this . . . you could start with the beginner package and add on later, or you could select two or three options now . . . or if you wanted, we have an extended payment plan that would help you buy the entire unit with all options immediately. Which would you prefer?"

"Do you really think this basic unit is going to take care of your needs, or would you like to go with the deluxe unit?"

"If you are in a big hurry, I could arrange for overnight service, or, if you can wait, I could bring it around next week when I am in this area. Which would be the best for you?"

The greatest thing about this tactic is the fact that you are infrequently turned down. Ask a man to directly buy and it is very difficult for him to say no.

— Tactic # 15 —

Use "Why and Why Not"

This dandy little tactic is almost a trick. Again, when all else has failed and your customer will not indicate why he will not buy, set up a simple balance sheet on a tablet. Draw a line across the top of the pages and a line straight down in the middle. At the top left, write "why to buy," and at the top right, put "why not to buy." Now, tell your customer that you will first list the reasons to buy and then you both will look at the reasons why not to buy. All you do is list every point covered in your presentation, getting agreement from your customer as you go along. After listing all the reasons to buy, say, "Okay, now, let's list the reasons why not to buy." Pause and try to think of a reason. Finally, give up, hand the pen and pad to your customer and say, "Look, I can't think of any, why don't you list them?" Most of the time, your customer will never list a reason. He will put the pen down and tell you to write the order, or he will give you the reason which could be personal. Of course, this is something you want to know.

— Tactic # 16 —

Work the Columbo "Oops"

In late 1979, I named this after the television show, Columbo, because we have all seen Peter Falk use this tactic on his suspects. I'm happy the program has been reestablished on television . . . it helps make this book current. Also, it serves as a periodic reminder of the tactic.

You can use the Columbo "oops" on your prospect. After you have tried to close and fail, begin preparing to leave. Then, suddenly turn to the prospect and say, "Oh, I almost forgot to mention something very important. If you place your order now, I can give you 60 days to pay. You will have this item sold, and the profit in your pocket before you pay us. That's a good deal, isn't it?" (By the way, there's no need to have a rumpled raincoat and a big cigar.) And, of course, you can use another important point that you have held back for just such a reopener of the door. The Columbo "oops" is an excellent tactic to use when you have "sandbagged" three or four extra features and benefits that would add to the value of the proposition. And remember this . . . customers cannot be expected to say "yes" after they have said "no" without additional information. In order to make a new decision, they need **new information**. That makes the Columbo "oops" tactic an absolute essential.

— Tactic # 17 —

Use "Here's the Future"

When a selling situation is going badly, use the future to make your close. Tell your customer you can see that he's just not ready to buy now, but you know he will be ready in the future. Write an order and date it three months away. Explain that he is to look so far down the road. Assure him that he has full control if his needs should change. This is much better than letting a competitor walk in later and get the order. You either ship or you have another chance to talk about it and, of course, another opportunity to close.

— Tactic # 18 —

Answer Quickly

Really grab your customer's mind and set yourself up to use sudden action by firing two safe questions at him simultaneously. Say, "Do you want the 80 gallon or the 100 gallon drum?" Follow immediately with, "Should I have it delivered Monday or Tuesday?" Your customer will be temporarily off balance and you will put the confusion in his mind. This helps you maintain control. While he sorts out his bit of confusion, write the order. When he finally responds, he has purchased the item.

— Tactic # 19 —

Use "You Deserve It"

Especially when selling tools or something an individual will use personally, paint a vivid picture of the prospect using the item.Say,"Imagine how you'll feel when you can do this job in half the time with this tool." This is another method of getting the customer mentally past the point of purchase. It does add, however, the aspect of pleasure and it allows the customer to mentally enjoy owning the product even before he has it.

— Tactic # 20 —

Just Suppose

This method of closing takes a customer's objection and turns it into one reason for buying. When your customer has one or two major objections for which you have answers, **delay responding**. Instead, indicate that you would like to get back to these points later and go on with your selling message. Once your customer has agreed with everything else, return to the objections or questions and simply say, "Just suppose, Mr. Customer, that I could take care of that . . . then we only have to decide when you would like to take delivery . . . well . . ." At this point, answer the objection and close the sale.

— Tactic # 21 —

Try "Dead Silence"

This is art. There comes a time when everything has been said. All points have been covered and a natural silence develops. Usually, because this silence is awkward, you, as the professional communicator, will say something to break it. That's wrong! Use dead silence to close. Simply sit back and stare at your customer with a wide-eyed, expectant look and slight, pleasant smile. Seventy percent of the time, you will close the order.

— Tactic # 22 —

Use Demonstrator Samples

If you watch television, you've seen how samples do the selling. Professional advertising agencies use samples of products and apply a little imagination to ask for an order. And, they do it all in about 30 seconds. Actors demonstrate toothpaste, razors, deodorants, fast food, etc. They show and demonstrate the products, using a lot of imagination to close sales. And we buy.

Try to use as many samples as possible. It's a real mistake to limit yourself to just two or three variations of your product or product line. When you decide in advance to show only one or two items, you are actually making a negative decision for your customer. Don't fall into that trap. Remember the sample you leave in you car is never going to help you close the sale.

One of the reasons that so many variations of your product exist is that buyers have different preferences. Ask any manufacturer . . . if they could just produce one type of product and not be concerned with preferences, they would do so. They know that simply isn't reality and so should you.

Having a sample will allow your demonstration to do the talking for you when you want to emphasize a strong **value building** point at the close of your presentation.

You will be able to use demonstration samples to make comparisons against your competitor's products. As you list the key points that show your superiority, point them out to the customer. As he handles the sample product, listens to your presentation, and sees what you say is true, you are helping him to more quickly get mentally past the point of purchase. When you're using a demonstrator sample, it certainly isn't necessary to discuss the value adding features and benefits in any particular order. You and your customer can simply be discussing these value added points as they come up in the demonstration.

As your customer goes from point to point, you have an opportunity to use reinforcement. When you see something he likes, you simply say, "Yeah, that's a great feature about this product, isn't it?" As you get agreement, you are nailing down the close.

Here's another extremely important point about demonstrator samples. Always handle the product with great respect. If you ever give the customer the impression that you don't have high regard for the product, neither will he. When that happens, your demonstration will eliminate a close. Jewelry salespeople know the truth of this demonstration tactic. If the product isn't already nicely presented in a velvet box, they will actually show it on a velvet cloth. I have worked with plumbing salespeople who have actually wrapped faucets in velvet before they display the item for a contractor.

Here's another point: Don't just go in and spread all of your samples out in front of the customer and ask him to plow through them himself. You should keep control of the entire situation, working with the customer to show him the items one at a time. Then, your samples will help close sales for you. You, however, must give your samples the verbal presentation that will get the results you want.

—— Tactic # 23 ——

Use the Penalty Close

I don't think you should make a practice of using this, however, there are certain circumstances when it is the only way to get a customer to move. It works on the principle that many people are more motivated through the **fear of loss** than they are through the anticipation of gain.

You simply tell the customer that if he doesn't take advantage of the offer now, he will lose. You would say such things as: "The sale ends tomorrow," etc. This type of close has a tendency to not "ring true" with many customers. Be sure when you use it, it is an **actual fact**.

— Tactic # 24 —

Use the "To-the-Bone" Close

This is an extremely effective close when a customer is asking for a discount. In this case, you would agree to check with your boss (or your paperwork if you happen to be the boss), then you would return stating that you have checked to see what you could do. Of course, you have found out that you really can't do anything about it. In that case, you tell the customer, "We're really to-the-bone on this one and we just can't do any better." In many cases, because a customer is simply trying to build the value of the product, he feels he has won. If he feels he has you to-the-bone and there's no more money on the table, he will buy.

I know of a circumstance where a salesman actually will run numbers on a calculator. He will run numbers two or three different ways. When he is finished, he will finally put the calculator down (turning it off) and say to the customer, "You know, we're so close on this one, we probably should raise the price." He usually gets the order.

— Tactic # 25 —

Use the Third Party Reference Close

Just about everybody likes to know that other people have bought a product and they are enjoying it. This close simply involves identifying the circumstances of other people who are in similar situations to your prospect or customer. In this way, the prospect can feel confident about going ahead and making a decision to buy.

Many salespeople carry several testimonial letters with them. They don't bring the letters out right away, but say something like this: "I understand your concerns . . . many other people have felt the same way. These people, however, tried the product and found out that they got everything we promised, and then some. They now feel it's the best decision they ever made. Here are letters from several of those people." And, then, of course, the salesman would show the testimonial letters, using the third party reference close.

— Tactic # 26 —

Give Him Something for Nothing

I am writing this at a time when in Pennsylvania there is a hundred million dollar lottery jackpot. People from all over the country are flying into the Pittsburgh Airport to buy tickets. I just saw, on television, one man from Chicago standing in line (holding up other lottery ticket purchasers) in order to buy 900 lottery tickets. They're all looking for something for virtually nothing.

Many people spend their lives trying to find, and never do find, "something for nothing." Does that keep them from trying again and again? Certainly not.

You may not be one of those people, but the desire to get something for nothing is the basis of one of the most powerful closing tactics. Everybody is interested when they feel they are going to get something and they're not required to put up anything to do so.

Most of your prospects know that they get what they pay for and generally, they don't get a bit more. Even so, they keep looking for an opportunity to get more. Because of this, we must be smart enough to use the very powerful irresistible "something for nothing" tactic. How do you do this? Simply promise the customer something extra. It could be something of very little consequence . . . a quicker delivery, a special color, a membership in a customer's club, etc.

The reason the "something for nothing" tactic works so well is that it requires the customer to take some action. It helps you overcome procrastination which is one of a salesman's greatest obstacles.

Most all customers and prospects will listen with great interest when you mention that he's going to get something for nothing or that by taking action now, he is going to receive something **free**.

The key to using the "something for nothing" tactic is to hold it until the very last moment. It is the final persuader to bring about action on the part of the customer.

I heard a story about this method that went like this:

> A woman went into a restaurant and requested a bacon and egg sandwich. Before placing the order, however, she asked, "How much is this going to cost?"
>
> The waiter replied, "$3.50."
>
> The woman asked, "How many eggs are you going to be using?"

"One egg," said the waiter.

The woman thought for a while and then asked "How many slices of bacon?"

"Two."

The woman thought for a while, shook her head no and started to leave. Before she was out of the restaurant, the waiter said to her, "Don't forget the bread is absolutely free."

She turned around and agreed to buy the sandwich.

Sometimes, offering the customer something for nothing is the only way to get him to agree to place the order. You must be different from other salespeople, then, over and beyond the normal company offering, you must find a way to present something extra to the customer that he feels he would not normally get. Many times, it simply means withholding a normal part of your package offering until the very end.

You are using an inducer. Essentially, you bring out this inducer when you feel the customer would like to make a decision, but needs to be pushed over the edge.

It is important, however, to make your inducer sound like the greatest deal available. The inducer doesn't have to be something that he can see or touch, either. It could be an intangible.

You can include the "take away" tactic as you present an inducer. For instance, you can show him that if he doesn't take advantage of the deal, he's going to lose prestige by not buying. Other people in his particular social level can not only afford to buy the product, but they wouldn't be without it. That is an inducer.

— Tactic # 27 —

Ask for a "No"

There are times when you should be asking your prospect for a "no." Yes, that's what I said. Ask for a "no."

We've agreed that selling has only one major goal . . . a positive agreement between yourself and the customer . . . getting him to say "yes." However, there are times when you absolutely must ask your customer to say "no." Does this sound as if we are going against all of the tactics we have discussed so far? Not at all. Not when you give the subject some good, hard, considered thought.

Most people hate to say no. This is an absolute fact. Many customers will simply say, "I'll think it over," or "Not right now, but maybe some time in the future . . . why don't you leave your card?" There's a joke in show business that I'm sure you've heard: "Don't call us, we'll call you." That's exactly what the customer is saying. You don't really think he's going to think it over after you leave, think it over during his breakfast the next day, think it over throughout the day, the week, or until he sees you next? Of course you don't. So why let the sales call end that way?

It may seem a bit strange, but the little word "no" is one of the hardest words for most people to say.

Think about it. "No" is such a final word. It's a complete turn down. After "no" there's really not much more to say. Most prospects and customers don't want that situation to develop because they are still thinking about the possible benefits they could enjoy. It's just that you as the salesperson have not yet gotten them far enough mentally past the point of purchase to say "yes."

Put yourself into this situation:

You are with a customer and you are on your second call. Your presentation on both occasions went very well. It's time to close, yet nothing is really happening that would indicate that the customer is ready to buy.

I'm going to suppose that the customer likes you and your company and he likes your products, but he just isn't indicating that he's going to accept your proposal. Perhaps he has a price from a competitor that is close to yours. He might have the thought in his mind that he has to say "no" to someone. He's thinking that if he can put you off, maybe he can **avoid** that unpleasant job for the time being.

Now, feel the psychology of this situation. With these circumstances, you have a problem. If you try to keep on selling, long past the logical point at which you should be asking the customer for the order, everything is going to go downhill. The sale will go up in smoke and you are going to lose all of the time and talent you have invested up to this point. You end up getting some kind of a loose agreement where you and the customer agree to "talk about it again" at some other time whenever that might come up.

You could make it easy on the customer. You could be a real nice, friendly person who says to the customer, "Look, I'll be around next week and see if you've made a decision then." Most likely, when next week comes around, you're going to walk out without the order because you will have opened the door for your competitor. The customer is eventually going to say "no" to you through the process of elimination. When you come around next week, he's going to have some lame excuse for buying it from your competitor. **You must force his hand now**.

You are in a situation of "heads I win, tails you lose." The best thing you can do is force your prospect to say "no."

This is a dangerous concept so let me make myself clear that what we're talking about here is only a **last resort** situation. It's a method you will use after you've tried the other tactics. Don't use this technique unless you are totally **convinced** that you are going to be a loser without it.

To force your customer to say "no," you simply bring up the matter of a clear cut decision. The best way you can do that is to clearly describe all of the benefits that you have already presented in a summary. Then tell the customer what his alternatives are. Compare your product, once again, to the competition. After that, you put the decision to the customer. Say something like this, "What do you say, Mr. Prospect, yes or no?"

One way or the other, you are going to get an answer.

If you can bring these doubtful types of closings up to this point, you will be amazed at the results you are able to get. Keep in mind that your customer really hates to say no. No is final and he has cut off the possibility of getting your product and that's the end of it. On the other hand, most customers and prospects like to be able to say "yes." It's the normal thing to do after he has engaged in a great deal of positive conversation about the proposal.

You have another factor working for you at this time. It's the prospect's mind. When you bring the prospect to a yes or no decision, you are going to be appealing to his basic makeup. Most people like to think of themselves as people of action . . . almost like some hero in a movie or a television show. Everything in our lives requires decision of some sort, and so, we like to think of ourselves as being decisive. Yet . . . let's face it . . . few of us really are. That's the point of this entire tactic.

If you can bring an indecisive customer to the point where he has to make a decision, just the action of making that decision will reinforce the customer's positive image of himself.

What we're saying is that the customer can feel better about himself for having come to a conclusion.

Think of it another way. The customer is forced to be the kind of person he always wanted to be. He will receive satisfaction for making a decision and he will feel good about his relationship with you. Customers are naturally drawn to positive, courageous salespeople. In the process, they like the way that type of salesperson makes **them** feel.

When you try this tactic, you will find out that you can't win them all. Sometimes, you'll get a "no" for an answer and you have to deal with it.

When this happens, you must realize that you have lost the sale. The chances are, however, you **didn't** lose it in the close. If the sale was lost, it was lost a long way back when you were involved in probing your customer for his needs and making a presentation. (This will all be covered in later tactics.)

In the process of using this tactic, however, you are going to gain a lot, also. By standing up for your right to a clean cut yes or no, you will add to your own self-respect. You will have gained the knowledge that whether you win or lose, you've done the best you can. And you will have also carried out your full responsibility to your company, to your family and to yourself. Remember, if you can't close, you can't sell. Part of closing is to get a response, even if it is negative.

And, there's something else you can do . . . when a customer says "no" you can ask him, "why not?" Given the right answers, you can improve your presentation and your close for the next prospect.

So, starting right now, make it a rule that you are going to use this tactic whenever necessary. Never leave a doubtful closing situation without some kind of clear cut, yes or no decision. Always ask for the order. And if you have to, ask for the answer in terms that the prospect cannot evade.

When you do this, many customers will give you the go ahead and save the "no" for the other guy. This is a real psychological advantage.

Do you want to be a successful closer of sales or not? What's your answer? Yes or no?

— Tactic # 28 —

Surprise Him by Giving Him What He Wants

Don't do it right away, but eventually give the customer what he's asking for. Do this, when you have already anticipated what he wants and you have opened your presentation, asking for more than **you want**.

For example, if you know a customer is going to be asking you for a discount, raise the prices when you discuss what he must invest.

Let's suppose the customer telephones you and indicates that he feels your price is five percent too high and that you are going to have to cut by that amount to get his business. Simply tell him that you will think about it, check with your management, see what you can do . . . or all of the above. Then, during your next call, you say, "The last time we talked, you mentioned you would do business with us if our price was five percent lower. I looked into the situation and because we anticipate doing so much volume with you, we've decided we would go ahead and make the concession you have asked. My boss has given me the authority to reduce your prices by five percent."

When you do this, make sure you give a legitimate reason for making the concession. If he can't see logic in it, he will suspect that your pricing was not appropriate to begin with. More than that, he won't feel that he has won anything.

— Tactic # 29 —

Make It Conditional

There's another way to use this concession tactic that will get the customer to commit.

When a customer asks for the concession, again, don't give it right away. Tell him you are going to do everything you possibly can to get your management to agree to the terms. But explain to him that if you are going to put your "neck on the line" in this way, you have to be sure that you are able to deliver the order. Tell him that you will go ahead and write up the order on condition that your management approves and that you would expect him to sign it right now.

When this happens, you end up with a strong negotiating tool to go back to your management and you pretty well have the agreement sewed up with the customer. Even if you aren't able to get your company to agree, you will have been working on the customer's behalf and you might be able to get him to compromise by "splitting-the-difference."

A reverse of this often occurs. Sometimes your customer isn't too sure he can get his boss to approve. In this case, you can write a provisional clause on the face of the order that will protect the buyer.

Don't feel that you are doing less of a selling job because you have to make these concessions to a prospect. Over the years, you are going to find that many of your larger orders come as a result of knowing exactly what you have to "give" in order to get the quantity and quality of business the customer is able to place with you. Beyond being a presenter of company policy, products, facts, etc., you have become a negotiator. As a representative of your company, you are properly giving them the opportunity of deciding whether or not they want to accept some slightly lower profits in order to increase their overall sales volume.

— Tactic # 30 —

Close Early, Close Often, Close Late

There are at least three times that you can ask for an order while you are communicating with a customer. First, you could write to your prospect a week in advance to let him know what you're going to ask him when you make a call. That's closing early.

When you make a call, you can ask the customer for an agreement every time you answer a question or handle an objection. This should occur at least three times. That's closing often.

If you don't close during the sales call, you could write ten days later and ask him in the letter if he is ready to make the decision. That's closing late.

Then, you can call him on the telephone and ask him if he got your letter. That is yet another attempt to close late.

On this further attempt to close the sale, of course, you must give the prospect some new reasons for going ahead with the new decision.

Surveys show that closing attempts are often relegated to a onetime effort. Forty-six percent of salespeople questioned asked for the order only once. Twenty-four percent asked for the order twice, but then they quit. Fourteen percent asked for the order three times and figured that was quite enough. Twelve percent of the salespeople surveyed asked for the order four times and figured they were pestering the prospect. The survey went on to show that 60 percent of the acceptance of an order came after the fifth try by a salesperson. Therefore, being persistent, closing early, closing often, and closing late is the only way to be sure that you're going to be counted among the ranks of the top producers.

— Tactic # 31 —

Go for the "Yeses"

This closing tactic is simply a matter of asking predetermined questions that you know will get the customer to say "yes" to each one of the minor questions. If you can get your prospect into the mental habit of saying "yes," he will have a mind-set that will be very difficult to break when you ask him to agree to the sale.

For example, you could ask questions of this type:

"I know you want to make all the money you possibly can, don't you?"

"Don't you think this type of advertising will give you the largest possible exposure?"

"You do like the product, don't you?"

"You mentioned that the warranty is exactly what you want . . . so, we are in agreement there, aren't we?"

"These quantity discounts really add up, don't they?"

"I'll bet you were really surprised by all the features that we have built into this product?"

"Isn't this the type of home you always wanted?"

"Now, didn't we discuss that this product would save you at least $8,000 in three years?"

And, finally, after you have gotten enough yeses that remind the customer of all of the benefits he's going to receive, you see that he is mentally past the point of purchase, he's already thinking about the W. I. I. F. M. (what's in it for me), it's time to ask the closing question:

"So, you want to go ahead right now, don't you?"

"Yes."

Use information gathering questions to close the sale.

I suppose you have heard this comment about Sampson who slew a thousand men with the jaw bone of an ass, that goes on to say, "More sales than that are killed everyday with the jaw bones of a salesman." It's true, isn't it? I hope you said, "yes," based on your own experience.

I'm as guilty as anyone . . . I like to talk, too. But we all have to learn a lesson. When the customer is talking, he is in the process of **buying**. When we are talking, we are not necessarily selling and the customer could become disinterested or bored. Then, it would be to our advantage to keep the customer talking, but to direct his conversation with questions.

Selling is not just telling. Of course you're going to be talking about your product and your proposal. It's essential that you do. However, some of the benefits your customer must know about are more effective when he discovers them through a questioning process. When you are able to carefully use questions, you can control your customer's mind and close the sale.

You'll have to adapt your question so that it fits your own product and personality and also so that these questions evoke a good, positive response from your customer. Here are some examples:

"Did you receive the brochure on our specials for the month?"

"What do you think about our new line of high-end products? Isn't it about time we offered these items?"

Just like the questions that are designed to get a "yes" answer, these questions are designed to get a positive response from the customer. You are seeking his positive opinions. In order to get a positive response, you must be very careful of the type of questions that you ask.

Of course, you will ask questions at the right tactical point during your presentation in order to gain information that you can use when you are presenting the features and benefits of your product. However, the most crucial time to ask questions is during the close.

Form your questions so that they will have the greatest impact on your customers; getting from those customers the best positive responses. In this way, your questions can close your sale.

Be sure when you ask a question that you listen very carefully to the customer. Don't be impatient and never interrupt the customer when he is responding. Also, don't have some preconceived idea about exactly how the customer is going to answer. Be careful that you listen so that you can use his exact responses when you are reinforcing all of the good points of your product at the close.

Support the customer when he says something positive. Let him know that he has made an extremely good point about your product.

After you've asked a particularly pertinent question, pause and let the customer answer. Even if the customer takes a few seconds to think about it, allow that time. If you rush on with your supporting points or try to close before the response, he'll think your question wasn't to be taken seriously at all. Worse than that, he'll think you don't respect his opinion and he is not going to give you the order.

Also, while you are using questions to help you close the sale, keep the pressure out of it. Make sure your customer is at ease at all times. Don't let him feel that you are using questions as a method of testing his knowledge or his intelligence. This, again, will build resentment and be a real road block to closing the sale. You can avoid this situation by making sure you form your questions so that they involve his wants, his needs, and his desires. They can relate to his welfare. When your questions are asked this way, the customer very quickly is able to agree with you. This leads to a closed sale.

— Tactic # 32 —

Use a Minor Point

Wouldn't it be great if all customers responded to sound logic. The questioning process, then, would work all the time. The fact of the matter, however, is that we don't live in an ideal world situation, and not everybody is totally logical, all the time. There are many times when the most logical reason for buying a product just won't convince the customer to go ahead. In these times, it's necessary that you close on some **minor points**.

Be sure you don't think of minor points as something that you are going to come up with in a moment of desperation. That won't work, either. These are the points that you have ready as backup ammunition to make the value of your offer overwhelming. They are reserves that you can fall back on. They are also psychologically sound reasons for a customer to buy. Why is that so? Because when a customer buys on a minor point, he doesn't have a **"big hassle."**

It is much easier for many customers to make a bunch of small decisions than to make the big one. The customer may not be able to say, "Okay, I'll take it right now." That's just what you want him to do, but it's against his nature.

The same customer, however, can easily make decisions about some minor points. These points are such items as:

- Product sizes
- Quantities
- Delivery dates
- Various financing plans
- Color, size, type
- Advertising programs
- Various models

These types of minor points are ones that will take that big hassle out of making the major decision. Minor points call for minor decisions. They can, however, close some big sales for the salesman who uses them in the right way.

Even though the point may be minor, it is up to you to make it a **big deal**. Most of your minor points are probably those features that you have exclusive of your competition. In this way, they become a big deal. Your major points are probably those that your competitor talks about, also. So, by talking about a lot of minor points, you are helping to differentiate your product. That's how they become a big deal.

—— Tactic # 33 ——

Use Your Experience

I was conducting a sales training seminar and I heard one older fellow say, "I don't know what he expects me to learn here . . . I've got 20 years of experience in this business." His buddy looked at him and said, "Henry, you have got one year experience, 20 times."

I really enjoyed the conversation. We can all learn more, can't we. I suppose that's why you are reading this book. However, no matter where we are in our career . . . just starting out, at midpoint, or in the autumn season, we can use what experiences we have already gained to help us close sales.

All customers appreciate the experience a salesman has based on his opportunity to travel and become involved in many situations with other people that are similar to the customer or prospect who is face-to-face with a salesman. Knowing this is true, you have an opportunity to make the most of your experience as you put it to work to close sales. Here's how you can do that:

- **Use testimonial information** in the form of case histories to get your customer agreeing. The best kind of proof you can have in any selling situation, is to use factual stories and examples that are true life and relate to your customer situation. They are especially effective when they detail what you have done as a salesperson to help other customers. When your customer or prospect hears these stories of how other people are "happily involved" with your product and service, he, too, wants the same result.
- **Suggest promotional programs** that have worked for other customers. Show a prospect how these promotional ideas will help him generate extra business or, increase his profitability. In the truest sense, when you help a customer increase his business, you are a consultative salesperson. Every time he sees you, he will think about how you helped him and he will be willing to buy more from you than your competitors.
- **Be an expert for your customer**. Use all of your experience to set aside any put-downs, any put-offs, or objections your customer might have. When you have handled the same objections, again and again with other customers, you are able to

handle them with this prospect as well. And, we have already established that every time you handle an objection, you have an opportunity to close.

Any time you establish your expertise with a customer, you become a stronger closer. You see, an expert is respected and his peers will listen to him and have confidence in everything that he says. When you become that expert and the customer knows it, he will want to work with you which will result in your closing more sales.

— Tactic # 34 —

Use Emotional Appeal

Think about the last time you bought an automobile, What about jewelry? How about clothing? What about furniture for your home? Was there just simply logic involved in all of these decisions? I doubt that very much. I am sure that there were some emotional reasons for buying the particular car you did or selecting some of the other items. It's the same way with all of your prospects and customers. **You cannot close every sale with pure logic.**

If all you had to do was use logic, all you would need is a calculator or a computer. As long as you're dealing with people, that's not going to be the case. Emotion in many situations is much stronger than logical reason.

The profession of selling requires you to be a real human being involved in working with various and diverse personalities who are subject to many human emotions.

Both logic and emotion must be involved if you are to consistently close sales. So far, much of what we have talked about has emphasized the area of logic. Now, consider some emotional appeal that will help you open more doors in the customer's mind.

Let's go to a selling profession we are all familiar with . . . insurance salespeople. If you're like me, you don't like to pay insurance premiums. None of us are paying the premium to receive **immediate value**. Yet we pay the premiums, anyway, don't we? What are we hoping to get?

The insurance salesman appeals to his prospect's emotional tie to his family, in the case of life insurance. He appeals to caring and love and concern and "doing the right thing." In this way, he gets the individual to consider buying "the right amount of insurance." When the insurance deal is closed, everybody has what they need. The family has their protection, and the father who bought the insurance is emotionally gratified.

Emotion driven impulse will influence more people to action than logical arguments. One of the best ways to build emotion into sales presentations, is to tell stories. Show how someone else has derived pleasure from purchasing your product, has improved their self-esteem, has been able to "keep up with the Joneses" (or move ahead of them), enhance their position at the job or in the community, or, in general, greatly benefited . . . do this and your prospects will relate. You are, essentially, using the third-party endorsement which will often become the turning point of your sales presentation. These "similar situation" emotional appeals are very powerful. For this reason, you will want to equip yourself with many examples that are going to appeal to a prospect's self-esteem, pride, or even fear. Your prospect will easily identify with the individual in your story and will draw parallels between the story person and himself.

You must practice your stories. Just like every tactic in this book, no matter how technically correct they may be . . . they require a great deal of practice to do them well. Your stories must be told well. Don't make them too long, and save the "punch line" for the end. In the case of a sales story the punch line is **what the customer gets**.

—— Tactic # 35 ——

Use Silence

Have you ever been casually watching television . . . not really paying a lot of attention . . . then, all of a sudden the screen goes blank? Now the television set has your attention. Silence, during the general hubbub of everyday noise will get attention. Silence is a very powerful influence in controlling others. You see, nature abhors a vacuum. For this reason, silence in a selling presentation must be filled.

Of course, sales are made through the spoken word. Rarely can new products, sell-up items, or services be effectively presented without verbal communication. Verbalizing, alone, however, is not all inclusive. You must combine words with **silent techniques** that will improve your close rate.

If you want to sell more to increase your volume, improve your profit and experience a good positive growth in your sales, add some **silent** selling tactics to your arsenal of techniques. Silence is more than golden . . . it is an essential tactic of persuasion.

Get into motion — Add action to all of your selling words. You can gain and keep your customer's attention if you handle your demonstrators in a way that requires a customer to follow your action. Disassemble an item, point to special features, move it from one area to another—keep your selling demonstrators in action. That is a silent way of keeping your customer's attention on any item you are presenting.

Handle your product with respect — An important silent selling technique is to handle your product as if it were a precious jewel, where such an impression is important to your customer.

Have courage — You must have the courage to stay with your prospect through the silent seconds after you have asked a question. Remember, earlier we said that someone always sells someone in a selling situation. Oftentimes it's the potential buyer that sells the salesman on not buying the product. Well, the toughest person in the world to sell is one who doesn't talk. So, you want to be that person. The prospect becomes ill at ease because he cannot stand the silence. Often, if you wait him out, buying signals will surface at that time.

Practice — Make sure you can use silence without a great deal of difficulty. This means that you must practice on just about every call. There is always a point where you can use some silence to "smoke out" what's on the buyer's mind. When you have done that, you will be closer to closing the sale.

— Tactic # 36 —

Personalize and Close

Don't be fooled into thinking that you can memorize a dozen of these tactics and apply them to every customer for instant success. The purpose of this book is to give you a virtual encyclopedia of information. However, it is up to you to take the tactics and use them so that they relate in a very **personal** way to each and every customer.

Too many salespeople place limits on their results by lumping all of their prospects and customers into one large group thinking that there is no need to separate one from the other.

It is true that people in similar situations generally react in the same way. That is a pretty strong basis behind the use of a set number of tactics.The danger in applying the tactics this way is that no one wants to be treated as just one of a group. Everybody wants to feel important. Everybody wants to be treated as if they were an individual with separate special needs, wants, and desires. If you forget that, you could experience a great deal of frustration in using these tactics. So . . . **personalize**!

Handle each of your customers and prospects as if that person was the only one with whom you are involved. Don't appear to be too assumptive; rather, focus on the needs of the individual upon whom you are calling at that particular time. Even go so far as to prepare personalized presentations, with a customer's needs clearly spelled out on the first page. Many successful salespeople I know do exactly that . . . they use page one to show that they fully understand the customer's problems, wants, needs and desires. It is all written out. They use a second and third page to describe possible solutions using their products. They will then put into a presentation folder a final page which contains the contract. Step-by-step, they walk the customer through a personalized presentation which is a strong closing device.

Understand that as a salesperson, **people** are your business. When you personalize your entire presentation all the way to the close, you will take advantage of a very powerful motivating force. Selling is personal and so should be your tactics.

—— Tactic # 37 ——

Obligate Your Customer

I haven't read a lot of the classics, but I remember one quote from Cicero who once said, "The greater the favor, the greater the obligation." That's an axiom you must understand and use with customers you call on frequently. When you use this tactic properly, you will have a tremendous advantage over your competitors.

On repeated calls to regular customers, the art of selling really becomes a matter of obligating the buyer to you. You do this by first making sure the customer thinks and feels that you have superior products, you offer superior service and you make sure that you establish with that customer an honest friendship, and even affection.

Think of your selling as an investment portfolio. In an investment portfolio, you put as many different securities in it as possible. By doing this, you receive more dividends. The best way to keep your customers loyal to you is to help them get what they want. The more you help them, the more they feel impelled to help you in much the same way. In other words, if you help them improve their business and their life, **they will want to return the favor**. Here's how you do that:

- Obviously the first thing you have to do is **determine the customer's wants, needs and desires**. The only way to do that is to ask. Then, think about everything you can do to help the customer.
- **Be a good recorder of pieces of industry information**. While you are traveling, collect and record tidbits of product, pricing and service information. There will always be a time when you can use this information to make it of some value to a customer. You see, your customers don't get around as you do. Simply traveling is a tremendous education that will be of great value to your customer.
- **Always remember the profit motive**. Every time you are talking with a customer, try to find a way that will enable him to cut his costs and keep more profits in his pocket. Show him how he can save money, or increase his income. This is a tremendous selling tool for the industrial salesman who calls on owners of businesses and purchasing agents. Even the purchasing agent wants to save money for his company so he can enhance his own position.
- **Plan ways to make your customer feel big or important**. Don't use fake flattery or any phony ego boosters because that's going to have a way of backfiring on you. Instead, build a complete inventory of ego boosting tactics that you know will appeal to each customer.
- **Solve your customer's problems**. When you become your customer's trouble shooter, they will look for you. Also, when the customer has a problem, you have an opportunity to solve it with one of your products and/or services. When you solve a customer's problem, you obligate that customer and help motivate him to look for you.
- **Act as if you are one of the customer's employees**. That doesn't mean you allow the customer to abuse you when he should be simply using you. It means that your customer must feel that you are trying to be on his team. In this way, an adversarial position will not develop between the two of you.
- **Keep in mind that genuine friendship is a personal obligator**. People buy from people they like. Your customers will buy from you if you feel they are a friend. When you act as a true friend, your true friend, the customer, will reciprocate . . . he will help you become successful.

— Tactic # 38 —

Use Prewritten Orders

I have outlined this tactic in my sales training seminars and invariably a salesman has told me that he thinks it is presumptuous. Well, if you can't presume the close of a sale, you aren't going to make many. To even call on the customer is presumptuous. If you are going to make a call, you **must** assume you are going to make the sale. For that reason, there is nothing wrong with having an order form all ready for the customer to sign.

I use this technique all the time. When I put a proposal together for a customer, I have everything worked out and all he has to do is sign his name. Of course, I include a paragraph that says I am entirely flexible and willing to adjust any part of the proposal. This tactic really doesn't have as broad an application as some of the others, but I think it is an excellent way of asking for an order.

Steve Jones, an electrical products wholesale salesman, uses prewritten orders any time his manufacturers come out with new products. Steve knows his territory very well and he knows the needs of his customer. He knows what each customer should buy and will actually write those quantities on his prewritten order form.

When I talked to Steve about this, he explained that, "It makes things a lot easier for himself and the customers. It also saves time." Steve admitted that he did have a few occasions where the buyer cut the order down. He thinks, though, even though the orders get cut down, it is still a great way to simply ask for new business. According to Steve, the conversation involves a discussion of how much a customer is going to buy instead of if he is going to buy. He went on to explain, "I only use this system on my new products . . . other than that, I stick to my regular presentations."

What did this do for Steve? He claims it added an additional $150,000 in sales in one year. As a million dollar salesman, that means Steve increased his business by 15% by having it "prewritten."

— Tactic # 39 —

Use "Magic Words" in your Closes

When you are asking for an order, you want to use everything you know to get the customer to buy. One of the things you should know is that certain words will trigger responses in your customer's mind. These words trigger responses because they appeal to the customer's point of view. There are five of them you should memorize and try to build into as many closing statements as you possibly can. Here they are:

- **You** — When you use the word "you", you are bringing the buyer into the conversation. Instead of resisting the presentation, he can actually help make the sale. Of course, you want to combine that word with such motivating concepts as "you **get**", "you **save**", etc.
- **Profit** — The word profit has power because it's the real reason that your customer is in business. Try to design your closing comments so that that word comes up. Anytime you are talking about price or the cost of the product, you want to make sure you use the word **investment** instead of **price** and then show him his **profit**. In this way, your customer never pays a price, rather he enjoys it by making a **profit**.
- **Value** — This is what the customer's trying to buy. Through out all of these tactics, you will see that we are trying to sell two things . . . **trust** and **value**. He must trust you and then see the value of the proposition. Your customer always wants to make sure that he is getting his money's worth . . . and then some.
- **Help** — Customers and prospects really only see salespeople who are going to help them in their jobs or their life. At the point of asking for the order, you want to let the customer know that you, your products and your services are going to **help** him.
- **Opinion** — As you construct your closing sentences, make sure you include the customer's **opinion**. This could be in the form of a question as you ask the customer his opinions about the things that you know he already likes. By doing this, you are appealing to his ego and he will help you close the sale.

These are magic words that help you along every time you are closing the sale. Oh, you don't have to use them all. It is important, however, that you work one or two of them in, each and every time. If you are the type of salesperson who constantly sees new prospects, you can use all five of these words developed into a closing conversation that will increase your orders by a very high percentage. Some salespeople who sell retail, tell me that they have been able to increase their close rate by a full 20%.

—— Tactic # 40 ——

Show Him Your Pen

You can probably tell from the tactics outlined in this book that I am all for the aggressive close. However, as a sales trainer, I have observed salespeople actually scaring the customer away by using the scientific methods contained in these tactics and not tempering them or softening them with the art form of selling.

Many prospects are scared off when you reach for your pen. A sudden move of this nature has a certain finality about it that is so scary that the customer will actually move back in his chair. They act as if you are just about to pull a gun on them. And, yet, you are going to have to use that pen at some point if you are going to make the sale. Okay, what do you do about it?

Get your customer used to seeing the pen before you are ready to close. When you are asking him questions about his wants, needs, and desires, simply take some notes. Write down what he answers . . . in short form . . . and get him used to the idea that you use paper and pen to help him get what he wants. When you are demonstrating profit, don't use your calculator. Use your pen to show him what he is going to save by buying your product or how much money he is going to make. When you're describing benefits of the product, write down exactly what he is going to get. This entire process will strengthen your presentation and it will hold the attention of the "pen shy" prospect. If you combine this with the tactic of a prewritten order form, you simply have to turn a page in your presentation and you are ready to close.

—— Tactic # 41 ——

Take a Note

During the process of using your pen to get your prospect acquainted with this "tool", begin making comments such as, "let me make a note of that."

Using the pen, using a prewritten order, and making the statement, "Let me make a note of that" is natural, smooth, and **powerful**.

When you are set up with these physical tools, the conversation flows very naturally. It will go something like this:

Customer: "Does this come with a 10 year warranty?"
Salesman: "Would you like the 10 year warranty package?"
Customer: "Yes, I want to make sure that we are protected."
Salesman: "Let me make of note of that."

At this point, you would simply write down what the customer wants. **PUT IT ON THE PREWRITTEN ORDER FORM!**

Customer: "Wait a minute . . . I'm not ready to order that yet."
Salesman: "Oh, don't worry, Mr. Jones . . . I simply like to take notes to make sure I don't forget anything. I always put comments down on the paperwork so that I haven't forgotten anything you told me. I want to make sure I write down the things you say you want and make a note of anything that might cost you time and money."

Once this comment has been made, the customer is working **with you** instead of **against you**. Following those comments, you would, then, simply proceed to the next tactic you had planned for the close.

—— Tactic # 42 ——

Use Alternative Committing Questions

You will have to time this so that you use it properly, but this technique can help you close the most reluctant prospect. Here's how it works:

Ask the major question regarding whether or not the customer wants to buy, but don't allow him to answer. Without much of a pause, go ahead with another question that involves getting the customer mentally past the point of purchase. Now, let me explain that:

Let's say you are involved in a conversation about how the product will benefit your customer. When you see that your customer is talking about things that he would do with the product once he had it, you know he is mentally past the point of purchase. At this point, you can pose the two questions.

Say something like this, "Well, I guess the only decision we have to make is how soon you're going to be able to enjoy using the product . . . and, by the way, will you be scheduling a training school for your people to show them how to get the maximum efficiency from the unit?"

You see, the alternative committing question begins after you use the phrase "by the way." Make sure you avoid any long pause between the first question and the alternative committing question in such a way that the customer has to reply to a situation that shows he already owns the product. In this tactic, then, the alternative committing question is one that indicates he is going to go ahead with your proposal. It requires the customer to make decisions about owning the product. This technique really requires a lot of advance preparation. For every customer there could be a different set of questions. Once you have worked out what you are going to say, you will want to memorize the words so that they are presented smoothly and naturally.

—— Tactic # 43 ——

When the Customer Says, "I Want to Think It Over"

How many times have you heard this? "I'd like to think it over." "We never make decisions right away." "Why don't you just leave your literature here and we'll talk about it." "How about checking back with me next week and I'll let you know."

Any time a customer uses those comments with you, you must immediately begin to close. You know a customer's not going to think it over. We've already discussed the fact he's just trying to "trap you in sunshine", avoid making a decision, or, simply, get rid of you for the time being.

Once you leave, the usual, everyday, operational details of his job or his life will interfere with his thinking. He will forget about your presentation. This doesn't say that he is insincere, but, even when you have a friendship established with a customer, everyday living and working will rapidly set aside the fact that he did intend to think about your proposal. When you come back next week and ask him if he has thought about it, he probably won't tell you, "No, I didn't have time." He will simply say something like this, "Yes, I thought it over and I'm sorry, we just can't do it. I'll tell you what, we'll keep it on file and call you when we are ready." In that situation, there is absolutely nothing you can do. You have allowed the sale to be lost by simply letting the customer do what he thinks he wants to . . . think it over. So, what can you do about this and turn it into a closing situation?

Get in step with the customer — The first thing you must do is use empathy. Don't argue with the customer, but also **don't agree**. Simply say to the customer, "I understand, you would like to make sure that you are making the right decision." Or, you could say something like this, "I appreciate that you feel you need time to think it over." Using the empathy transition phrases, "I understand" or "I appreciate" gets you in step with the customer, but it does **not agree**.

Get denial — Now get them to deny that they are trying to get rid of you. Say something like this, "let me make sure that you're not just saying that to get rid of me . . . are you?" Have a nice smile on your face and look at the customer in a questioning way. Most of the time, with this direct approach, they will say something like, "Oh, no . . . everything is okay . . . I just wanted to take some time."

Question and press — Do this gently, but you must press the customer by questioning him. It's time to ask this type of question: "I just want to make sure I'm clear on this point . . . what is it you want to think over . . . is it the product itself?" Be sure you don't allow the customer to answer the question "What is it you want to think over?" You see, it is the second question to which you want to get a response. This is called using the "is it's." The second question simply asked if it was the product. When he answers that, you have a chance to do the "smoke out." You simply go down the list to ask if it's the product, the quality, your company, or the price. What you are actually doing is summarizing all of the benefits that you have talked about before . . . benefits that he agreed he wanted. You are not arguing with the customer, all you are doing is asking. Throughout the process, you are allowing the customer to think about reasons why he should buy. Also, you are giving him an opportunity to realize that there is no reason to wait.

This whole process tells the customer that you think his idea is a good one. You're indicating that obviously, he wouldn't be taking his time to think it over unless he was really interested. You then summarize all of the benefits and make them good closing points. You see, you're going to be reducing the statement. "I'll think it over" to a specific objection or problem. When you do that, you can handle it much better than you can handle an intangible that is going to be extended over a long period of time.

Here are some specific comments you can make when a customer tells you he wants to think it over:

"I understand, what **exactly** do you feel you want to think about?"

"Well, let's think about it now while it's still fresh in both of our minds. Are there some things I left out? What are some of the items you want to know more about?"

"Mr. Smith, you have always been an excellent decision maker. Why don't we save both of us a lot of time and go ahead and work this out right away?"

"I'm sure you have some very good reason for saying that. Do you mind if I ask what it is?"

"I'm a little confused over that. I know if you take longer to think this over, you're going to lose some of the profits that you could make. I know you like the product a lot. I'm wondering . . . what is holding you back?"

So, you don't have to chalk up the sales presentation to wasted time when the customer says he wants to think it over. With the right attitude and using the proper tactics, you can change that comment into a close of the sale.

— Tactic # 44 —

Make it Ridiculous

Customers are always saying things that they feel they must, simply to test the value of your proposition. One of their favorites is to, in some way, let you know that the price is too high. If you can't overcome that particular comment and immediately change it into a close, you're going to severely limit your ability to get others.

When a customer tells us something costs too much, we have a tendency to look at the entire investment that customer has to make. That's the wrong approach. You want to rise above the field of mediocrity . . . be different from all of the other salespeople. When they think the total price is too much, it is your job to break it down into how much it is actually going to cost . . . **reduce it to the ridiculous**.

In order to do this, you first have to find out how much is too much in the mind of the customer. Simply ask the question, "How much too much do you think the product is?"

Now let's suppose you're selling a product that costs $50,000 and the customer has only budgeted $45,000. So, it looks like you are $5,000 too high. Well, let's think this through. First, you know the customer didn't expect to get your product for nothing. So they do have some money to spend and the problem is only a $5,000 problem, not a $50,000 or a $45,000 problem. So, that's where you start. Start with the $5,000 problem . . . not a **$50,000 problem**. You start on the difference . . . on the smaller amount. In order to do that, you must remember not to talk about the total investment. Even say something like this, "so it's not the $50,000 were talking about, but we're having a bit of trouble with the $5,000 difference . . . isn't that right?" **Get the customer to agree.**

Then, work through an example and have the prospect help you. Hand your prospect your calculator and then say something like this, "Let's say that you have already bought our product. Do you think it will last for ten years?" Since this is the warranty period for the product, your customer will probably say, "Well, I hope it does . . . that's how long you guys are going to be responsible for it." Again, you agree, "That's right . . . and if we divide $5,000 by ten years, we get $500 a year, don't we?" Again, you get agreement from your customer. Then you simply continue: "I suppose you're going to use the equipment about 50 weeks a year . . . so if you take the $500 and divide it by 50, you will get $10 a week . . . isn't that right?"

I am sure the figures you will be working with won't come out so neatly, so that's the reason you're going to have your customer use a calculator. Continue on by saying this, "There's probably a lot of weekend work and some overtime so my numbers are probably off on the high side. It would probably be a lot less than $10 a week. Anyway, let's assume that you are going to use it for just five days a week. Dividing 5 into 10 simply gives us $2."

At this point, you want to pause, lean forward and directly ask this question, "Isn't everything we've talked about worth a lot more than simply $2 a day? Do you really think you're going to let $2 a day stand between having this product and not having it?"

"How much does coffee cost a day to supply your employees?" "What does it cost at minimum wage to have the lowest paid employee?" "Don't you think this is worth a lot more to have it working for you full time than

$2.00 a day?" "Why, if you broke that down into eight hours, that's only 25 cents an hour, isn't it?" "Why don't we go ahead?"

So, you see, a $50,000 price ended up simply being a 25 cent an hour investment. This is a very powerful technique, especially when you have the customer doing the calculations.

—— Tactic # 45 ——

Establish a Chain of Closes

Every time you have a contact with a satisfied customer, you have an opportunity of closing sales. A satisfied customer provides you with the following closing possibilities:

- Sell the same item you sold the last time to the same customer.
- Sell another, ancillary, add-on item to that same customer.
- Sell the same article to another customer that could be an acquaintance, friend, or business associate.
- Get a recommendation from the current customer and sell another article to another customer based on this recommendation.

This chain of selling is one that exists in every industry, but one that is not often used by salespeople. Give it some careful thought and you will realize that it is often less expensive and easier to sell to an existing customer than it is to spend a lot of time prospecting for new customers. To close more sales, you must constantly look for every opportunity to establish a chain of closes. Through this process, you will sell more and your work will be a lot easier.

—— Tactic # 46 ——

Use the "Limited Offer"

You have seen the limited offer tactic used by many retail salespeople and by television salespeople. Any time you hear the expression, "Only one to a customer" or, "This month only," you are hearing the limited offer close.

The idea, of course, is to stimulate the customer to think that he must buy or lose. By using this tactic, you will create a feeling of "emergency" in the mind of your prospect.

Make sure that when you use this tactic you can back up your offer. Don't bluff. If a prospect comes to you after the limited offer has expired, make sure that you don't make a concession. The next time you have an opportunity to use this tactic, he will remember that there was no real "emergency" and the tactic will have no effect. Your prospect must know that by acting now, and **only now**, he can gain some sort of an advantage; but, if he does not take immediate action, he will **lose**.

— Tactic # 47 —

Close with Every Buying Signal

Don't think that there's only one buying signal. Anytime the customer indicates he's mentally past the point of purchase, he is telling you that he needs a reinforcement to that point of view. This reinforcement should always come in the form of a close.

You must be able to recognize a buying signal in order to make this tactic work for you.

Anytime the customer says something that indicates that he is talking about using the product . . . when he is describing "application" . . . he is giving you a buying signal. Here's an example:

The customer says to you, "I was thinking about buying your equipment, but I decided my men would just mess it up when they tried to install it. For this reason, I have decided not to buy it."

Well, is that a buying signal or is that a turn down? I hope you recognized it as a buying signal. In fact, in that example, the customer actually told you that he was thinking about buying it. He simply has a problem with his men. His men don't know how to install the equipment and he is afraid that he is going to suffer some loss of reputation or money or both. He has indicated that he is mentally past the point of purchase and he just needs someone to teach his people how to install the product.

Obviously, your job is to get his people involved in a training program.

There are many times in your presentation when you'll have an opportunity to add up all of the benefits you have been presenting to your customer. This, also, is a good time to close. You see, when a customer allows you to add up these points, he is giving you a buying signal because he has mentally agreed to the "ownership" of all of these benefits. Once you add them up . . . ask for the order.

Another time to close is when you have overcome some sort of an obstacle. You see, once again, the customer is giving you a buying signal when you have handled a problem for him, overcome an objection, or answered a question. He is indicating that he accepts your comment. That's a buying signal . . . go ahead and ask for the order.

Anytime your demonstration ends, you should ask the customer if he would like to have the product. That's a very natural conclusion to any demonstration. Simply say something like this, "I'm ready to talk terms if you are."

Look for those buying signals. They come frequently and should always be used as closing opportunities.

—— Tactic # 48 ——

Ask the Customer "Why Not"

Once you have tried a series of tactics and you have not been successful, ask the customer why he doesn't buy. This is a lot better than simply leaving. Say this, "I know you probably have a real good reason for not going ahead. Do you mind if I ask you what it is?" All you're doing is asking him why he isn't going to buy.

Most customers will respond to such a direct question. You have let him know that you understand that he has made his mind up against your proposition. Your customer is feeling that he probably looks stubborn or unreasonable to you. He will begin to justify his reasoning. In the process of his explaining, you simply find out that he may have been misinformed, misunderstood what you presented, or he has an objection that you can easily overcome.

By asking the "why not" question, you accomplish many things:

- You will be putting the prospect on the defensive because whatever he tells you must sound logical or he will look somewhat foolish.
- You will be able to learn exactly what obstacle you have to overcome if you are going to close the sale. If you find out you can overcome the obstacle, you have a renewed opportunity to get the order.

- Whenever a customer tells you why he doesn't buy, he is letting you know, at least to some degree, that he is interested in some parts of your offering. He is telling you that there is only one or two reasons that have to be overcome.

Many salespeople have found the "why not" close has led them to an alternative product that would perfectly satisfy the customer's needs. In fact, salespeople have reported to me that the alternative product may even be an upscale product. The customer simply wanted more than was being offered in the ordinary, usual product or service.

— Tactic # 49 —

Use the Customer's Question to Close

When the customer asks you a question, you have the perfect opportunity to close the sale.

Let's suppose you're making a presentation and your customer stops you and asks a question. Further, let's suppose that you know if you answer the question completely, you will disrupt your normal presentation and lose the impact of a preplanned close. Of course, if you don't answer the customer's question, he could be upset and you would lose his attention. In this case, you have to do something that will enable you to answer the question and still retain control of the situation.

The idea is to simply ask a question of a customer's question and put him somewhat on the defensive. Let me give you an example:

Customer: "Which of these products do you think I should use?"

In a situation like this, you may not know what the customer's experience has been with the type of product. You want to make sure that you don't fall into the trap of recommending a product that he doesn't feel entirely meets his needs. Be careful how you answer. Ask him a question.

Salesman: "Just exactly how will you be using the product?"

When a customer answers this question, you can then present the right product and close. You can do this with selection, delivery, price, or other alternatives.

— Tactic # 50 —

Know When to Stop Talking

Although I've given you many tactics on closing, I have tried to make each one as short as possible. The first reason is because I want you to read them and the second is because I want them to be effective.

I like the advice Mark Twain gave when he told the story about a preacher asking his congregation to give him some money for missionaries. Mark Twain stated that the preacher made a wonderful presentation and that he was moved to donate $25. The preacher went on with his talk for another 15 minutes and Twain cut his contribution down to $10. That wasn't enough . . . the preacher continued to talk, so Twain decided to give him $5. As the pastor continued to talk on behalf of the missionary service, Mark Twain became bored and decided he was only going to give him a dollar. The preacher went on for an hour and a half and finally closed his talk. When the collection plate was passed, instead of getting $25 from Mark Twain, he got only $1.

Many salespeople go beyond the point of close. The customer has already mentally bought when he is indicating he is "buying" the individual segments of the presentation. **When a customer indicates he is mentally owning the product . . . close!**

— Tactic # 51 —

Use a Customer List

We have already talked about third party reference as a closing tactic. One of the most effective forms of this method is to have a customer list ready to show your prospect.

One of the most effective salesmen I know is one who carries a list of people who have bought certain products. That's right . . . he keeps a list of people under **every product category.** As he shows the list, he simply says to his prospect, "I am proud of everybody who has bought these products. Just look at the names of some of these people. They are industry leaders and they know a good buy when they see it."

Another method of using this list is to simply say, "Here are the type of people who have taken advantage of this offer. There are people like . . ." and then you simply read some of the most prominent names your prospect would recognize.

Most of the time, customers will close themselves in this type of a situation.

— Tactic # 52 —

The V.I.P. Deal

Everybody lives at the center of their own universe. You do, I do, and so do your customers. For this reason, many of your buyers and potential buyers believe they have to have a special deal before they will buy. Give it to them. They deserve it.

Often, all you have to give up is something that is rather trivial. While you simply say, "Since you are such a big buyer and important customers of ours, let me show you what I can do." Once you have said that, you show him something that was not included in your original presentation. It may be something that you do for most people, but you simply left it out anticipating having to use the V.I.P. close.

In my own situation, I have had customers who insist that they will not accept my offer unless I lowered the price. Knowing this in advance, I made sure that my opening price was at least 20% higher than I really wanted. I let the buyer know that others are paying the higher price and quoted him a lower one . . . the exact price I intended to get prior to beginning the presentation/negotiation. Deception? Yes. Like I said . . . the V.I.P. buyer deserves it.

— Tactic #53 —

Use the "What If" Tactic

If you're going to use the V.I.P. tactic, combine it with the "what if" to make sure that your V.I.P. customer is going to buy when you finally **give**. Say this: " What if I were able to get the price down by 8% . . . please understand I don't know if I can do it, but if I can, would you go ahead with my proposal?"

This type of question makes your prospect want to close the deal as much as you want to close the sale. He thinks if he doesn't say yes now, he will lose the opportunity to take advantage of the "negative leverage" he has used on you up to this point. This puts you in an excellent position of being an effective negotiator. The customer is no longer thinking he's going to ask for more, but he is going to be way ahead if he now accepts the offer the way he has convinced you to change it.

When he finally signs the contract, he's going to feel that he's a pretty smart guy and that he drove a pretty hard bargain. That's great, because you always want to leave a customer feeling that he has won.

—— Tactic # 54 ——

Use a Lot of Tie-Downs

Anytime you get a customer to respond to a closing question, you want to tie down that response so that your sale stays sold. The tie-down is a matter of getting confirmation on a point . . . it is a positive reinforcement that keeps your customer committed. Here are some examples:

- You would say to the customer, "We only have five of these left and the orders are noncancelable. Why don't we go ahead and send you three of them right now?
- Or, you might say to the customer, "Before we begin production for next month, we have to have firm orders. Why don't we go ahead and get yours in right now?"
- Another tie-down would be, "It's customary for us to get a deposit when we send in the order. Can I have your check for $200 right now?"

You don't have to tie-down every sale, but there are circumstances when this technique will get a customer to move. Get these types of tie-down comments and questions in mind, practice them and use them where they are necessary.

—— Tactic # 55 ——

Close Customers Who Won't Talk

What do they do with incorrigible prisoners to further punish them? They are already in jail. That's right, they put them in solitary confinement. Therefore, we can conclude that solitary confinement is our society's worst form of punishment. That's what customers and prospects are doing to you when they won't talk. What a frustrating experience!

Many salespeople give up and simply go on to another prospect. That's not necessary. Many customers who don't say anything, simply have a problem they don't want to talk about. Others, of course, are just playing games. Are those the only reasons customers don't talk? No, here's a partial list of reasons a customer or prospect would remain silent:

- He is simply testing you.
- He doesn't trust any salespeople.
- He wants to see if he can intimidate you.
- He has a negative self-image and doesn't like to express himself.
- He thinks he's being a smart businessman.
- He really has no authority to make the decision.
- He wants to see if you will become embarrassed, flustered, or otherwise unsettled.
- He might just be stupid.
- He's trying to be John Wayne . . . the big, strong, silent, man who is going to command a situation with his "strong, silent type" posture.
- He may be simply listening, absorbing, and not aware that he isn't contributing anything to the conversation.
- He may just be a nice, patient, polite man who is allowing you to present everything you want.

Well, in any given circumstance, you may not know the real reason. The important thing is to have a tactic to handle this situation.

I like to think that even the most taciturn of prospect will open up when you simply start writing up the order. That's right, one of the best ways to get a silent customer to talk is close the order and threaten him with shipping the product. If he doesn't talk, he has bought. Don't try to psychoanalyze these guys. That isn't your job. Even if you do spend extensive time figuring their psychological orientation, you're not going to be able to change it. One psychologist said the only way you change human nature is through a deep religious experience, psychiatry, or through a frontal lobotomy. As salespeople, we're not qualified to handle any of those three. **Use tactics!** Close the sale! Good closers do it all the time. Here's how:

- **Don't think of silence as a rejection** — Just because a customer won't talk to you doesn't mean he isn't going to buy. It also doesn't mean that he is saying "no." Get him to open up.

- **Ask a question and wait** — With a proper mental attitude, you ought to be able to have some fun with this. Ask the prospect a question that cannot be answered with a yes or no. That means you have to use questions that begin with the words: **what, when, where, why, who** and **how**. These are the words that ask the open-ended question that grabs the customer's mind and causes him to think. Once you have asked the question; **shut up!** Beyond that, look directly at your prospect and hold your gaze firmly on his eyes. Don't move . . . don't squirm in your chair . . . don't flinch, and control your complexion. Don't let the red grow from the collar up into your cheeks.

In this situation do look expectant so that he sees it is now his turn to contribute. **Wait as long as you have to**. Something has to give. All of a sudden, you're going to find out that he's actually a human being and that maybe he really wanted you to go ahead and try to close the sale. He might simply answer by saying, "Well, in answer to your question . . .". Then he might go on to say, "So, why don't you go ahead and ship it?"

I am not describing an ideal world situation. It's a fact. Many silent customers close themselves when they are forced into the position of responding.

Try this technique. You're going to find that you will be able to close prospects that most other salespeople walk away from.

There you have it. You have exactly 55 closing tactics to practice and make your own. Remember, **you can't sell if you can't close**. Practice these tactics one at a time until you "own" them. Practice does not make perfect. Practice makes **permanent**. You could be practicing the wrong things up until this point. By practicing these closing tactics, you will make them a permanent part of your selling skills.

SECTION II

Overcoming Objections, Answering Questions, and Negotiating

Selling is never a one way situation. Nor should it be. You want to involve your customer or prospect as quickly as possible in the selling conversation or demonstration. As you involve him, you will get him mentally past the point of purchase . . . he will begin to **mentally own** your product. When a customer has an objection, or begins to question what you are presenting, he is involved. Objections, then, are nothing to be feared because they become **selling helpers**. **Questions** from the customer are his way of letting you know what's on his mind. **Negotiating tactics** give you an opportunity to move quickly into the close.

All in all, this chapter will give your sales presentation the sparkle that is needed to make sure the closing tactics in the previous chapter work smoothly and consistently.

Tactic # 56

Welcome Objections

In any conversation, where there is interest by both parties, there is give and take until the individuals involved come to a common understanding. That's communication. The give and take is a process of questioning, agreeing and disagreeing. All of these communicative devices are actual helpers in the conversation . . . an exchange of ideas.

It's the same way in selling situations. The helpers are the objections that are raised by the customer as he stops you from time to time, to have a point clarified, or give you an opportunity to support your statements with more facts. Most customers who raise objections are actually seeking more information about your product or your service. As your customer raises an objection, there is interest. You must think that he is trying to justify his interest in buying. He is actually **helping** you to sell.

If you do not give your customer an opportunity to express his objections, you will find yourself working in the dark. A sincere objection, at any time during your presentation, will make it possible for you to gain a better understanding of your customer's needs.

— Tactic # 57 —

Determine If It Is a Sincere Objection or a Mere Excuse

For you to make a "selling helper" out of a customer's objection, you must qualify the customer's comment to determine whether it is a genuine **objection** or a **mere excuse**. Excuses cannot be used as selling helpers. They must be dealt with quickly to remove them as obstacles from your selling conversation.

Every salesman I've worked with, with any experience, knows that excuses are commonly used by customers to hide their real reasons for not buying. You must look at these excuses as smoke screens behind which your customers hide in order to conceal the real objections or to simply put off the decision to buy.

Some of the most common excuses heard are:

"I'd like to think it over," "Business is bad," "I want to talk it over with my men," "I have other plans, " "It costs too much," "I want something else." and "I have enough," etc. These are not real objections because they cannot be considered selling helpers. They ask nothing of you. They contribute nothing to the selling conversation. Since they contribute nothing, they can easily be identified as excuses behind which your customer has some genuine reasons for not buying. It is your responsibility to separate the excuses from the actual objection so that you can use them as effective selling helpers.

How else can excuses be easily recognized? Aside from the fact that they contribute nothing to the selling conversation, there are certain precise indicators that make excuses easily recognized. Put it to a four-part test: **the qualification of the customer, the customer's attitude, the time** in the selling conversation when the excuse is raised and **the frequency** of comments.

— Tactic # 58 —

Testing for Excuses

Customer Qualification — Customer qualification, in this sense, means that the buyer has already been qualified based on his need, his ability to buy and his authority to purchase. If you have qualified your prospect in this way, you can assume that the objection raised on the above criteria is simply an excuse. He's telling you he doesn't have any need or he doesn't have the ability to buy it, or that he doesn't have any authority. . . he is trying to put up a smoke screen.

Look at his attitude — How is he behaving himself in the selling interview? The customer's attitude is going to reveal if the objection is real or if it's just an excuse. Listen for an uninterested tone of voice, an offhand manner or a general attitude of indifference. That is certainly going to indicate that the customer is merely making excuses. Your sincerely objecting customer, on the other hand, will be more positive and direct in his approach.

The time — Carefully pay attention to when the excuse is being raised. The time in the interview will indicate that it is not a sincere objection. Most excuses are made early in the sales conversation before your customer could possibly have enough information about the product to raise a real objection.

Frequency — You can be sure what the customer is saying are not real objections when his utterances come at a fast and furious pace. Relatively few sincere objections are raised in a selling conversation. The customer who is constantly interrupting you with one negative comment or another is offering a series of excuses.

You must be closely in tune to the time in the interview when a customer comments, the way it is worded, the qualification of your prospect and the manner in which he is making a comment. In this way, you are going to be able to identify customer resistance as an excuse or as a sincere objection. In most cases, customers give excuses. For this reason, your problem is simplified. Try this . . . assume that all objections are excuses and dispose of them. How do you do that?

Ignore them! Bypass them! Comment briefly!

Use them as a reason for buying. Whatever you do, **don't defend**.

—— Tactic # 59 ——

Don't Defend

Successfully handling and overcoming objections involves working **with** the customer to eliminate an obstacle that is going to prevent the purchase of your product. This means you are not going to argue with the customer. However, You must not become too aggressively involved in convincing the customer to buy.

A lot of aggressive salespeople feel that answering the objection means that they've got to wear down the customer's resistance. This is a dangerous attitude. Remember, objections are **selling helpers**. You are not going to let them get in your way, nor are you going to let them cause you to become overly aggressive, defensive, combative, or even obnoxious.

On the other hand, don't let them intimidate you. Some salespeople go so far in the opposite direction . . . away from handling an objection . . . that they feel any attempt to try to overcome them, amounts to pushiness. Properly handling an objection is actually a **customer service**. Don't you see that?

Assume that the customer has a desire for what you sell. Otherwise, you wouldn't have been accepted into his place of business. In retail sales, the customer wouldn't even have come to see you. With this as your basic premise, it is extremely logical that you are looked upon as someone who is there to help that customer get what is wanted. If you don't try to overcome a customer's objection, you are working against that fundamental idea. To not overcome the objection, is to withdraw your help from the customer.

— Tactic # 60 —

Realize That Objections Are the Lack of Trust or Value

Remember, customers object or give excuses because they are looking for help. I realize this is a broad statement that covers a variety of circumstances, but many customers aren't sure what an item will do or, if the objection is to price, the customer may not yet have seen how the benefits will compensate for the initial investment.

Keep in mind the relationship that you have developed with your customer. If you call on the individual frequently, he may not want to say "no" and will, therefore, object to something about the product or service, just to shut you down. Whatever the case, you must find the ultimate reason for a customer feeling that he is not going to buy the product. You must discover this before you are able to go on in your presentation.

— Tactic # 61 —

Use Empathy

Before handling any customer objection, you must **listen to the entire objection**. Many salespeople tend to interrupt and begin defending the product, the company, or, even themselves, before the customer has had a chance to finish his comments. This is a big mistake. When customers are given a chance to fully express themselves, they will often answer many of their own objections. Other customers just need to moan and groan a little bit before they spend their money. If you don't let the customer finish his conversation, he'll be frustrated and you'll never find out the real reason he doesn't want to buy.

The first step, then, in handling an objection, is to show your **empathy** for the customer's position by acknowledging or offering some "agreement." Notice that I have put "agreement" in quotations. This is because I don't believe you are going to actually agree . . . you are simply going to get in step with the customer to show that you **appreciate** his point of view or you **understand** what he is saying. You are actually putting yourself into a position of working **with** the customer and not **against** him. You are letting the customer know that you care, you are on his side and you are taking into consideration **his concerns**. This agreement step then simply means that you will verbally repeat the concern back to the customer. Here are some examples that show you exactly how to do that:

Customer: "I'd better think this one over."
Salesman: "I understand that you would like to think it over . . . it is a big decision."

Now please realize that we are not going to leave it at that point. We are simply using empathy to establish a transition from the customer's objection into the position of being able to go on with the presentation and close the sale. You will see how this works in subsequent steps. Here's another example:

Customer: "I think I'd better look around first."
Salesman: "I appreciate you would like to see everything that is available."

Do you see what's happening here? We are saying things that allow us to mentally walk side by side with the customer. Now, you can see the next logical statement is to let the customer know everything that is available, but you're going to do it for him right at that particular time. He isn't going to have to leave the situation in order to look around.

There is a fine line between agreeing with a customer and acknowledging his concern. For example, you are never going to say, "You're right. You should really shop around first." Or, you're not going to say, "I agree, this one is too high priced for you." Always be careful how you word your acknowledgment. Remember, you are simply getting in step with the customer . . . showing **empathy**. Now, you can go on to the next step which is to smoke out the real objection.

—— Tactic # 62 ——

Find the Real Objection

Please remember this, **more than 60% of the time when customers object, they give you a false reason for not buying.**

That's right, 60% of the time the customer's objection is simply an excuse. For that reason, it's absolutely crucial that you "smoke out" the truth; the "real" objection that the customer might have buried deeply in his mind. You do this by asking a series of questions that narrow down all of the possibilities through a process of elimination.

— Tactic # 63 —

Get Permission to Ask a Question

You have already gotten in step with your customer with your empathy statement. Now, you get the customer to give you a "yes" to a very simple question that I have never heard anybody answer with a "no." You simply ask the question, "MAY I ASK YOU A QUESTION?"

Now all you have to do is wait for your customer to respond. Ninety-nine percent of the time the customer will say, "Sure, go ahead."

— Tactic # 64 —

Use the "Smoke Out"

After you've asked the customer, "May I ask you a question?" and you have gotten permission to go ahead, the next question you ask in the actual "smoke out" process is: "DO YOU LIKE THE PRODUCT?"

You see, this is the easiest question of all to answer in the affirmative. Most times, the customer will say that he does. If he doesn't . . . you want to know it. Here you will have an opportunity to go back and find out why not or present another product.

Let's see what we've done so far. I'm going to suppose that you tried to close the customer and you asked him this question, "How about setting up delivery of the unit for next Wednesday?"

Customer: "I really would like to think it over for a while."
Salesman: "I understand you'd like to think it over . . . it is a big decision."
Salesman: "May I ask you a question?"
Customer: "Sure, you can ask me a question."
Salesman: "Do you like the product itself?"

Okay, so far, so good. Where do you go from there? After you ask, "Do you like it?", go on to ask additional questions which cover specific points that you discussed during the demonstration. For example, the conversation could now go something like this:

Salesman: "What do you think about the efficiency rating on the unit . . . you did say you liked it, didn't you?"
Customer: "Oh yes, I like the efficiency rating. I think it's probably the best I've seen."
Salesman: "How about the contractor friendly panels that are on it which lets you service it more easily?"
Customer: "That's a good feature too. It certainly would save my men a lot of time."

You go on and on like this until you have covered most of the presentation points. Be sure that you include all of those positive points that the customer agreed he liked whenever you did your demonstration. Once you have gone through five or six (or as many as you want) of these points, then it's time to narrow down the questioning to the matter of **customer investment**.

—— Tactic # 65 ——

Ask About the Price

You must get to the price. You must get the customer thinking about his investment so he can realize that he is going to get a return. He must be thinking about benefits. He can only get the benefits when he buys. He can only have the product when he pays for it. This is where you want to be, finally, during the smoke out process.

So, in this smoke out process, the final question is to ask the customer, "How do you feel about the price?"

You see, a price objection is always based on one of two considerations. The first consideration is **value**. This is a case where the customer has failed to see why the product should cost as much as it does. The second consideration is **budget**. In this case, the customer feels that the investment he would have to make (the price) is higher than he can afford. It is very important for you to determine which of these two reasons is actually holding the customer back. Only then can you go on with the proper response. Only then can you use this objection as a selling helper. You see, these are two different reasons and they must be handled differently. If, based on your initial question regarding price, your customer tells you that the price is a problem, then ask this question:

Salesman: "Is the price of this particular unit too high **or** is it more than you want to spend right now?"

Do you see what you've done? By asking the question that way, you are going to find out if it's value or budget. By asking him if it's more than he wants to spend **right now**, you determine if it's the current budget and you leave an opportunity open for the future sale of this product. Sometime in the future, the customer may be better able to afford it.

Let's see how this goes by an actual example:

Salesman: "How do you feel about your investment in the product. . . the price?"
Customer: "Well, it seems a bit too expensive."
Salesman: "I appreciate you feel the product is expensive. Tell me, is the price of this particular unit too high or is it more than you want to spend right now?"

Now that's not too difficult is it? You should be using this frequently. Now, if the answer is budget, simply ask the customer how much he **did** want to spend and then go ahead and demonstrate something in that price range. Or, if you have nothing to demonstrate in that price range, then use the tactic under closing that teaches you to work it to the point of ridiculous. You would show him that what he wanted to pay in the actual cost of the product, is the only difference under consideration. Then you will prove to him that the "little bit of difference" is well worth the product when you spread it out over the lifetime use of the item.

—— Tactic # 66 ——

Give Him New Information

The final step in handling an objection under this smoke out system, is to realize this fact: No customer ever changed his mind from a "no" to a "yes" based on the information already given. Now think about that for a moment. If you ask a customer to buy after he has raised an objection and you don't give any new information, he cannot make a logical decision to do so. In fact, if he was to say yes just based on the sheer force of your personality, he would lose face. That isn't going to happen very often. If you want your customer to make a new decision, you must give him a new reason.

When a customer objects, he is making a decision not to buy. To make a new decision, you must have new information. The new information comes in the form of additional features and benefits that the customer will get. So, what do you do? You explain some things that you "forgot" to tell him about in your original presentation. That's right. Sometime there are insignificant little features of a product that you normally wouldn't present because most of your competitors have the same items. Drag them out. Use everything you can that will allow the customer to make a new decision.

Much of your success in handling and overcoming customer objections hinges on your ability to provide that one extra good reason for him to buy. This means you should, during your presentation, hold back some "ammunition" for handling objections.

Let's recap what we talked about so far, in this segment on objection handling tactics.

- Listen to the entire objection before you attempt to handle it.
- Use empathy to give "agreement."
- Ask permission to ask the customer a question.
- Ask a question to get the customer responding (Do you like it?).
- Ask a series of "smoke out" questions to find out the true objection. ("How to you feel about. . .")
- Ask about price. "How do you feel about your investment?"
- Give a new reason to buy . . . new features and benefits on which the customer can make a new decision.

With all of this in mind, you can handle most all objections. Use these first few tactics to get the customer ready to buy, convinced that he is getting a great value for the exchange of his money.

—— Tactic # 67 ——

Handle the Price Objection

Price objections are, probably the most often heard and can be the most difficult to handle. We have established their price as one on value or budget. Also, a price objection can merely be an excuse. Many customers put them up as stumbling blocks to end the presentation. Customers are well practiced in simply saying, "Your price is too high." If you have anticipated this objection by discussing quality features of a product and showing how the quality relates to benefits to your customer, the criticism might not arise as frequently.

Successful salespeople have reported that they answer price objections by using one of the several following methods:

- **Direct comparison** — Look at the higher priced and lower priced articles. Make a direct comparison between them. Establish the quality of the higher priced products and deemphasize the price. Compare the lower priced item with the quality of the higher priced product and justify a greater cost. It's really a matter of showing value received by the customer and showing that value is greater than the price that he has to pay. Here are some examples of how that's done: "I understand our competitor is much less. What does that tell you? I am sure they know how much their product is worth. Let me show you the differences between my product and theirs."
  "It has been well known by most people in the industry that our quality is the highest you can find. Actually, you're going to pay less over the life of the product than you would for our competitor's product. Doesn't it interest you to know that our product will still be serviceable when you have to replace the competitor's with a new unit, once again, having to pay for it?"
  "Think about this . . . it only costs 10 cents an hour to operate. That's actually less than the cigarette you are smoking. I'm sure you can afford that, can't you?"
  "I'm glad you brought up the question of price. Have you ever really figured out what it would cost you to not have the high quality that we build into our product? Just think of the wasted time on the job, the cost of breakdowns . . . and what about repair bills? It is always true that better quality really saves in the long run. Why don't we just go ahead and have this shipped next week?"
  So using comparisons can convince your customer that he's going to lose a lot when he down-scales his purchases.
- **Customer Ownership** — Remind the customer of other high priced items that he owns. These items will show evidence of his willingness to pay for quality products. Sometimes you can refer to such items as the automobile he owns, quality

furniture in the office or other items that you know are possessed by your customer. These conversations go something like this: "Mr. Customer I know the car you drive is one that you're proud of . . . isn't that so? Obviously, you do appreciate quality. I'm wondering about something . . . why are you trying to buy something cheap now?"

"I can tell you are someone who appreciates the better things that are available. It's hard for me to understand why you would hold back on quality, now. Does that make sense?"

Be careful how you do this, you don't want to get too personal and insult the customer. Talk gently, smoothly, and with a pleasant smile on your face.

- **Shortcomings** — Describe the lower priced product and talk about all of it's shortcomings. In this way, you can show the customer what he is going to **lose**, while at the same time, show him what he will **gain** when he buys your quality product.

  Say something like this, "Have you ever thought about why our competitor's are so much cheaper? Do you think it's because they cut some corners in the production process? What about the materials they use . . . do you think they cheapen up there? Do you suppose our competitors cut back in their quality control department? Why should we even worry about what they do when we can come to an agreement right now for you to buy the best product!"

— Tactic # 68 —

You Must Be Convinced

If you are a salesman who feels your prices are too high (and there are a lot of salespeople like this), you are defeated before you begin. You will never be able to convince your customers otherwise. You need a "facts-of-life" quickie course on basic business economics. Sit down with your manager and isolate a product as a specific example. It could be one with which you are having some pricing difficulty. Go through the step-by-step process of purchasing, warehousing, promotion and selling, delivery, etc., adding the expense for each element of the marketing mix. Look at the necessity for the add-on to cover overhead, discuss a reasonable profit, and work out a final selling price.

Experience has shown that when a salesman is asked to suggest a reasonable profit, he will, in most cases, suggest a profit margin larger than that normally enjoyed by his company. Basically, that is a proof to you that your price is right.

The next step is to convince yourself that your customer will receive value equal to or greater than the price that he pays for the products he purchases from your company. Review all of the extra and often hidden benefits that are offered through service, credit, inventory, consumer selling aids, yourself as a salesperson, factory assistance, in-house engineering and layout, etc. These valuable services must be thoroughly understood and must be part of the information that you have available for occasions when you are required to talk of the overall advantages of your company. Now comes your product knowledge.

— Tactic # 69 —

Product Knowledge Means Better Price

I have consistently stated that people are generally **down on the things they are not up on**. This applies in a very direct way to you as a salesman. If you are not up on your major product lines and competing products, you cannot properly present them in a sales conversation. You will end up being sold by your customer on the negative points your customer has about your product. Instead of **you** selling the customer, you will leave the selling situation down on your products, your company and, eventually, down on yourself.

From the above, you can see that there are three keys to preparing yourself for the price battle. They are:

1. Know the economic side of your business and believe in your company's offering.
2. Know the value of services offered to your customer doing business with your company, particularly unique offerings.
3. Be thoroughly schooled in the major product lines and know your competing products.

Armed with this information, you can do very well against your competitors. You will be far ahead of the "field of mediocrity" and will have the opportunity to improve daily as you win one price discussion after another.

— Tactic # 70 —

Talk About Quality

Price is determined by what is built into a product. Superior material, workmanship, design, construction, built-in conveniences, and durability, are all points to be covered which show a product offers value to your customer. You should have this product knowledge organized in a manner that will enable you to tell the full story quickly and completely around those **six points**, all the while, relating the conversation to the needs of your customer.

— Tactic # 71 —

Explain That You Supply Cheaper Products Too

Give examples where actual experience proves that the lower cost item does not perform as well and that the better unit gives complete satisfaction. Product failures are very costly to your customer and he knows it! It is a cliche, but it works, when you remind your customer that "the bitterness of poor quality lingers long after the sweet taste of low price has been forgotten."

— Tactic # 72 —

Zero in on All the Negative Aspects of the Inexpensive Item

Detail the costs of complaints, breakdowns, and return calls. Use "horror" stories as impact makers. There are a lot of stories and, as a sharp salesman, you will keep a file of these case histories for such use. The sale of a quality product, then, includes a built-in "insurance policy" against such disasters. In this regard, an enterprising salesman captured the attention of his customers by designing such a policy as an impact maker. He would always have it ready when the price objection came up.

Imagine such an "insurance looking" policy form that is set up to say on the outside cover:

CERTIFICATE OF INSURANCE

Against product disaster

for

____

When the salesman opens the policy, he has the customer read the printed information inside:

> "This insures ____________________ against the following disasters:
> Item A — Performance failure within the stated terms of the manufacturer's warranty;
> Item B — Costly call backs such as . . .;
> Item C — Angry home owners due to . . .;
> Item D — Loss of profits because of . . .;
> Item E — Damage to image . . .;

The closing line of the salesman's insurance policy"' describes that this policy remains in force as long as the customer (whose name is written in the blank spaces) continues to use top quality products as supplied by his company.

Of course, the policy is not a legal document but it is a "tongue-in-cheek" attention getter that will pleasantly focus the attention of the customer on the subject of **full value**. This little gimmick (that's what it is) is the type of thing that can make you stand out from another salesman. It will help you rise above the "field of mediocrity" and help you to organize a "miscellaneous mind." It will help you put your "selling helpers" to work which will enable you to produce more volume and profit dollars.

—— Tactic # 73 ——

Build the Customer's Prestige

In every type of business, there are first class operators and those who function on the basis of low price, low quality. How a salesman is known to his community is important. If he does not want to project an image of the "fly-by-night" and is interested in word-of-mouth testimonials, he must always give his customers the best that is available.

Higher priced items are prestige builders for your customers; therefore, they are long-range business builders. In this day of consumerism, where the home owner is very much aware of resource for satisfaction, heads-up businessmen are looking more and more to proven quality items that will keep them in the ranks of prestige businesses. High-grade performance **can be sold** and is a very timely response to price objections.

—— Tactic # 74 ——

Answer the "I Can Get One Like It Cheaper."

Of course, there are cheaper Brand X products. Your customer is right. He can get a **similar** product that is cheaper. The key in this situation is not to allow your customer to feel he can get the **same thing** for less money. Two products may look alike and be designed to serve the same function, but they are very different in quality and in performance.

Walter Gierlach is a salesman who always practiced a technique of overcoming the price objection. This is a very down-to-earth example that I have borrowed from him to point out the "similar but, oh, so different" aspect of a product. When a prospect would tell Walter he could buy one like it, but cheaper, Walter would dramatically close his catalog, put away the literature or set aside his demonstrator sample and look at his customer squarely, eyeball to eyeball. He would then ask, "When do you plan to paint your living room next?" The customer, a little off balance, would give some indication of when this would be done. "Well," asks Walter, "Are you going to use the $8.99 per gallon special or one of the best paints at $16.00 a gallon? Now, remember, they both cover the wall and come in all the colors . . . they do perform the same function."

When the customer states he's going to use the better paint, Walter helps him list the reasons why:

"It's easier to work with."

"It will last longer."

"It covers more evenly."

"You need only one coat."

"The same type of difference exists between my product and this other one offered by my competitor," he explains, as he gets right back into his sales message.

There are always differences in lower and higher priced goods. You can sell those differences. You can build a strong message around them. You must get attention to the subject as Walter did with his paint example, and then supply the product facts that prove the difference. You must go through the advantages of special features, point out exclusive benefits and fully discuss the additional pluses of guarantee, better service, easier terms and the reliability of your company.

To capsulate, and by example, you are structuring your reply to say, in effect, "You are probably right that you can get a security system similar to this for $200 less. I won't argue with you about that point. They certainly know what their product is worth. Like them, I know that our security system is worth more . . . I especially know that it is worth more **to you**. At the price I have quoted you, I also know this is a better buy than you can get anywhere no matter what the price. There are security systems much more expensive and there are some that are even cheaper than the $200 you mentioned, but for what you need, this is best because . . ." (here, the salesman explains all of the benefits the customer is going to get and shows how the benefits of his product match the customer's wants, needs, and desires).

This is just an example. As in all cases in this book, putting words into your mouth is the last thing I want to do. But, putting an idea, explaining tactics, and giving examples of "how to" is the purpose of this book which is designed to give you an arsenal of persuasive tactics.

—— Tactic # 75 ——

Let's Make a Deal

No one who has been in the business of selling for a while is so naive as to not know that deal making occurs. Ethical borderline activities can result in short-term gains, but in the long haul, will create a salesman who has lost the respect of his customers, developed an eroding self-image, and will eventually become a tool of his customer, a burden to his company and join the ranks of industry sales "hacks."

I realize these comments are strong. I intend them to be, because this activity is just plain unhealthy! I'm not even talking about the under-the-table stuff, just this business of chiseling and using one salesman against the other. For example:

A building contractor was accepting bids on a bill of materials for 16 apartment units. Charles Brommer submitted his bottom price and so did a competing salesman. Within three days, Charles was told by the contractor that his competition had resubmitted their bid, which was now considered lower than the original quote. He wanted to know if Charles, too, would like to have the opportunity to requote.

There are two ways to go at this point, but only one right way. This is what Charles did: He reminded the contractor that originally he had been asked to give his lowest price and he had done so. He went on to say that if he were to give a lower price, that he would be making himself a liar. Therefore, even if he could cut his price, he would not, for then that contractor would no longer have faith in him.

"You see," Charles said, "If you can't trust a man, you will not want to do business with him. You certainly can't trust him when his word is not good. When I told you I gave you our best price, I did. I will stand on that quote!"

Charles got the job and his company made a reasonable profit on the material. There is a plus to be gained in this situation. Charles is perceived as a man of integrity and for the long haul, wins the respect of his customer. This is of great value and will result in many orders for years to come. There will be opportunities when the same contractor will need material quickly, and he's not going to have time to get competitive bids. He will call the man that he knows deals with him in a sincere and up-front manner.

Here are several examples of how you can handle that same situation:

"Mr. Smith, the price I gave you is based on the highest quality of materials, the best workmanship, the longer durability of the product and the superior design of this new unit. If I'm to give you a discount, it's going to have to come from some of those product advantages. Believe me, you're going to save a lot more than a few hundred dollars because of fewer repairs and overall better operation of these products. I don't want to have to take anything out of this proposal by substituting cheaper products. I don't want to cheat you."

"Fifteen years ago, I started my business on the basis of integrity. I decided I would always quote my best price first. I decided it would be better to explain my commitment to quality once than to have to apologize about poor performance of products forever. That's why I quoted you the best products at the best price."

"Think about this a minute . . . would you rather we build our products up to the best quality or would you like to think that we build them down to the lowest price? We know how to produce lower priced items so that we can beat our competitors, but we also know that it's not worth it. It's not worth it to us and it's not worth it to you. I have quoted you a price for the best products that are going to give you the satisfaction you want."

"I can appreciate you would like to make sure you are getting the very best deal. I wonder, how much would you trust a doctor that offered you discounts? What about a lawyer who was representing you in court? You probably wouldn't trust cut rate professionals. We feel we are the same way. We have produced the best product, and we price those products so that it is fair to our customers and to ourselves. Then, we always follow up with the best service. That's what we are promising you and that's what we will deliver."

"I understand you would like me to meet my competitor's price. I'm not a hard man to get along with, so I'll do that. We have to review the proposal, however, and I'd like you to tell me what we can cut out so that we can meet the pricing level."

— Tactic # 76 —

Think of Price as a "Figment of the Imagination."

I heard an unusual comment from a salesman who successfully sells high-quality items with big price tags. He said this, "Price is a figment of the imagination." Well I had to investigate this concept. When I did, the salesman explained that he means that price diminishes relative to the value received. Now isn't that exactly what we have been pointing out as we illustrate these tactics?

When you keep an eye on the value your customer receives as a result of the purchase, you are able to speak in terms of what is truly important to that customer. Keep your eye on value in this next example as you listen to Tom Evans talking about price with his customer. In this situation, he is introducing a new pipe bending machine with a built-in threader and cutter that has been proven to be ideal as a mobile unit. This equipment, as agreed by the contractor, could save that contractor as little as $10 to $15 a day when in use, or as much as $50 to $60 a day. It is expensive, however, being priced at $4,000. The customer has just said "no," to the order, claiming the price is too high. Here's how Tom responds: "Mr. Contractor, were you sincere when you said this would save you as little as $10 to $15 a day? Okay, now I'm going to agree with you that $4,000 is a very high price to pay for a pipe machine, but won't you agree with me that this tool is built to last a lifetime and that you should never have to replace it? Now, let's suppose that you do not buy this machine and tomorrow you could use it . . . could you use it tomorrow? Or, next week?" (All along, Tom gets positive response.)

"You will lose the $10 it would save you, wouldn't you? If you had this machine, would it work for you 100 days out of the year? Probably more! Well, at 100 days at a loss of $10 per day, your cost for not having bought the machine is $1,000 for the year. In four years, you will have paid for this machine . . . but . . . and this is very important . . . **you will not have it**.

"Now, if you are going to pay for something, don't you want to make sure you are going to own it? Don't you want to know that when it is paid for, it will keep on earning money for you? And, don't you think I've been fair using the very least amount this machine will save you? You know, if I had used a higher figure, we could see where you would be losing more money much sooner, and, therefore, would have paid for this machine more quickly and still not have it. Should we look at those figures, or can we go ahead and have it delivered?"

Please note that Tom concluded his conversation with a subordinate question, giving his customer an alternative choice. The choice was to either write an order or give Tom an opportunity to further explain the situation. In this way, Tom is still in control of the selling situation.

Tom got his order. As he gave the contractor the order pad, showing him where to sign, he quietly explained, "We feel it's better to explain our price just once that to have to defend our poor quality forever." (That's putting our previous example into action.)

This is precisely why you should constantly be engaging in the price discussion. Your customers are only interested in price **temporarily** . . . at the moment of the decision to buy. They are interested in **quality** and **total value** from that point on, for the full life of the product. Because of this interest, they will listen and respond **to the total value story**.

—— Tactic # 77 ——

Use Fear of Loss

The desire to gain is a powerful motivator with everyone, and it is certainly uppermost in a customer's mind when he objects to price and attempts to negotiate a better deal. You should know, however, that the fear of loss is always psychologically stronger than the desire for gain.

You should incorporate this psychological fact into your approach when you are handling price objections. Point out the hazards of lower price products, showing what your customer stands to lose, and compare that with a relatively small gain of a slightly lower price.

Use words to this effect, "You are right. If you buy that other product, you will save $10 now, and I agree that is important. But do you know what you lose? First, you will lose the backup of an experienced company in the business of producing that product for years. We are not just a fly-by-night operation. We have been around for years, producing top quality, selling products at a fair price."

"You will lose the service offered by my company as a producer of this product . . . we handle repairs in the field for you. Most importantly, you lose the assurance that can only be guaranteed by installing the very finest. This insurance is protection against the possibility of costly replacement. You risk losing future jobs that could be yours through testimony of having installed the superior product. Also, you are putting your reputation on the line and you risk damage to that reputation."

"Now all of this is hardly worth $10 . . . it is all truly priceless and you have been working all of your life to establish this positioning. Mr. Customer, this is what you get for $10 more. It's a bargain, isn't it?"

Henry Brock upgrades products through a simplistic demonstration that converts many of his customers into users of sell-up items. During the course of his selling conversation, after he has fully explained the benefits of the better product, he asks his customer, "Will you lend me $20 for five minutes?"

When the bill (or two 10's) is handed over, he continues, "You know, when you sell the home owner a cheap product, this is what is happening."

Right in front of this customer, Henry slowly rips the bill in half. Without speaking, he tears it again in fourths and throws it into a convenient trash can.

"Now, I know that the destruction of that $20 was painful and I did it just this once. That is what happens every time you buy the cheapie. You will lose that extra $20 you could have had. Multiply that times the many opportunities you have to sell a better product and this destruction of $20 occurs that often. Doesn't it make more sense to put that $20 bill in your pocket instead of the wastebasket?"

Henry is successful with this sell-up tactic. He always replaces his customer's torn bill with a fresh one and retrieves the pieces to turn into his bank, which takes care of the taped pieces and processes them back to the Federal Reserve as mutilated money.

Drastic? Yes, but sometimes necessary to make the point that low price means missed opportunity for the customer.

Pricing is an attitude or at most, merely a number . . . a measuring point around which you can rally to proudly proclaim that you have the greatest value package in town. Properly handled, price and the discussion and all that goes into it becomes one of your greatest **selling helpers**.

— Tactic # 78 —

Understand That There is a Difference Between Business Buying and Personal Buying

You must understand that when price is being discussed, a lot of emotion is going to be involved. That emotion will range from the customer wanting the item to the degree that they'll do anything to get it, to cold analytical considerations by purchasing agents who simply want some recognition from their boss for buying high quality items at a low price.

Business items are different from personal items. Know this before you begin your pricing discussions.

— Tactic # 79 —

Personal Item Purchases

Any time a customer feels he is going to get good value and benefits, a price can be relatively high. In these cases, customers are simply asking themselves the question, "Can I afford it?" When the emotional involvement is strong . . . when the customer's wants and desires have been firmly established, he will try to find ways that he can afford the product.

All prices are high until you explain the benefits the customer is going to receive. Your customers will emotionally reject a product if they don't think they are going to get compensating benefits for the dollars they are going to put out.

In personal buying, emotions, not logic, will dominate. The prospect really can't make decisions as to whether or not the product is worth the money he is paying . . . he simply needs to know that he is going to receive the personal gratification that he is looking for. In many cases, the prospect isn't even conscious of price. The price, merely, has to be justified based on how well the product and service satisfies the wants, needs, and desires of the prospect.

This means that if the price of your product is higher than a competitor's product, you must justify the extra benefits, showing how much more satisfaction the customer can expect to receive. Once the prospect accepts the justification, he also will see the need for and be willing to invest in those extra benefits that are produced by your product.

Think about this . . . most people really don't have a strong motivation to hold onto money. Money does nothing for anybody sitting in a drawer. Money is simply a means to an end. Actually, people who have money are looking for a way to convert it into personal gratification. You have heard the expression, "it's burning a hole in your pocket." This is proven when you look at the savings patterns in various nations. The statistics for the United States show a mere six percent savings of earned income. Canada is slightly higher at nine percent, and Japan tops it all with approximately 35 percent. Even in Japan, that era of savings is changing as more of the Japanese are finding ways to receive personal gratification. They want to spend their money. They want to get something for the efforts that they have put into making that money that is sitting in savings. Other than this changing situation in Japan, all the patterns for all the countries remain relatively constant from year-to-year.

If people only spent money for the things that they absolutely need, spending habits would probably fluctuate wildly from time-to-time. Spending habits don't fluctuate like that which means most people are spending for the things that they want and desire . . . they are spending down to what we call the comfort level of savings.

This results in the knowledge that spending is a constant . . . people will put out money for the things they want based on the highest priority at a particular **moment**. They will do this all the way down to their comfort level of savings. All of this comes together when we think of an individual buying a Rolls Royce and another individual buying a basic Chevrolet. Both people are spending down to their comfort level. Both automobiles provide transportation from point A to point B, however, the Rolls Royce is perceived as having greater benefits, therefore, commands a higher investment and requires somebody to buy it that can afford it.

Essentially, when you are selling personal items, price is not the greatest factor . . . **satisfaction** and helping customers get what they want and desire . . . that's what you need to talk about.

— Tactic # 80 —

Business Buying

Corporations always attempt to remove any emotional considerations from their purchasing function. And it works. Emotional responses in business purchasing is very low whenever the purchasing agent is not going to be the end user. Purchasing agents want to be perceived as having done a good job by their boss. They have a desire for recognition for a skillful purchase, but they are not going to be heavily motivated by end-user type of benefits. Now, of course, there are some exceptions when a purchasing agent is buying something for his office or is purchasing a piece of equipment that he is going to be using, such as a computer. In that case, emotion would play a stronger role, but again, tempered with logic. Again, this could only occur when a business person is allowed to purchase without any regard to peer pressure.

The place where a business prospect's emotions are involved is at the leader level. But even here, the boss feels that he has to eventually justify his purchases to his staff. Of course, business leaders have preferences and they are entitled to them. Still, peer pressure on the leader, either real or imagined, is going to have a tremendous impact. In all cases, up and down the ladder, peer pressure can be the deciding factor.

If you are selling to businesses, comparisons of price, value and quality is the way to go. Most of the tactics in this book have been written around those points.

— Tactic # 81 —

Pre-empt Your Price

In both business and personal situations, you can soften a price that tends to be higher than your competitors by pre-empting it. This simply means that you don't wait for the customer to ask about the price, nor do you save it as the last item to be discussed. You must deliberately bring it up as a **benefit** and justify it before your customer has any opportunity to question the difference between your price and the competitor's. When you do this, you are going to minimize the price objection. Here's how you would do this:

"If you don't care at all about quality, you will probably think this product is high-priced. If, however, you want to make sure you are getting the very best . . . this is the product for you."

You see, if you have any perceived negative characteristic about your product, you want to recognize this first and explain how this perception is not necessarily true . . . it's really a benefit for the customer. Do you remember the slogan that Listerine used for its mouthwash? They advertised, "The taste that you hate." What were they doing? They were simply pre-empting a perceived negative. They told us it tasted like medicine and that it did a tremendous job . . . just as medicine should.

— Tactic # 82 —

Be a "High Price" Guy

Retail concepts of pricing is beginning to influence salespeople everywhere. In retail, a discount is not considered a good bargain unless it is 20 percent or more off the "original" price. But, in retail sales, most of the time, the product was bought with the 20 percent discount in mind or it was originally priced that way. Further, a lot of goods are reduced because they are being dumped before they are out of season. Industrial pricing practices can't stand that type of discounting. The type of discounts used in retail selling would certainly be the death of business selling.

When you check with the small business administration, you find that every year at least 50,000 business fail. A closer check of that shows that the failures are rarely because of high prices.

Anytime a salesperson cuts the price, he is giving away pure profit that is necessary to keep his company in existence on into the future. A company is much better off investing in properly training their salespeople to know how to sell "high price."

You should remember this: Anytime you're trying to sell strictly to a **need**, you will have great difficulty trying to get a high price. A need is simply a necessary evil. Customers don't want to reward you because they **have to have something**. There is no emotion to satisfy. When there is no emotion to satisfy, there are no benefits that can be presented to justify a higher price.

You must make sure the product you are selling appeals to the wants and desires of your customer. Only in this way are you going to be able to inject yourself as a "high price" guy who is able to satisfy the customer, his own company and himself.

—— Tactic # 83 ——

A "Secret Ingredient"

You can win the price battle. The worst kept secret (it's rarely openly discussed, but well known) is that effort rarely meets the "academic illumination" of the type of material contained in this book. That simply means that this written material might be read, but nine out of ten salespeople **will do nothing about it**.

Please don't feel that is negative. It isn't. It's great news! **The field of mediocrity** still exists, and it means opportunity for you; that is, if you will begin right now to develop your skills to handle the price objections.

See yourself as one out of the ten! Know that you are the exception. This is the "secret" ingredient that you can use to your advantage. Take action today and become a true professional using these Tactics Of Persuasion.

—— Tactic # 84 ——

The "No Need" Objection

Second, only to the price objection, your customer is most frequently heard saying that he has no need for the product that you are selling or that a competing product is quite satisfactory. He may also state that the product offered does not take care of his requirements. Many times this objection is made before you have an opportunity to explain your product or service.

You should determine that your customer has a need for your product **prior** to making your call. This need can be determined through general knowledge of the customer, by observation, by asking qualifying questions, by listening and by investigating the customer situation on prior calls.

Once you are convinced that your customer has real needs, it becomes your job to point them out to that customer. There are several helper tools that you can use:

- **Surveys** — Use survey information that you gathered from other customers who are in similar situations. Show by numbers, charts or graphs, how these customers are buying and using the product.

- **Testimonials** — Testimonials of other customers in the same situation can be used to show where the product has specifically satisfied a similar need.
- **Description of Benefits** — A description of the benefits derived from either owning the product or using it can be effective with the right type of prospect. Of course, if it's an item for resale, the profit motive should be used.
- **Prove the Demand** — Proving the demand for your product can be used to overcome the objection of a customer who says there is "no sale" for the item. Use records of inquiries from home owners and other evidence of demand. Where a program is available, offers should be made to the customer to help him merchandise the item through cooperative advertising, consumer oriented literature and displays.
- **Show Competitor Inadequacy** — Your customer must be convinced of the inadequacy of the competing product. One of the most prominent phrases heard in selling circles is, "I don't knock the competition." If you know that the competitive product does not represent the total value package as does your own, you have a responsibility of informing your customer. This is the purpose of knowing your competition. The technique with which this is handled determines whether or not the "knock" is a boost to the competition or a selling point for you. The best method is a direct comparison of the features and benefits of your product to that competition.

— Tactic # 85 —

What If He Says, "I'm Not Interested?"

When a customer lets you know he feels he has no need for the product by saying, "I'm not interested," you should be prepared to answer that immediately. In most cases, you will question the customer to draw him out. Here are several examples:

"I appreciate you feel you are not interested. Can I ask you why?"

"I understand. . .there really is no reason why you should be interested at this point. I haven't yet had a chance to show you how this product will make more money for you and solve most of your problems. Can I show you that, right now?"

"I certainly understand that! I have a list of 150 people who were also not interested in this product. (Bring out the list.) The amazing thing is that once I had a chance to show them what they get by buying this product . . . they all decided it was the best decision they ever made. May I tell you why?"

"Does that mean you're not interested now, or will you never be interested? I thought you wanted to find a way to make more money? That's what I'm here to talk to you about. Are you interested in making more money?"

— Tactic # 86 —

How to Handle an Objection to Product

When your customer is not objecting to price or is not objecting on the basis of "no need," he may object to product. This type of objection generally concerns quality, design, construction, size or type, raw material, color and performance of the product.

Many of these product objections can be anticipated and handled before your customer has an opportunity to object. Product objections are usually the result of having failed to establish a need in the mind of your customer. You can avoid the product objection by discussing the product features clearly, distinctly and in a way that you relate specific benefits to a customer.

When your customer does object to products, however, his objections can be turned into selling helpers as follows:

Since you have already determined that your customer has a need for the product, you must discover the real reason for the product objection. You will do this by **asking questions**. You must draw out your customer. If the customer says, "I don't like the quality," you then ask, "What is it you don't like about the quality of the product?" Or, you can use a reflective question in which you merely restate the intellectual content of your customer's objection. You could say, "Oh, you don't like the quality?" Then, you should pause with a quizzical look on your face and wait for your customer to expand his remark. Oftentimes, your customer will not have a sound reason, and the objection is automatically eliminated. You then must take this opportunity to explain all of the quality features of your product.

Use demonstration. One of the best methods of overcoming product objections, is to use a demonstration of the product itself. Where it is not possible to show product performance, laboratory test results can be used.

Trial use of the product is another method of demonstration. Many industries, such as office equipment, use the "on approval" method of selling equipment. Of course, not all products will lend themselves to this technique, but hundreds of them do, and you should employ this system to boost sales hundreds of thousands of dollars over a period of years.

—— Tactic # 87 ——

He Thinks Your Competitor's Product Is Better

Sometimes a competitor salesperson has been in before you. In this case, the customer is already mentally enjoying some of the benefits presented by that competitor and he might already have made a decision to buy in the near future. He may listen to your presentation, but halfway through make the remark that he feels your competitor's product is better. How do you handle that? Well, the same way we have been handling most of these objections . . . get into the customer's mind with a question and uncover a new opportunity to present your product, comparing it favorably with the competitor. Here's an example of what to say:

"Of course, you have probably had a chance to look at the competitor's product. We very rarely hear anyone say they think it's better than ours. You probably had a good opportunity to compare both products. Could you give me your unbiased opinion of both of them?"

"That's the first time I have heard that. For years, we have had the reputation of being the best in this industry. What is it that you could possibly think is better with the competitor's product?"

"What do you mean by that? Is it service you're talking about, the quality of the product, how long the product will last, or is it just something the competitor told you?"

"You say our competitor's product seems to be better than ours? Probably that is because you have seen some of the obvious features in their product. Let's take a deep look beyond some of those obvious features and see how we compare item for item . . . is that okay?"

"I'm wondering about something . . . have you talked with people who have owned both of these products? I have a list of people who have bought from me after they own my competitor's product. Let me tell you what they said, and if you want to, you can call them."

"I'm glad you looked into my competitor's product. Some of my best customers are people who have used it. Could I use your phone to call just a couple of them right now?"

—— Tactic # 88 ——

They Think Your Product Is Too New

Some people just don't want to be the first to try something new. They feel that after a period of use the "bugs" will be worked out of the product and it will be better. In many cases, this is based on good, sound logic and historical fact. Take into consideration the $1200 VCR that had relatively few features. I bought one. Today, a VCR with twice as many features costs approximately $450. It's true, your prospects are afraid of new products. For this reason, you should be prepared to answer this objection in this way:

"Please don't think that with this product our customers are in a position of field testing. We have already field tested this product for the past two years. It's only new in your area. You can be the first to take advantage of this new line."

"I understand your concerns. However, this is really not a new product in the sense that it has been designed using all of the basic parts from our proven models. The words "new and improved" certainly apply here. Let's review the reasons you bought the other model and I believe I can show you how those reasons are magnified with this new product."

"Yes, that's right . . . it is new. That's the reason you ought to get one right away. If you buy a month from now, the product will be 12% more. You see, we are having an introductory special that you can take advantage of. And you know, we always stand behind our products and back it up with the best service available . . . wouldn't you agree that's so?"

"I understand your concerns. However, several people have already bought the product and they think it's the best thing this industry has produced in years. Here are some letters. You see, they haven't had any problems and they are very happy. You can call any one of them."

"Lately, I have heard that quite a bit. I think we should all be concerned about new products. Think about this, though . . . everything that was ever manufactured was new at one time. This applies to computers, VCR's, automobiles, airplanes . . . well, just about everything. Many businesses took full advantage of all the opportunities presented by these new products. Most of those businesses grew as a result. Other businesses stood by the old technology and went out with buggy whips. This is the same position we're in today, isn't it? Either we become agents of change, or we become victims of the changes that are occurring around us. Give it a try . . . you know we stand behind all of our products. Let's begin with a small order today."

"Well, some day this product is going to be old. I don't think you will want to wait until then, do you?"

"I wonder if you have ever bought a new product that you really liked? Well, why did you do that? This is the same situation we have here today and I am sure that just like you enjoyed that other product, you will like this one too."

"Do you always buy used cars? Well, we come out with new products just like the car industry does . . . and for some of the same reasons . . . to make sure our customers have the advantages of the latest technologies. Doesn't that make a lot of sense?"

—— Tactic # 89 ——

What if the Customer Says, "What We Have is Good Enough?"

Here you are trying to sell people updated models of your product, when they assume that the old one is just going to go on forever. Or, they say to you simply, "What I have is good enough." What a shutdown. How do you handle that? Here are some suggestions:

"That's exactly why you should buy a new model. If your machine is still good, it has some trade-in value. Let's discuss the difference between the trade-in value and what you are actually going to pay for this unit."

"I understand that. You wouldn't have bought your old model if it didn't take care of your needs. I wonder, though, have those needs changed? A lot of our customers feel exactly as you do, yet they switched over when they found that our new product is much more efficient and more productive. Would you like to at least take a look at what these other customers have found out?"

"I have your maintenance bills on the older model. Look at this, it is costing you more per month to maintain than the payments would be on this new unit. Doesn't it make sense to get rid of those maintenance bills and have the money go towards the investment in something that is up-to-date and has more features?"

"You make a good point. That model is still working for you and so it still has some value . The longer you wait, though, the less value it will have when you finally decide to trade. Now's the time to really make the change . . . wouldn't you agree?"

"I know a little something about the aviation industry and you know, they change their engines at a certain overhaul time even when those engines are running well. Do you know why they do that? They do it because failure is just around the corner. That's probably the same way with this product. It might look good, but inside it is wearing down. There are probably a lot of weak parts in there that are going to fail. Probably, like most things, it's going to happen when you really need it. Why not avoid that . . . just like the airline industry, we want to make sure we safely stay in business . . . doesn't that make sense?"

"I can't think of any real good reason why you shouldn't have a new machine . . . is it the price? If that's the case, why don't we look at a way that you can afford it by talking about some credit terms ? Could I use your phone to call our credit people right now?"

"You know, some people still have outhouses . . . they work. Also, there are people that use pencil and paper for all their mathematical calculations. This works too. But, our society is changing and as new things come along, most people use them. I'm wondering why you are resisting modern technology when it comes to my product? As long as you have this type of product, don't you want the newest and the best?"

"I know you are satisfied with what you have. In this way, you can actually avoid putting out more money, can't you? Isn't it true, however, that your business depends upon improvements? I wouldn't even have come in here today if I didn't know that I could help you improve your situation. You see, many times we become satisfied with things because we don't have any chance to compare it with what we could have. Here's three good reasons why you should change."

— Tactic # 90 —

Objections to Service

If the customer is not objecting to price, or if he's not objecting to the "no need" for the product, the customer could object to service. Service could make or break a salesman and/or his company. Criticisms of deliveries, invoice adjustments, repair and contact by the salesman, when left unchecked, can quickly drive a customer to the competition.

When your customers come up with these types of objections, you must get right to the point by asking for more facts about the unsatisfactory situation. As you begin to question your customer, a tactful approach will also give you information as to whether or not the customer has had the same experience from other companies such as yours. This will enable you to make comparisons.

— Tactic # 91 —

Delivery is Lousy

One of the most common service objections is delivery. Let's suppose one of your customers has said, "Your delivery is lousy." You can meet this and other service objections in the following manner:

First, get a clear understanding of the situation by asking "how" and "why". Once you discover the reason behind the reason for your customer's objection to deliveries, you can usually answer it in a convincing way.

Describe past satisfactory delivery situations and give example where your company has given the customer low cost service.

Demonstrate prompt service by listening to your customer's complaint and immediately solving his problem with the use of the telephone.

Illustrate the service package offered by your company to include trucks, warehouse capacity, lines carried and the personnel who stand behind you to provide a complete package designed specifically to service your customer.

Have a portfolio of testimonial letters available. These letters should be from customers praising the service of your company from the standpoint of reliability, promptness, courtesy of your company's people, and the attention given by you. These letters can be obtained, from time-to-time, when a customer is particularly pleased and expresses his satisfaction. A courteous request will generally produce such an item. Offer a trip to your place of business. Let your customer see your company's facilities that exist to service his needs. Have him visually inspect your inventory, meet your people and see the activity of your business. By showing your facilities and the investment your company has made, you can easily overcome criticism of service.

— Tactic # 92 —

Handle Complaints Efficiently

Salespeople must have a positive mental attitude towards adjustments. Know that claim situations make you a more necessary part of your company. You are the individual that most appreciates the importance of keeping customers happy and your customers are confident that you will take care of it. With this attitude, use a four-step process when a customer has a complaint:

1. Listen.
2. Express sympathy.
3. Get the facts.
4. Take action.

We will look at each of these areas.

— Tactic # 93 —

The Advantages of Listening

Even small problems can become emotional issues. A customer can become extremely frustrated because of a product or service failure, and by the time you make your call, he can be quite angry.

Tension will have been built that will need to be released. You will do no good trying to talk to your customer when he is in that frame of mind. No matter how right you may be, how easy the solution to the problem or how logical your answer, you must hold back your comments until your customer has a chance to express himself. When he has done this, he has released tension.

Often, by letting your customer blow off steam, he will calm down enough so that he actually minimizes the complaint, making it easier to handle. The chief advantages to listening are to let your customer cool down, give him an opportunity to minimize the complaint and give you facts from your customer's point of view. Your listening also allows your customer to have a feeling of importance.

As you practice your listening technique, you will find that there are certain natural obstacles in these emotionally charged situations that can become pitfalls. You will often feel your customer is wrong and you will want to jump in and correct him. That is the wrong tactical approach. Many times, your own anger will be triggered. Most times, you will want to defend yourself and your company. Again, that is the wrong tactical approach.

All of these reactions are natural if you are indeed a professional salesperson and you believe in yourself, your products, and services, and in your company. Your tendency will be to interrupt your customer, especially when he is wrong. Don't do it! That is the wrong tactical approach!

The advantage of hearing your customer out far outweighs the self-satisfaction you can get from correcting him. Realize that listening may do much of the job of handling your customer's complaints.

In some cases, for the reasons mentioned previously, listening might do **all of the job**. Listen well. That is the **right** tactical approach. Wait until your customer has wound down, then go on to the next step in the four-step process: **express empathy**.

—— Tactic # 94 ——

Use Empathy

There's a big difference between empathy and sympathy. When you sympathize with a customer, you are agreeing with him. When you empathize with a customer, you are letting him know you understand how he feels. This does not, however, mean you agree. That is an important distinction.

You must not fall into the trap of "feeling" just as your customer does, because then someone else will have to solve the problem for both your customer and **you**.

Empathy means expressing your understanding . . . putting yourself in your customer's shoes and letting him know you have done so.

By way of an example, assume one of your customers is angry because your company has failed to deliver products on time. He shouts his comment to you, "We had to walk off the job because you didn't deliver! You are costing me money. Can't you get your people to ship on time?" How should you respond to this?

So often, salespeople attempt to take the heat off themselves personally and pass it on to their company by saying something like this, "Damn it, you're right . . . they messed up again . . . I'm mad, too!"

When that happens, the customer cannot logically expect to get much help from you. That is the wrong tactical approach. You will have isolated yourself from the very people whom you must draw upon to help you solve the problem. You have shown yourself to be in complete **sympathy** with your customer when you really want to show him that you **empathize** with him, but are in control of the situation and will be able to draw upon the resources of your company to effect a solution.

The right tactical approach is to make yourself a part of the situation by saying, "I understand how you feel. Late deliveries can cause a lot of problems. I'm sorry, **we** have given you these headaches. Let me see what we can do about it."

Using the "we" approach, draws your company support system into the situation, implying that **they** will be part of the solution.

So, regarding empathy, once you have listened and have expressed an understanding, you have prepared your customer for the next step of the process: **get the facts**.

— Tactic # 95 —

Fact Finding

If you listen carefully, you will probably have already gotten most of the facts necessary to handle your customer's complaint. By empathizing with him, you will have defused the situation. You are now ready to draw him out; to find the right solution to the problem.

If you have doubtful areas that remain . . . those not made clear to you when you are listening . . . you should ask your customer several questions. Suggested questions in the example given above might be: "Was your entire order delayed, or just part of it?" "Do you have a copy of the packing slip or invoice that I can look at while I call the warehouse?" "Can I see the equipment you received?" "When exactly did the shipment arrive?" "Where was the delivery made?"

As you get more facts, you will be able to determine where your service system has failed, and talk to the proper people to make sure it doesn't happen again.

When you are in the process of determining the cause of a service or product failure, you must discover that the responsibility actually lies with a customer and not with your own company. Or, the responsibility could be fixed on a third party for the transaction, such as the consumer, a contractor, a subcontractor, or you might find joint responsibility with two or more parties involved. Let's look at some of these areas of responsibility.

— Tactic # 96 —

The Buyer's Responsibility

Many times a customer will make a mistake and be responsible for a claim. What is your tactical approach in this case? Some of the most common errors made by a customer are simply mistakes in ordering, a misunderstanding regarding price or terms, the improper installation of products, improper storage, violation of manufacturers' guarantees, and taking discounts that are not earned.

One of the most common claims that requires much handling is the excessive return of merchandise by some customers. As a salesman, you are required to make sure your customers receive proper adjustments for these returns.

Customers return merchandise to your company for many reasons: the same products can be bought for a lower price elsewhere; he has overbought the merchandise; the dealer's customer has changed his mind; the merchandise has become a discontinued item; the customer finds he really is unable to sell the item; the product has become "shopworn"; the stock has become unbalanced by size, color, models, etc.

Consumer customers are sometimes at fault in returning products to your dealers. Many dealers resist any argument with the consumer customers, hoping to pass damaged product claims back to you. Beyond this, many dealers will admit that their consumer customers asked for the wrong size, merely changed their minds, or simply ordered several items on approval and returned those that were not selected.

Probably most claims of your customers are honestly made. However, some of your customers may not be aware of the responsibility for mistakes. Further, many of your customers may not be aware of the cost of rehandling merchandise. Because it is convenient for them to order and return, they tend to always be in a position of expecting adjustments.

Your tactical approach to all of this is to carefully consider the possibility that your customer could be at fault and investigate the cause of this claim before solving his problems. It is not true that, "the customer is always right." Often, he is wrong and it is your responsibility to resolve the situation to the benefit of your customer and **to your company**.

— Tactic # 97 —

Your Responsibility for Claims

You may be responsible for a customer claim. Your company might be responsible for making an error that results in a complaint from your customer. Before you can do creative selling, you know you have to overcome this obstacle. Acknowledge this responsibility and make a prompt adjustment. That is the surest way to win your customer's good will and get more orders.

— Tactic # 98 —

Third Party Responsibility

A trucking company could be the third party responsible if you are shipping some distance. Carriers are often at fault when goods are received damaged or a shipment is delayed. In cases of this nature, since shipments are well documented, it should not be difficult for you to determine the dates of shipment, transportation charges, the condition of the goods at the time of shipment, etc. In this way, you will be able to fix the blame for delays or damages.

Other third party irresponsibility could fall on the shoulders of an installing contractor for merchandise sold to a home owner. Again, it will be necessary to produce the proper documentation showing performance on the part of your company.

— Tactic # 99 —

Joint Responsibility

It is possible that you may find upon investigation of a claim that your company and your customer are both to blame. For example, a furnace could be sold to a home owner. Three weeks later, the home owner could complain that the burner is not working properly, that it is smoking badly. Upon investigation, you might find that the installing contractor did not regulate the burner properly, and that the home owner is burning a poor grade of oil. The responsibility then lies with both the contractor and the home owner. What is your tactical responsibility in this situation? You are the consultative salesperson that must make recommendations to correct the situation. Your responsibility is to make sure that the eventual end-user gets everything he was promised, and then some. The "and then some" in this situation, is the problem solving service you offer.

— Tactic # 100 —

What about Your Responsibility

As a salesman, you certainly cannot control mistakes made by manufacturers, shipping errors, credit department errors, or mistakes made by end-user consumer customers. You can, however, avoid errors that might lead to complaints and costly returns, as well as a great deal of customer dissatisfaction. Tactical action, in this case, is preemptive.

When you detect that your customer is trying to buy more merchandise that he can logically sell, inviting an excessive return goods, it is your responsibility to advise him. Explain to him that where your company will be responsible in accepting returns, it becomes too costly to do so on a frequent basis.

You also have an on-going responsibility to explain your terms, prices, delivery charges, discounts, various allowances and promotional programs to your customers. Mistakes made in these areas are frequently responsible for customer complaints and objections when you are trying to present a product or new service. Carefully, go over all of these areas as you close a sale with your customer.

Trying to use the tactic of "sale on approval," where your customer has the privilege of returning merchandise, is often responsible for many returns and adjustments. Though this is a good selling tactic to use occasionally when introducing new products, a continued practice will result in a lot of costly returns and claim adjustments.

One of the most frequent reasons for complaints and adjustments is carelessness by salespeople when booking orders.

You must be sure that you put in the proper quantities, sizes, colors, styles, prices and terms when you take your order. You must be careful not to make promises to your customers which do not conform with the policies of your company. That is an incorrect tactical approach.

As you affix responsibility for a customer complaint or claim, keep in mind that you want to resolve problems in such a way that you will be building a sounder relationship with your customer. Your customer's complaints will represent opportunities for you to provide service.

So, the tactical approach to this entire area is to listen to your customer, express empathy and through the questioning process, affix responsibility. Once you have done that, you will want to come up with some recommendations for action which could eliminate the same type of problem in the future. This simply means that it is time to take action. Don't give your customers excuses for nonperformance.

Too often, salespeople tend to answer a customer's complaint with such comments as, "This is our busy season," "Our manufacturer is on strike," "We have some new people in our accounting department," "Well, we just weren't able to get to it," etc. Those types of answers will only earn you more customer anger and leave your customer still wanting some action. And, of course, it is very likely that you could lose the account.

— Tactic # 101 —

Taking Action on Complaints

To properly service your customer, you must be a selling manager. You must be able to draw upon all of the resources of your company that support you. When your customer is objecting to service and it becomes a roadblock, you must draw deeply inside your company, upon all of the talent that your sales manager, credit department, warehouse people, truck drivers, and service department can give you.

In these situations, you must keep in mind that you are never alone. You represent the total weight, the total talent and the total capacity of your company to solve a customer problem. Your major task, then, is to apply yourself and the capabilities you represent, in such a way that you not only solve your customer's problem, but you return a profit to your company.

Returning a profit to your company does not necessarily mean that the responsibility for the claim must lie with either the customer or the customer's customer. I am talking about the return on investment over a reasonable period of time, doing business with a particular customer.

As a salesman, you are responsible for making sure that you combine customer good will with your problem solving service activities. In the long run, however, all of these activities must eventually help return profits to your company as a result of your sales activities with your customer.

At the same time, on an individual basis, all of your customer's complaints and objections about service must be settled satisfactorily, or they could become major disasters. When you have to present a decision to your customer, review these guidelines and structure your presentation in such a way that you and your company gain the greatest benefit from your presentation.

Always be courteous — Every person you speak with deserves courtesy. This especially applies when handling a customer on an emotional subject. In this area of servicing claims and overcoming customer objections on service, you must realize the customer could be concerned about his self-respect every bit as much as he is concerned about the mechanics of the subject at hand. So, treat him like a prince. You might want to invite him to lunch, buy him a cup of coffee or give him an unusual novelty gift. Attempt to find a place where you can talk in private. This is often beneficial. It is an excellent tactic. When your customer has listeners, he will tend to conduct himself in a way that protects his ego.

Be sure you let your customer talk first. Keep in mind that you are an ambassador of good will between your company and your customer, and it will be easier to permit your customer to blow off steam.

Courtesy is often the foundation for personal success. **Courtesy is an excellent Tactic of Persuasion**. Even if your customer is wrong and you know it, don't beat him down. You won't be able to return a profit to your company if you win an argument and lose your customer.

Detail your explanations — Once you have tackled the problem and found the cause, give your customer a detailed explanation of how you intend to handle the situation. Leave nothing up to his imagination. Be sure that he believes when you leave his place of business, that his problem is going to be solved. Once you have explained how you are going to handle his problem, ask him if your solution is acceptable. Be sure that he agrees.

Show your customer a gracious attitude — A good tactic is to let the customer know you really care. I have heard it said that many customers

care what you know, but more importantly, they want to know that you care. You see, sometimes, it is not so much what you do for a customer, but how it is done that will determine if the relationship is to be short-term or long-range. If a customer detects that an adjustment is being made grudgingly, that customer will remember the mood long after the incident has been handled. If you have to give, **give with a smile**. You will gain stature in the eyes of your customer and he will continue doing business with you and your company.

—— Tactic # 102 ——

Put Yourself into the Adjustment

We have already determined that you must represent all the resources of your company. Often, many people will have to be involved when making claim adjustments to a customer. However, you want to use the service opportunities as if this is a service that you are making, using the resources of your company. When you do this, your customer will gain confidence in you. Handled this way, every time an adjustment has to be made, you will become more and more valuable to your customer.

—— Tactic # 103 ——

Be a "Straight Arrow"

Sometimes your decision is "yes" and at other times it is "no."

No matter what the decision must be, you must speak honestly and in a straight forward manner. Don't beat around the bush. Don't delay response. Sweeping something under the carpet is going to leave a visible lump that you will continually trip over on future calls for your customer.

Of course, it is easier to give a "yes" than to give a "no." When you have to give a "no," use a very sympathetic manner; give a full explanation of why your answer is "no." Never force your customer into a position of "take it or leave it." Use all of your good selling skills to sell the negative decision to your customer.

— Tactic # 104 —

Be sure to Follow Through

Once you have handled a customer objection regarding service, or a customer complaint resulting in a claim, you must make sure that your customer remains satisfied. A follow-up will let your customer know that you are interested in keeping him. If your customer is not fully satisfied, you have further opportunity to become involved . . . a further opportunity to sell your solutions.

— Tactic # 105 —

When the Customer Says, "It's Not Time to Buy."

Price, need, product and service . . . all are objections that you can get your teeth into. A more subtle and oftentimes more difficult objection, is when your customer says, "I don't want to buy right now." "I think we're going to have hard times ahead." Or, "I'll wait for the next model."

This situation can be extremely difficult . . . sometimes more difficult to handle than the other objections we have discussed, because it is often not a "selling helper," but an excuse that is used to discourage you. This is more often used whenever you have not established the need for the product.

Most times, this objection is just plain unwillingness on the part of your customer to make up his mind. Some people find it very difficult to make a decision on anything. In fact, most people will procrastinate making a decision on the very things that they know are good for them.

This does not mean that all objections of this nature are excuses. There are times when your customer has a real reason for not wanting to buy immediately.

As with all of these situations, it is your responsibility to find the real reason. If the customer is merely giving you an excuse, there's nothing to be gained by discussing it. Bypass it, ignore it, and get on with your selling message.

When the customer says, "Let's wait for the next model," you should respond that he will not gain that much by waiting because the changes on the new model are not necessarily that important. On the other hand, your customer can save money by buying now. You may even have a closeout special on the existing model.

When your customer says, "I want to look into it further," you immediately know that your customer is convinced of his need for the product, but his mind might not be made up regarding price, or the source of supply. The first thing you must do in this situation is find out, by asking tactful questions, which of the problems still exist in the customer's mind.

Try some of these approaches:

"I can understand that you would like to delay in making this decision. I am interested, however, on the exact reasons against buying right now. Could you tell me those reasons?"

"Before I go, let's review what we've talked about. Here are some of the reasons you said you liked the product. Why do you want to wait?"

"Something just struck me as being a little strange . . . if you think about this for a long time, I know you're going to come up with the same decision. For instance, if I ask you what type of car you like and you told me, you would probably come up with the same answer next week . . . or next month . . . or next year. That's the same way with this situation. You could think about this product for ten minutes or two days or a week. You will probably come up with the same idea. You're going to remember the things that are good about it. The only thing that the delay is going to cause, is a period of time when you won't be able to enjoy the product. Let me make sure I get the product to you right away . . . you don't have to wait."

"I appreciate you'd like to wait. However, you did tell me you liked the product and everything about it. If you wait, you won't be able to enjoy it. All we have to do is condense three months into one minute if you say yes now. Can I go ahead and send it?"

"You have invested a lot of time thinking about this. Why bother spending any more time malling over something you know you want. Haven't you thought about it enough already?"

—— Tactic # 106 ——

The Customer Thinks That Tough Times Are Coming

This is something that is going to come up again and again. There are always peaks and valleys in the economy that worries people. Business customers are especially affected by the "doom-sayers." This kind of an attitude is a bit difficult to argue against, because you really don't know if their fears are justified or not. So, what kind of a tactical approach can you have for this situation? Try this:

"That really surprises me . . . I wonder who told you that? No one can accurately predict the future. How would this purchase affect that future, anyway? Wouldn't it make you more productive and make your job a lot easier?"

"I guess I agree with you and that's exactly why I'm recommending that you buy now. I know that you need the product and taking care of this now is going to enable you to have it before the crunch hits?"

"If you were the pilot of an airplane, you wouldn't turn around and go back just because there was a little rough air ahead, would you? Well . . . your company is just like that air carrier. You have a precious cargo and as the leader . . . the pilot, I'm sure you don't want to stop making progress. Why don't we see how we can work this out and get the product to you right away?"

"Well, if we've got tough times coming, maybe you ought to cut back a little. You see, I wasn't suggesting in the first place that you fill up all the shelves in your store. But, does it really make sense to do without the entire product line?"

"What do you think your competitors are going to be doing? According to what they tell me, they're going to try to get a bigger market share. They aren't going to do it by cutting back . . . they're going to do it by more aggressively going after your business. Let's you and I develop a plan where they won't be successful."

— Tactic # 107 —

More Specific Tactics for Handling Customer Objections

As we analyze your approach to overcoming objections, it becomes very clear that this part of the selling process is one best developed "under the gun" and through long practice.

The instruction given here is intended to short cut your trial and error process of learning. Further, it is my intention to take the experience of seasoned salesmen and give it to the new man who can then benefit by it, cutting the time that it takes the new salesman to learn and bringing him up to the level of an experienced professional. For this reason, and because so many "young" people have asked for a survey of techniques that work for the "old" pros, I offer the following tactics that should prove helpful:

1. **Before answering an objection, it's important that you listen, ask questions, and get feedback.** It is essential to get in step with the customer. Obtain an accurate understanding of the real meaning of his objection and then create a favorable climate in which to answer his questions.
2. **Offset the Objection.** With this technique it is entirely possible to agree with the customer's objection while at the same time mentioning other benefits that are known to be of greater importance to that customer. This, essentially, is the old "yes, but . . ." method. Now that is okay as far as it goes, however, you will find yourself tending to get into arguments with the customer. An up-to-date version of this method is to use empathy transition rather than simply agreeing with the customer by saying "yes." Here's and example:

   "I understand, others have felt the same way. However, they tried the product and they found . . . (list several benefits), they now feel that it is the best decision they ever made."

   Do you see what has happened? Instead of using simply the "yes, but . . .", you have used "I understand" as **empathy transition**. You have gotten in step with the customer. Then, you have used the words **felt**, **found** and **feel** to bring in some emotional aspects. After you tell the customer what somebody else has found, you list several benefits that customer will also get. By doing this, you are helping him find new information that is of benefit to him. So, the up-to-date version of offsetting the objection with additional benefits is a tactic in which you become a consultative salesperson, helping your customer make a decision about the things that are good for him.
3. **Use the "boomerang."** Many experienced salesmen use this technique for nearly every objection raised by the customer. I am not suggesting that it should be used alone, but with convincing application, it is very powerful. The idea is to show your customer that what he thinks is and objection to the product is actually a benefit. This, of course, presupposes that you know your product and competing products thoroughly.
4. **Use the "third party" method.** Report to your customer that another individual, despite his objection, bought the product and was glad he did. Use testimonial letters.

5. **Postpone the objection.** There are many occasions while talking with a customer that an objection could be postponed to your advantage. It could be done when an objection is really unrelated to the subject or when you intend to answer it later in your presentation. Postponing an objection can also be used **as an effective close to your presentation.**

   You may know the customer's only objection to your product is the one he has just mentioned. You may also have the answer to the objection. If this is the case, **you do not**, at this point, want to answer. It is much better for you to get your customer's permission to set the answer aside and continue with your presentation. As you continue, you get agreement on every point. As you prepare to answer the one objection that was postponed, ask your customer, "Mr. Customer, you have agreed with me on every point except . . ." You will then state the objection. Your next question is, "Then, if I am able to answer your question, are you ready to buy?" Get your customer's agreement and proceed to answer the postponed objection.
6. **Acknowledge the objection and continue.** It is not necessary for you to jump on every objection that is raised by your customer. You know many customers raise objections just for the sake of argument. Industrial salespeople who call on the same customer over a long period of time recognize the game the customer plays. Many customers, particularly professional purchasing agents, sometimes like to "get the fun out of" the salesman.

   Some customers just want to "pull your chain." This is just a part of the business of selling. For this reason, the best thing you can do is acknowledge a trivial remark and then just keep moving on with your presentation.

— Tactic # 108 —

The "R x R x S x S Formula"

There's is a formula that you can keep in mind as a good tactical approach to handling objections. It is the R x R x S x S formula which is a workable, general tactic for overcoming obstacles given to you in the form of objections or questions. Here's what the initials stand for:

R = Reveal
R = Reduce
S = Satisfy
S = Satisfaction

In order to use the R x R x S x S formula, you must first be able to relax when your customer raises an objection. Even sit back and physically indicate to the customer that his objection is heard and that it is being taken under serious consideration. The obvious physical relaxation also indicates to your customer that you are in control.

Even though you may not have the answer to your customer's objection, you have begun to work on the first part of the formula. You are allowing the customer to respond. You are allowing him to elaborate.

The second "R" stands for **reducing** perceptual differences. The first "S" stands for **satisfying** the objection and the last "S" in the formula means **satisfaction** in the mind of the customer.

To repeat, you are in the first step of the process when you **reveal** the objection your customer has. You must now quickly move into the second step which is to **reduce** the perceptual differences that always exist in every sales situation. Here, you begin to question your customer . . . to get him to talk all about the questions that he has raised. You may even know the answers to the questions your customer will ask. The idea is to get him talking. You want to get involvement because you are not just looking for an answer from the standpoint of information; but as you get your customer involved, you will learn certain things about the point under discussion. You will find out just how much knowledge the customer has in this specific area. You will be taking a reading on your customer's attitude and interest level, and you will determine whether the customer is strongly negative or slightly positive.

All of this information is immediately put into the computer of your mind and you are preparing yourself to respond to your customer's good valid objection. It is at this point, between reduction of perceptual differences and the attempt to satisfy your customer, that the objection becomes your "selling helper." You must be careful, however, that you have satisfied the requirements of the second stage before moving into the third. You must remember that reduction of perceptual differences means that you are interpreting everything that your customer says.

You must ask questions. You must listen carefully. You must interpret. You must ask more questions about the information you receive. You must listen again and subject the new information to further interpretation. Then, and only then, can you go on to **satisfy** the customer's objection, the third step in the process.

In the truest sense, you are now using the customer's objection as a selling helper. At this point, you must employ your skills of concentration. You must be able to stay with a specific item long enough and in enough depth so that it will influence your customer's behavior. In order to stay with a specific point in depth, you must draw upon your knowledge.

For example, the essence of your customer's objection may have been about delivery. At this point, you must concentrate all of your questioning and all of your responses to that area.

If the customer's objection is related to product features, your questions and answers must be focused in that area.

If your customer's objection is related to backup inventory, again, your questions and responses must stay in the area of adequate supply of his needs.

The categories I have mentioned, are merely suggested as illustrations. When you are selling a product, representing your company, you must be sure that you have adequate knowledge in all areas that relate to your products and services, and that would be of interest to your customers.

This third area of the formula could very well be the nut of your entire sales call. It could take a few seconds or could dominate the entire selling situation. It is through this R x R x S x S formula that you are able to change your customer's objection from a fearful comment to a selling helper.

Of course, once you have satisfied your customer's needs in the third area of the formula, you will automatically move into the fourth area . . . the final "S" . . . **satisfaction**, or writing up the order. The last area, then, is a perfect opportunity to change an **objection** into a **close**.

—— Tactic # 109 ——

Anticipate Objections

One of the best ways of being able to handle objections is to know what a customer is going to say. How do you do this? By presenting products, working with customers, fielding objections and handling them. When you are presenting a product, many times to several different customers, you will find that some objections or questions are common.

Suppose you had a common objection to your product because it was foreign manufactured. In that case, you would want to anticipate the objection and be prepared to say something like this, "I know a lot of people that feel the same way. Most of those people, however, buy a lot of Japanese equipment when they buy electronics. Also, they drink French wines and Columbian coffee. Here's the point . . . we do live in a world economy and every one of us use products from foreign countries every day. I suppose you might even have some sweaters that are made in another country. If all of a sudden you are targeting our product because it's not made in America . . . that is sort of inconsistent with the way the world operates today. Really, we have a great product at a great price. Does it make any sense to just let your competitors buy it."

"I consider myself to be a very patriotic person, too. It is true that this particular product is one that was manufactured overseas and is being distributed by my company. However, over 3,000 Americans depend upon my company for their living, They work for us. That's about as patriotic as you can get, isn't it? By buying this product, you support those Americans."

"I appreciate how you feel. I think I know who you are thinking of buying from . . . it's our competitor, isn't it? Well, do us both a favor and find out how their product is made. I think you're going to find out the only American part of it is its name and that all of the component parts were manufactured overseas and simply assembled in the United States. Now, since both of the products have foreign parts in them, I'd like for you to consider the most important part of all . . . value. Let me show you how you can get the most value from our product."

You see, when you are fully prepared to discuss an objection you know a customer is going to bring up, you've got a great chance of handling that objection and changing it into a strong selling point.

— Tactic # 110 —

Ignore the Customer's Objection

When I recommend this tactic, many salespeople give me a sideways look with a raised eyebrow. Keep this in mind, however; people act abnormally in selling situations. Most buyers are scared to death that they will buy. For that reason, their resistance is very high at the beginning of selling conversations. They are likely to throw out all kinds of resistance statements at the beginning of your sales call. It's very much like a person shopping in a retail store who is actually there to make a purchase. A clerk could approach and ask, "Can I help you?" The immediate response is often, "No, I'm just looking."

You know they don't mean that. That's just a defense mechanism . . . selling resistance. What they really mean to say is that they haven't yet lowered their resistance to having a conversation with a salesperson. They're also saying that they need a little time. They want the salesperson to be patient. They want to take a few moments to learn about what is offered. Your customers are the same way.

I have a Pomeranian who is one of the most pleasant, playful pets anyone could want. Yet, if anyone invades her barrier, such as another dog, she gives the appearance of being vicious with her barks and showing of teeth. She feels that the other animal is trespassing on her territory. This type of resistance or attitude is displayed by prospects all the time when a salesman seems to be invading the customer's territory . . . a barrier is raised.

When you detect a customer or prospect is simply defending his perimeter, back off a little bit. Don't try to answer the objection at that point . . . you could even cause an argument. Know that the initial "barks" are worse than the imagined "bites" that they are trying to project. Smile, simply state, "Let me get back to that" and go on with your presentation. It it's important to respond to the customer's comment, then **do** get back. If it really isn't important, drop it.

—— Tactic # 111 ——

Get Permission for a Late Answer

Whenever you delay responding to a customer's objection, you will be taking some of the strength from that customer's concern. Sometimes, you will handle it permanently as a result of the delay. You will find that your prospect eventually becomes very much involved in a discussion of the benefits he is going to receive and totally forgets the resistance. Most times, when you delay answering a minor comment of resistance, the customer will never mention it again. All of the features and benefits described by you will increase the value so much that it entirely cancels out the customer's concern.

—— Tactic # 112 ——

Answer the Objection Right Away

An opposite approach to the above is to get on the objection right away and provide an immediate answer right away. Do this when you think the objection is of major concern to the customer and might lose the sale if left unanswered. In these cases, if you hesitate or delay, you will simply magnify the problem in the customer's mind. You can use any of the tactics that have already been described.

—— Tactic # 113 ——

Six Quick Tactical Steps

There are six quick steps you can use to handle most customer objections. Combine this with the R x R x S x S formula, and you will have a winning tactical plan that will get you through some of the toughest situations.

All you have to do is memorize the six tactical steps and mentally follow your outline. Here they are:

1. Hear the customer out.
2. Get the customer to repeat his concern.
3. Rephrase the customer's objection to show you understand.
4. Focus and isolate the objection.
5. Tell a story.
6. Move the customer to action.

Hear the customer out — Think of what happens when an automobile tire gets a puncture. Eventually, it's going to go flat. That happens with customers, too. Once they have had an opportunity to express their objection, that objection tends to deflate itself. You can help this process along by being a good listener. Let the customer talk. Lean forward, indicating that you are extremely interested and concerned. Wait for the customer to wind down . . . to deflate. Now's your chance to go on to the next tactical step.

Get the customer to repeat the objection — The customer has already stated what was on his mind, but you want him to elaborate so that you fully understand exactly what he is thinking. Also, you will be demonstrating your interest when you ask him to repeat the objection. You want to say something like this to him, "I think I understand what you mean . . . but could you say it just one more time?"

Many times, when the customer does repeat, he will answer his own objection. You couldn't ask for anything more.

Rephrase the Objection — After you have heard out the customer, restate the objection to show the customer that you do understand. It also will make it very clear that you do not necessarily accept the objection as being the final statement. Beyond that, it gives you an opportunity to do a little more thinking about how you are going to handle the situation.

Now that you are in step with your customer or prospect, the two of you can work together on his concerns. You change from being a salesperson trying to put across your point of view into an "assistant buyer", there to help the customer with his problem. You are simply going to suggest a solution to that problem, instead of engaging in any kind of an argument with the customer.

Let's suppose the customer has expressed concern about service after the sale. You would simply say to the customer, "I believe I understand you . . . you are concerned about service after you buy our product . . . isn't that right?" When the customer agrees, you have an opportunity to talk about your excellent service, both past and present. You will be taking an objection and turning it into a selling helper. Before you do that however it is important that you focus and isolate the objection.

Focus and Isolate the Objection — We have already discussed the fact that there are two reasons the customer objects. One is the reason the customer gives you that sounds good and the other one is generally the real reason behind the "smoke screen." To quickly focus on the real reason and isolate that point in order to handle it effectively, ask the customer this question: "In addition to that, what other reasons do you have for not going ahead with the order right now?"

If there is no other reason given, then you go ahead and work on the objection the customer has brought up. By focusing on the objection and isolating it from all other concerns, the customer has told you that he is pre-sold and merely needs some help in this one area.

Tell a Story — It's always a good idea to remove yourself and the customer from your immediate situation by discussing a similar situation in the form of a story.

Remember that more objections are overcome by emotional responses than through logical conversations.

An example story will allow you to create situations in which your prospect can see himself based on another person's similar experience.

We are all imitative people. If a story relates, we seem to follow its conclusions.

Abraham Lincoln was noted for using stories to move people, persuading them of his point of view. One of his most famous examples was the one he used when he explained how he felt after being defeated by Douglas in a senatorial race. He said, "I feel like the boy who stubbed his toe. He was too big to cry and it hurt too darn much to laugh." See how easy it is to relate to that example?

Choose your stories very carefully in anticipation of your presentation. Try not to use them until your customer comes up with a common objection that you expect. When you do this, you will stand out from the field of mediocrity and you will close more sales as you handle objections.

When you have the customer in a good frame of mind after telling an example story . . . stimulate some action.

Move the Customer to Action — What is the only reason to answer the objection? Of course, it's to get on with your presentation and make a sale. The first five steps we described, if properly executed, will have moved you into a position where your customer is more willing to go ahead with your proposition than he is to turn it down.

It's at this point that you must have an **assumptive attitude**. The customer must see that you expect him to buy.

This doesn't mean that you suddenly turn away from being his assistant buyer and become a pushy salesperson. No, it means that you are indicating to him you understand all obstacles have been overcome and you are very happy to help him get what you know he wants.

—— Tactic # 114 ——

Handle the Hidden Objections

Hidden objections are some of the most important to anticipate. They are also objections that must be uncovered and handled. Often, these objections may not seem very important to you . . .but to the customer, they are **very important**.

So, how can you detect a hidden objection? When do you know that it's there, for sure? Well, if you've been selling for any length of time, you've probably seen dozens of examples in your own experience. Hidden objections usually follow a pattern something like this:

The sale is moving along smoothly, and everything seems to be falling into line. As you begin to reach the closing stages, however, peculiar things start to happen. You may notice a subtle change in your prospect's behavior.

Your prospect's voice may lose some of its firmness. He may get shifty and avoid your look. He may get fidgety, nervous, even contradictory. When you see this type of customer behavior, be alert. There may be a hidden objection.

Often, your best clue will come from something your prospect will say. He might begin to raise trivial objections, such as, "Well, what you say sounds good, but I'm not too sure that we have room for it on the shelf." He may doubt your ability to deliver and say something like this, "We're on such a tight schedule, right now, I doubt you could get the product here soon enough for your fall sale." Or he might not even be that definite. He might say, "I really can't put my finger on it, but somehow, I'm just not sure this is what I want to do."

When you hear these types of comments, your own good judgment will tell you that there's something wrong. Chances are, there's a hidden objection. In other words, rather than come right out and tell you what he is concerned about, the customer, for some reason known only to him, is throwing up the old smoke screen.

Let me make this one point, right now. If you are faced with a hidden objection that becomes a series of excuses, the very worst trap you can fall into is to treat these excuses as if they were real and valid **objections**. If you answer one excuse, the prospect will come up with ten more. If you answer all ten, he will think up a hundred others. Yet, you are duty bound to listen to your prospect and to take what he says seriously. What are you going to do?

The answer to that question is that obviously, you first must get the objection out into the open. How you do this will depend upon the nature of your relationship with your customer.

If the customer is an old friend, someone you have sold to several times before, go on with your presentation, but slow it down. Make an **obvious** effort to listen carefully to what he has to say. After three or four evasions on your customer's part, you must suddenly stop everything. Become perfectly frank with your customer. Come right out and speak honestly. Say, "Mr. Smith, you've enjoyed buying from us several times before. But I can tell by the way you're acting that there's something wrong. What is it? Just let me in on it maybe I can help."

Very often, you'll find that this simple sort of open honesty on your part will open up your customer. Of course, he doesn't want to hurt your feelings, but by re-establishing the man-to-man basis of your friendship, you'll find that he'll often talk fully and honestly. You have given him an opportunity to open up and let you in on what he is thinking.

Of course, all of your presentations won't be to old friends. Even in those cases, however, you can use a variation of this straight-forward honest approach on a new prospect when he is hiding an objection.

— Tactic # 115 —

Capitalize the Objection

This tactic is very similar to the "boomerang" method. You convert the customer's objection into a reason for buying the product . . . you reverse the conversation entirely. Here's an example:

Customer: "Your product is sold to all of my competitors."
Salesman: "You're right . . . that's why you really should consider carrying the product. It is well accepted by everyone, particularly consumers. They are looking for it. When you carry this product, you're going to sell more of it."

You see, you are reversing the customer's thinking. You are capitalizing on the objection he made. You can do this with many common objections that your customers and prospects have. This is not a difficult situation to create. Disadvantages to some people can easily end up advantages to others. It just depends upon your point of view. Here's another example:

Customer: "I'm already loaded up with the same type of product you're asking me to buy."
Salesman: "That's probably the best reason I can think of to consider buying our products right now."
Customer: "Why in the world would you say that?"
Salesman: "Well, you've already agreed that the reason you're so stocked up is because the product you're carrying doesn't move well. Just ask any of my current customers . . . they're finding they have to order more frequently than they ever did before. Our products are advertised and they are the most popular. You really deserve a line that's going to move for you and help you make money."

Customer: "I think you're right. Look, I'll go ahead and order your products and I'll get them on my shelf. At the same time, I'm going to make arrangements to return this other stuff."

— Tactic # 116 —

Simply Deny the Objection

Sometimes your customer isn't going to be too nice. He's going to make some comments that may be derogatory about you, your company or your products. He might even say something nasty about all three. When this happens, deny it very quickly and emphatically and get off the subject. Here's an example:

Customer: "I have heard that your company has a terrible service reputation."

Salesman: "Thanks for being so straight forward. For sure, that comment hurts me but I want you to know that it's absolutely not true. I'd certainly like to know where you heard that. Our service level is 97 percent against an industry standard of 91 percent. Even with that, having the best service level in the industry, we are striving to be better. Since you have this concern, I'm going to ask my company to send you all the statistics on our service level as we compare to the industry. How about that . . . will that help?"

Customer: "Well, sounds to me like you're pretty confident about your service . . . maybe the guy that told me that just had an ax to grind."

With all the tactics we've discussed so far, I'm sure you have enough ammunition to go out there and do a super job. However, your education would not be complete unless we took up some specific objections that I know you have either heard or are going to hear in the near future. We will list these objections and then give you some short comments full of tactical information you can use to handle the objections.

The answers I'm going to give you have been tested in field situations, numerous times. Use them with confidence.

— Tactic # 117 —

When the Customer Says, "Your Line Is Too Extensive . . . I Can't Handle It."

You say:

"I'll bet you haven't seen my line recently. If you haven't, then you can't possibly know how we have streamlined it to make it easier for our customers."

"Our line is actually merchandised in groups. You can buy it that way."

"I can help you select certain products so that you can make up your own line. That's why I'm here, to help you."

"You certainly don't have to buy all of it. I can put together a program that will help you merchandise just those items that you feel best relate to your customers."

— Tactic # 118 —

When the Customer Says, "I Suppose I Have to Buy a Certain Number for Inventory?"

You say:

"A very small minimum is the only restriction, but you will be able to sell that almost before your invoice is due."

"That's right . . . you only have to buy a minimum of one to get started. That makes it easy, doesn't it?"

— Tactic # 119 —

When the Customer Says, "I'm Too Busy."

You say:

"I knew you would be busy so I worked several hours to condense my comments to five points that I want to discuss with you. It will only take minutes to do it. Can we go over them right now?"

"I'm glad to hear that . . . that means you're the person I should talk with. A busy executive is one who's going to know the value of what I have to offer. I know you'll be glad you invested just five minutes of your time. Can I begin right now?"

"I understand . . .let's make an appointment right now for later."

"If we don't talk for five minutes, you're going to be too late to get in line for the best deliveries."

"I'm just like you . . . I believe in the value of time. I also believe in the value of my product and I know it can save you a lot of money. If you can just give me 15 minutes, I know I can show you how my product will save you $15,000. Do you have just 15 minutes?"

"I appreciate you feel you don't have time to talk with me. I'm wondering if you would say that to a customer that came to you with a big purchase order? Of course you wouldn't. What I have to say to you can make you just as much money as that purchase order would. In fact, I could probably help you make more money than you could make with your next 10 customers. Let me tell you how."

"If an investment broker said that he would give you a 30 percent return on your money and your investment was perfectly safe, would you give him a few minutes to show you his portfolio? I've got something that will do exactly the same thing for you."

"You would rather have me send the information? Well, I could do that, but it would take you two hours to read it. I can give you all the points in 10 minutes. That would save you 50 minutes over having to read the material. Let's discuss it now and save you time."

— Tactic # 120 —

When the Customer Says, "You Sell Too Many of my Competitors in My Trading Area."

You say:

"Because we do, we do extensive advertising and you can benefit from that."

"Our product is well accepted and you have built in demand that you can rely on."

"We don't oversell an area. Because there is so much demand for our product, we are able to create a velocity stream of products for all of our customers. We are going to open more accounts, and we were hoping you would be one of them."

"How many other major sources of supply do you have? I'm sure we are not the only supplier you are going to buy from."

—— Tactic # 121 ——

When the Customer Says, "I'm Busy, Talk to the Purchasing Agent."

You say:

"If my offer saves your company $15,000, should your purchasing manager be making that decision or should you?"

"Mr. Smith, if you received a letter marked, "Personal and Confidential", would you have your purchasing manager open it? Well, what I have is intended only for your consideration . . . believe me, this isn't something you want to share with anybody else right now. Can we talk?"

"We have always found this kind of decision cannot be made by a purchasing manager. It is always an executive decision and I'll need to cover it with you."

"This proposal involves the bottom line profitability of your company and it cannot be decided upon by a purchasing manager. In fact, it's my company policy that we do not talk with purchasing managers because it would be unfair to top management."

"It seems to me that what you're really saying is you don't think what I have to say is worth your attention. I guarantee it will affect your bottom line, and I know that is your key responsibility. If after you've heard me you still want me to talk with your purchasing agent, I'll be happy to do so, but past experience shows that that is never necessary."

"Well, I understand that you would like to put me off onto your purchasing agent . . . what I had to talk about is going to affect the bottom line of your company. If you still want me to talk to your purchasing agent, please have him give me a call."

"That's strange, when I talked to your purchasing manager, he said that this is something you should hear about."

— Tactic # 122 —

When the Customer Says, "I Want an Exclusive on Your Line in This Territory."

You say:

"That sounds fine with me if you are willing to absorb our total business in your area to maintain that exclusive."

"If you're afraid of competition, I can show you how you can beat them with an aggressive selling program."

"Okay, that's fine. Let's make arrangements where I can also be your only source for this type of product in your company."

"We have good years, sometimes bad years . . . just like in your business. For that reason, all business people need more than one resource. Don't you agree?"

— Tactic # 123 —

When the Customer Says, "Your Product Is Too Technically Complicated."

You say:

"Today's automobiles are extremely complicated, yet teenagers drive them. What exactly do you think is complicated about my product?"

"I know our product looks to be technically complicated, but it is actually very easy to use. It's my job to show you how easy. It will only take me about five minutes to do that and I'm sure you will be very comfortable. Can I go ahead?"

"At one time, people thought flying would be impossible. When the first airplane was invented, they thought it was too complicated to operate. Today, people are even flying ultralights. People even thought indoor plumbing was a marvelous, technical wonder. We both know all of these things are really simplistic. When you look at our product, you're going to find the same thing is true. You certainly wouldn't go to a business meeting on the West Coast on a horse and buggy. And I know you don't want to go back to outdoor plumbing. Let's look at how simple my product really is."

"We rarely ever hear that comment. What makes you think it's complicated?"

"You know, I'm not the smartest guy in the world. I learned to use this product in less than a half an hour and I'm sure it'll take you much less time."

"When you said that, I immediately thought of Mr. Jones across town. He thought it would be difficult to learn how to use our product, too. He learned it in less than an hour. I'm sure you would learn it much faster and in the process, you'll discover why it's the best value on the market today."

— Tactic # 124 —

When the Customer Says, "I Want You to Make Sure Everybody in Town Prices Their Merchandise Just as I Mark Mine."

You say:

"Both you and I would go to jail if we did that."

"Our products are nationally advertised and a list price has already been established."

"There is already a suggested retail price on the product. You can give discounts as you see fit. We are fair with all of our customers, when they buy our product, they own it. That is the American way . . . that is the free enterprise system . . . anything less would be unfair to everyone and un-American."

— Tactic # 125 —

When the Customer Says, "I Don't Like to Take Risks."

You say:

"I don't like big risks either. For that reason, we have designed our line of products to keep you virtually worry free. We guarantee our products . . . if something should happen, we service those products and you can talk to any of our customers . . . our products make them a lot of money."

"I'm glad to hear you say that . . . your biggest risk is not taking our products and losing everything you could get out of them. Let me explain what you get."

"I appreciate that. What would make you feel more secure?"

"It could be more risky for you not to get in step with the industry. What is the risk of falling behind your competitors?"

"I know it seems like a high risk to take on my line. For that reason, I'm going to give you my personal guarantee that I will work with you to make sure that everything goes smoothly and you are perfectly satisfied. How about that? Can we go ahead, now?"

—— Tactic # 126 ——

When the Customer Says, "I Just Buy Items. I Can't Take on Your Entire Line of Products."

You say:

"Good . . . I'm glad to hear that. We have a lot of items and they all go together."

"That's exactly what I want to hear. We have a lot of individual products to buy . . . you ought to look at every product in the line . . . let me show you."

"You really aren't going to be able to do justice to the line just by merchandising it as individual items. You can make more money by selling the basic product and then selling all the ancillary products and accessories that go with it. In fact, these accessory items will make you at least 30 percent more. Let me show how you can start out slow and then build up a real profitable business with our entire line."

—— Tactic # 127 ——

When the Customer Says, "Your Company Is Too New."

You say:

"This simply means that we're going to have to work harder to be as good as the companies you have been doing business with. I'm prepared to do that. Let's look at this one item where you can try me out."

"I know I can show you five good reasons why you should try us out. If you agree with those reasons, would you be willing to make a change?"

"I'm glad you are very loyal. That means once we start doing business, I can count on you to work with me as long as I take care of your needs **better than anyone else**. There are a lot of differences between my product line and the one you're buying. We have the best service record in the industry and, quite frankly, people who buy our product say everything about us is much better than the company you're doing business with now. Maybe we can start slow. Here are two products I know you would be interested in."

— Tactic # 128 —

When the Customer Says, "What If Your Products Don't Sell?"

You say:

"We don't sell on consignment, mark downs are just a part of doing business. I can help you merchandise the product. I can work with your salespeople and help you develop a promotional program."

"Merchandise the products with accessories. Sell them as a package. Overall, the total sale will be higher volume and more profit. I'll show you how to do that."

— Tactic # 129 —

When the Customer Says, "Your Quality Isn't as Good as It Used to Be."

You say:

"Give me some examples." (Get to the specifics and handle the problems.)

"What do you mean by that? We pride ourselves in making sure that our quality is the best in the industry. Could you give me an example?"

"You remind me of Mr. Jones in New York. He said the same thing and when we looked into the situation, it wasn't my product at all. He took the word of one of his tradesman who had been installing another product. Let's look into this and find out what the problem is."

—— Tactic # 130 ——

When the Customer Says, "I Tried Something Like Your Product and It Didn't Work Very Well."

You say:

"I know what product you're talking about. It was new and it wasn't tested. Our product has been in existence for 15 years and has proven its reliability. In fact, we have so much experience that our new models are virtually bullet proof. We unconditionally guarantee our product."

"I'm sorry that happened to you, but I can understand how you feel. Of course, that product is not ours. Let me explain the differences between the two."

"I've got hundreds of letters from satisfied customers. Let me show you a few that are right in your area. These people wouldn't praise our product if they didn't mean it."

"Haven't you heard that we are the Rolls Royce of the industry? Most people don't even try to compare us to the other products. Let me show you all the differences."

"I know you wouldn't like it very much if your company's products and services were compared with the worst offering in your industry, would you?"

"That's the position I'm in right now, so, would you please give me a chance to explain the differences between my products and everything else that is out there?"

"The product I'm going to show you today is far superior to what you tried ten years ago. Let me show you what's available today."

—— Tactic # 131 ——

When the Customer Says, "I'm a New Buyer Here and I Really Don't Like Your Company."

You say:

"You must have a reason for feeling that way. What is it?"

"Well, I respect your point of view. I'm sure you've looked at my company and others before you made that decision. I'd be interested in knowing why you decided against us."

"Are you telling me that your company doesn't need to keep their cost down and make more money?"

"Well, that's okay. Actually, we have more business than we can handle right now. Also, your closest two competitors have sent me an inquiry. However, if you want to change your mind, please give me a call."

"Well, I can understand that you must have a reason for feeling that way. Why don't you at least get to know me. We can get started right now."

— Tactic # 132 —

When the Customer Says, "Business Is Just Too Slow."

You say:

"Boy, I'm glad I came here. I know a way that will help you make more money."

"Do you think your slow period is going to go on forever? Well, fine . . . then maybe you'd be interested in talking to me about ways to increase business. Probably you need my product more now than you ever did . . . let me show you how you can increase your volume, improve your profit, at the same time 'reduce your hassle factor' and, in general, increase your business. Are you interested in all of that?"

"I work with customers who are in the same boat. I've got a program here that will help you improve your productivity. Are you interested in that?"

"That's one of my specialties. I've got a list of customers that have used our product to improve their overall business. In fact, all of them are busy right now when you are having your slow period. Would you be interested in learning what they're doing?"

"You know, even big companies have slow periods. Would you like to know how they overcome it? One of the things they do is selectively purchase. They cut back on unnecessary items but make sure they have the ones that are needed to keep their volume and profits up. Let me show you how our products do that?"

— Tactic # 133 —

When the Customer Says, "I Have to Talk to My Boss."

You say:

"What do you think you'll be telling him? I can help you out. In case he has questions, I can answer them."

"You know, making this decision is going to save your company an awful lot of money. Your boss will probably be very proud of the fact that you showed some good judgment in making the decision yourself. Why don't we go ahead and write up the order subject to his approval?"

"Do you think you should bother him with this? It isn't a real big decision. Can't you make this one yourself?"

"Okay . . . I'll just wait here . . . if he has any questions. I'll be able to answer them."

"There comes a time when everyone should surprise their boss with something that is good. This is one of those times. Why don't you go ahead and place the order and while we are preparing to ship it, you can explain to your boss how much money you are going to save."

— Tactic # 134 —

When the Customer Says, "I'm Not Interested."

You say:

"Well, I appreciate you think you're not interested . . . but I'm interested . . . in your reasons why not."

"Aren't you interested in making more money and cutting your costs at the same time?"

"You say you're not interested. That's something I don't hear very often. In fact, five executives bought this product last week and they all told me they weren't interested. They bought the product because they found out it would save them money and help them run their business more efficiently. Would you like to know why they made that decision?"

"I don't blame you . . . I wouldn't be interested either if I didn't have all the information. Let me explain some of the benefits you're going to get from this product."

"A lot of people say that just to get rid of salesmen. And sometimes I pass up a tremendous opportunity. I've got something that will help increase your bottom line by a couple of percentage points. I know you're interested in that. Is there a time when I should call back when it's more convenient for you to talk?"

Now you're armed. I'm sure that we haven't covered every objection that your customers are going to come up with for your particular product or service offering. However, this segment of the book has given you many tactics of persuasion that, when practiced, will create habit patterns. When these tactics become habits, you will be able to adapt them to new situations as they arise. And practice, you must. Start now. Get some customers in mind that you know have specific objections. Go back through the material you have read and design the answers. Then, go out and use your own tactics of persuasion.

You Must Be A Good Negotiator

For years, during the presentation of my seminars, I have been making a blunt, negative statement. Most people agree with this statement, but, of course, they want to know what to do about it. When I begin talking about negotiating skills, I try for shock value and state, "When salespeople know the cost of the product, the price will eventually degenerate to the lowest level possible to eke out a living."

Most salespeople **do** agree. Of course, they point fingers at the "other guy", commenting that he initiates the price cuts. Still, they also admit that they are looking for the bottom line because they ask the boss to give them cost and he frequently gives it. Then, they ask the question, "Is that the cost you're using, or is that 'cost, cost'?"

How long can we go on as salespeople using this type of tactic . . . selling the boss on cutting price? "How low can we go?" seems to be the negotiating skill level of many salespeople. It also sounds like a TV game show . . . one in which everyone loses.

—— Tactic # 135 ——

Don't Be an "Unskilled" Negotiator

The very second you were given the authority to make a concession to your customers, you accepted the role of a negotiator. Understand this does not simply mean price. You became involved in items such as specifications, terms of sale, delivery, and many others . . . where profits are made or lost. Today, the importance or negotiating effectively is so critical that companies literally succeed or fail on the basis of day-to-day sales negotiations. So, the first tactic is to get set . . . train yourself to be a negotiator.

— Tactic # 136 —

Someone Else Has What You Want, or Has Authority to Give It to You

The previous tactic was a matter of mind set, and so is this. You must realize that anything you want from a negotiation is owned by someone else or is controlled by another individual. We are not living in times where there is access to land through the Homestead Act, nor is there much opportunity for many people to go panning for gold, simply because it is lying around on public lands. In these modern times, the land is owned by someone and the mineral rights go with it or are assigned to another. This simply means that you must spend some time learning how to get what others own or control. How can you do this? Simply by making sure that in a negotiation, we help other people get what they want while they help us get what we want. It becomes a situation where both parties win and are happy with the outcome. So, in this tactic, realize that other people own or control what you want and you must help them get what they want in order to achieve your objectives.

— Tactic # 137 —

You Must be Sold on Negotiating

Even with the "mind set" goals of the two previous tactics, many salespeople still ask me, "Why do I need to learn negotiating methods? I'm hired to sell products and services."

Think about your customers and think about your suppliers. Do they practice negotiating? There's the answer. No matter how unsophisticated your customer, he has undoubtedly learned early in his business career to use "negative leverage" at the drop of a hat. It hasn't been too difficult for him, either. Basically, he's up against an **unskilled** individual who feels it's his task to do the bidding of the customer. A salesperson who continues using **just** persuasive communication regarding the features and benefits of a product or service is not dealing with the reality of the two previous tactics. He will eventually find himself going to his boss to cut the price.

— Tactic # 138 —

Make a Mental Commitment

Make a mental commitment to be an agent of change in this area of negotiating. If you'll do that, I will give you information that will help you become an excellent sales negotiator. The tactics I'll be describing in this chapter are used specifically to help improve sales volume, but just as importantly, you can use them to improve your net profit margin on each sale you make. Once you begin using sales negotiating skills, they will not only help you achieve the best possible deal for your offering, but they will also provide you with ways of doing that without causing win-lose situations to develop with your customers. **A mind set is necessary**. You must be committed to becoming a good negotiator in order to successfully complete all the tactics of this segment.

— Tactic # 139 —

Know the Difference Between Selling Skills and Negotiating Skills

Negotiating skills are never in conflict with tactics of persuasion selling skills. They are different, however, from the standpoint of emphasis. I've been able to identify three areas that should be given careful consideration before going into a negotiating situation with customers:

Area number one: Have goals — To be an effective negotiator, you must be highly motivated to set goals and achieve good results. You must feel that it's just as important to withstand the pressures of "negative leverage" being used by the customer as it is to present features and benefits of your product. You must start with the idea in mind that you are to achieve a **quality** sale as well as a **quantity** sale. You must consciously resist the tendency to lower your goals too quickly as you engage in a negotiation. This simply means you must be prepared. That's the next point.

Area number two: Be well prepared to negotiate — A critical element in successful negotiation is to make a commitment in terms of goals and then to have an extremely high "aspiration level."

In many cases, salespeople fail to achieve anything near their potential results during negotiations because they just do not set their sights high enough. A part of preparing for negotiations is to have a goal with high anticipation and to combine that with **knowledge**.

Area number three: Knowledge and skill — To be a good negotiator, you need certain fundamental skills. You need to grasp the difference between real bargaining strengths and assumed strengths. You should decide in advance how far you are going to bend and develop a feel for just when you should "give" in a negotiating situation.

— Tactic # 140 —

Commit to Learning These Five Skill Areas

Let's get very specific. In order to be a good negotiator, there are five action areas that you must learn to control. As we go on,, we will make each of these action areas an individual tactic for discussion. They are:

- Make an opening offer (or demand).
- Gather and use new information during the discussion.
- Establish credibility in the eyes of your customer.
- Use some effective counter tactics.
- Get a commitment.

— Tactic # 141 —

The Skill of Making the Opening Offer (or Demand)

This tactic is simply a matter of positioning the proposal you want to make. During my seminars on sales negotiation, I teach five basic points that I require the salespeople to memorize. With this outline in mind, they can prepare a sales negotiation **on the spot**. Simply having it written down on a piece of paper somewhere means that they can do a pre-call sales plan. Of course, this is something they must always do, but negotiating oftentimes means on location adjustment of a plan. For this reason, I insist these points be memorized. You must memorize them in order to visualize them as an outline in your mind as you negotiate:

- **Point One** — Open high.
- **Point Two** — Don't offer a detailed cost breakdown. To have opened high, you must have established a lot of cushion in your proposal.
- **Point Three** — Establish some elbow room to make concessions. Don't give away anything until it's absolutely necessary. This is true even if the "give" is a small item. It could be something that is needed as a bargaining point, later.
- **Point Four** — Mention an awareness of a customer's require ments and his needs.
- **Point Five** — Boost the customer's ego. Even during disagreement, never wound their ego.

So there's your outline, memorize it and apply it during every negotiation. Before we go on to the next tactic, however, I think you should also keep in mind two other important points:

- **Additional Point Number One** — Never narrow the negotiation down to one issue. Try always to have more than one topic to talk about. If you narrow the issue down to price, only, someone will win, someone will lose. But if you narrow it down to price plus various services that could be offered, you have the option of exchanging a lower price for the withdrawal of a service, or, holding your price and adding value through service.
- **Additional Point Number Two** — Understand that people don't want the same things. You will never be able to set up a win/win situation if you think your customer wants the same thing that you want. Don't assume price or delivery or terms or type of product is the only thing your customer wants. Many times, there is a matter of ego, long-term benefit, reduction of "hassle factor" and/or the overall growth of the business . . . all factors which motivate customers to buy or not buy.

—— Tactic # 142 ——

Get and Use New Information

It is very difficult to prepare everything you would need to know about a potential buyer's objectives and to know the tactics that he is going to use. Some of the information you gather in advance will be wrong, incomplete or may have changed by the time your negotiation is to take place.

Part of your advance planning must include some questions that are designed to gather tactically useful information. Often, negotiation is a matter of gathering and mentally processing information on the spot.

One of the things you must know about a buyer is whether or not he has a "**hidden agenda**" that could affect his willingness to sincerely negotiate. Now, by hidden agenda, I mean items of interest to the customer that do not necessarily relate to the business situation. They may not relate to the negotiation, but they could affect his attitude or his willingness to deal with you. A hidden agenda could be a personal matter such as his boss having "chewed him out" because of a previous negotiation. Internal politics could be involved where someone in his company might dislike someone in your company. There could be bad past history that you're not aware of between your two companies. Or, simply, some information could have been given to mislead you about what the customer really wants, needs or desires.

This type of hidden agenda will be as critical to the results of your negotiation as any of the logical business related objectives. Proper questioning will help you find out just where the customer stands and will go a long way to uncovering hidden objectives.

— Tactic # 143 —

Work on Establishing Credibility

It seems to me that a lot salespeople are so customer oriented they have become the "**customer's man**." In many cases, they are no more than servants on the job to do the bidding of the customer. Under these conditions, it is difficult, if not impossible, for a proper business climate to develop in which a salesperson can become an effective negotiator. To become a negotiator, the salesperson must have **professional credibility**.

One of the most critical aspects of success in sales negotiation, is your customer's perception of you, your company, and, ultimately, your proposal. Your customer must believe that you can actually **benefit him** through the process of negotiation. He must believe that the proposal is realistic and is of value.

So, how do you go about establishing credibility? Here are some "how to" tactics that are being used by salespeople all over the country who have become successful negotiators.

Facts and statistics — You always have the responsibility of **testing the validity of any fact or statistic that the customer will present**. Of course, the reverse is also true. (Customers have no problem with this.) Customers are always testing the validity of what you, the salesperson, has to say. You must equip yourself with any factual support materials available which could give credibility to the proposal you are making in the eyes of your customer. Support materials simply mean charts, graphs, testimonial information and other elements of proof that you can gather.

Sometimes you will find it difficult to predict the type of information that will cause a response in your prospect. For this reason, you want to have a collection of information that you could present and/or you might want to have the same type of information in different forms as a graph, or a series of testimonial letters.

If you find a prospect or customer is not impressed by graphs or charts, that would be wrong material to use. Some are more impressed over testimonial information in the form of collected comments or letters. Consider this, however, regarding the individual who is not impressed over statistical information . . . he might need some of this "overkill" just to get him to move at all. So, while showing your testimonial information . . . add the charts and graphs.

A salesman presenting a new line of kitchen products might say something like this. "Mr. Jones, I have a series of charts with supporting information which will give you the ten year history of the key indicators in kitchen products." In this case, the salesman would use information that is comprehensive and complete enough to help the customer adjust his thinking. This is done in an effort to give him the support he needs to get a decision from his boss to buy upscale kitchen products. He would then present the features and benefits of his own line and show the greater value of his products, using testimonial information.

As an effective sales negotiator, you will always carry more facts and statistical support than you will probably ever need.

Use the Industry Standard — "Yes, this is the standard warranty for this product according to the American National Standards Institute."

"Well, Mr. Customer, that is the standard discount policy in this particular line and we're really obligated to adhere to that."

By the two above examples, you can see that using the "industry standard" quickly establishes authority and credibility for the salesperson. It pretty much causes a "dead end" in the conversation, but it does allow for another type of concession . . . delivery, premiums, etc. At least, it protects price and profits. Use this when you want to eliminate price as the only negotiating point. Remember, when it narrows down to price as the only negotiating point, someone has to eventually lose. "Industry standard" or "company policy" will help you make a transition to the other negotiating points.

Keep this in mind, too . . . the issues in the above "credibility" comments might end up being negotiable. However, you have at least taken a negotiating stance without simply giving. Many times, your customer just needs a rational reason to back up or justify a price to which he has agreed. He may need to take this rationale back to his boss. He needs you to provide him with the negotiating stance necessary for his internal presentation. If standard industry practice is an acceptable rationale for him, then you should be using it.

Use Media for Credibility

"Mr. Customer, before we meet next week to discuss this job, I have an article from Forbes Magazine I though you might want to look over. It has excellent material describing the future demand for upscale building products. Some of the market research our people have been doing in this area is contained in this article."

An article from an industry magazine, or from some general business publication, about your company, your product, or service, will often impress a prospect. Any sort of information from respected sources such as a highly regarded independent research company, as well as some especially prepared presentations, should be used during your negotiations. These pieces should be introduced during a time when credibility is needed.

If you have done proper research, you could find out which trade magazines your customer frequently receives. Then, research those magazines for back issues containing articles that would support your company's position, your products, etc. Now, I don't think you should spring this on the customer right away, but use it as a "hold back" and bring it up when the conversation turns to the most opportune time. Just imagine the customer coming up with a specific point and you immediately say, "I'm glad you mentioned that . . . here's something I know you'll be interested in . . . I know you receive this magazine . . . here's an article that **exactly** supports our position, and . . ." This tactic is even more powerful when you use information from several different trade magazines that all support the same idea.

Establishing credibility is extremely important in negotiating.

Printed Documents and Labels — I really love this negotiating tactic for getting an initial stock order or moving excess inventory. It is a credibility item that causes action.

Suppose you have some excess inventory and you have called your customers that you know could use some of the capacity on a "contract" basis. Let's make this even more difficult . . . you are in a buyer's market and there is similar inventory available from a competitor. Let's make it even more difficult . . . your customers know of the similar inventory.

With all things equal, you must just be a better negotiator. Arm yourself with a tool . . . a printed document. Approach your customers with a preprinted, "standard contract" form. Have the terms and conditions spelled out in advance . . . **a blanket order**.

Be flexible. Your terms and conditions must be **negotiable**. The whole thing, however, adds a feeling of credibility to have the proposition presented in a "standard contract format." Whether it's excessive product, excessive services available, or simply a matter of trying to get a commitment for pre-season sales, a preprinted contract may just be a starting point for negotiation. It provides a solid base for credibility for product discussion.

When you have some product to get rid of, don't pass up the credibility value of using a "standard price" as a negotiating starting point. There's just something impressive about a preprinted form, contract, blanket order, or **price list** that makes it look official. It looks official, therefore, **credible**.

— Tactic # 144 —

Using Counter Tactics

So far, we have looked at some sales negotiation tactics and action. Now, it's time to look at the other side . . . the customer's side . . . and put emphasis on counter tactics.

Please note that I am separating **tactics** from **counter tactics** only for the purpose of illustration. In sales negotiation, the negotiator uses both according to the situation at hand.

Now, let's look at some situations that involve customer tactics, then we will look at a few of the counter tactic possibilities that you can use.

Time Pressure—Let's suppose it's late Friday afternoon. You have a heavy negotiation to sell a big order to a large commercial customer. You must reach a commitment within the next half hour or lose the opportunity. Let's be more specific . . . you are a refrigeration salesman and you are selling refrigerant. You have reduced your price from $1.40 a pound to $1.38 a pound and, yet, the buyer's threatening to conclude the negotiation if you won't reduce it to $1.36 a pound. This would be a penny below your minimum acceptable level. What do you do? Of course, I just selected a commodity product in the refrigeration industry. The same situation exists many times every day with commodity products in every industry. Play the role of the salesman.

If you decide the customer is bluffing, your counter tactic could be simply a patient rephrasing of your request for a commitment, taking care to avoid any blunt demands that could upset your customer. Or, if you decide the customer is going to place the order somewhere else, you could try for a combination of counter tactics. First, if there's a way to change the package as far as terms of payment, delivery schedules, future commitments, temporary warehousing, handling, containers or any other aspect, however minor, as long as it does not involve major expense to you, as the salesperson . . . now is the time you should offer it. Remember, earlier we said that we should not assume the customers all want the same thing. As you start offering some alternative "giving", you might find that one area is of interest to your customer.

Also, when you encounter this type of tactic . . . when the customer is trying to force you to make a major concession as a deadline draws near, it is often effective to make some kind of rational appeal. Talk about the damage that giving into his demands would cause between you and your sales management. Talk about how your sales management would feel about him when future situations require that you really go to bat for him with your own management. Let him know that this could develop in negative relations developing and that it's not really worth that happening.

Another counter tactic is to play on his ego. Simply state that you have always felt that he had a good "reputation for reasonableness" and that you are truly surprised over his demands at this time.

In general, there are two things that should be avoided in this type of situation with commodity products:

1. Don't make a concession before the briefcase has been closed and before the "final" handshake has taken place. You see, you can always turn around when you are walking out the door and agree to some small concession at the last moment. This just might do the job. The small concession could help the customer "save face" when he really did not want you to go.
2. Don't avoid holding something back for the last minute concession if it is necessary as a counter tactic against the heavy time pressure tactic.

Here are some other ways to respond to the deadline that an opponent dictates . . . it's a checklist.

- **Never laugh, smile or grimace**. Your customer could interpret your body language as a put down to their demands.
- **Always look seriously pensive**. To be a sharp negotiator, you must write down the deadline the customer imposed and say, "Let me make a note of what you said." You want to convey to the customer that you are taking his demands seriously. Of course, at this point, you will not try to change the demand, or the deadline.
- **Talk to yourself**. Say something like this to yourself, "There it is, the deadline." When you say that, you will not panic or become terribly effected by the time limit imposed by the customer.
- **After responding to the deadline, continue negotiating in another area**. Once you have responded to the dead line and written it down, use body language and quicken the pace of your presentation to suggest that you are speeding things up . . . talk about other areas that could be considered in the negotiation.
- **Wait Til the Last Second**. No matter what the time demand involves . . . minutes, hours, or days . . . don't put your re sponse counter tactics to work until just before the deadline.

In general, you will want to let your customer expect that you intend to honor his demand one way or another before the time runs out. Keep building the value of your proposition and then use your counter tactics at the very last moment.

High Opening Demands—You always want to make a high opening offer. Customers also use this tactic. So, what do you do? Your customer makes high opening demands in the form of low price, specifications that are nearly impossible to meet, or near-impossible demands on service. When this happens, it's time for you to use the counter tactic of **emotion**. You should express some frustration to indicate to your customer that you feel that he is a bit out of line.

Emotionalism works in many cases as a counter tactic where a customer is just testing you. Of course, you have to come across as being totally sincere. It will only work if your customer has a sense of fair play and, of course, other issues in your relationship are basically good.

One of the best ways to counter tactic this type of approach is to have your own high opening demand. In this way, you can negotiate with an attitude of "Let's explore this thing together." No matter how hard-nosed the customer appears to be, if he could be persuaded of the value of your proposition, he will generally settle on some mutually acceptable agreement.

Changes in the Package —You need some good counter tactics for this situation because it's one the customers love to spring on you.

Here's something the customer might say, "John, we like your product and we think the price is at a good level. However, we have to have a faster delivery schedule and you guys don't seem to be willing to do that."

Your counter tactic would go something like this, "We definitely want to work that out with you, Henry. I see you have three phases to the job. We could deliver the first phase out of our inventory and then within three weeks, take care of phase two, and in six weeks, phase three."

Get the customer to agree that your proposal would suit him just fine. Then you go for a little extra. "Okay, the delivery out of stock will certainly take care of your immediate needs and the service charge is only an extra five percent. Shall I call in and have it shipped immediately?" Now, you're not negotiating on special delivery terms so much as on how much extra it is going to cost the customer. And, of course, if the customer totally wins this last negotiating item, he's going to feel great. There's nothing wrong with that if you can afford it. He will still feel good if he negotiates you down to three percent or two percent.

Many times your customer will use this "package change" tactic at the last minute, once a deal has been set. He will often surprise you by continuing the negotiations in many unorthodox ways. Here are some examples:

"How could I have been so stupid . . . I counted on a big order, spent thousands of dollars on setup charge and the buyer called to cancel. He said one of his officers had a cousin in China who cut our price by 50 percent."

"I gave up a good job I had for ten years to take a position with a company as their sales manager. Then, the company was bought out and I was asked to leave."

"It was the biggest order I had ever gotten. I counted on my commission being $25,000. I counted on their promises . . . I believed in them. I bought a new car that I can't pay for."

"Everything was signed, sealed and delivered. Then the customer called and said they couldn't pay for it. The customer said, 'So, sue me.' Of course we're going to sue, but meanwhile, our cash flow in going to suffer, putting us into a disastrous position."

Okay, how do you handle these last minute package changes? I know these are real "horror stories" but they come from actual incidents that did occur. It would seem that you can do practically nothing about these situations, however, there are some counter tactics that could be used to get yourself in a better position.

I'm going to get personal here. Throughout my years as a salesman, a marketing executive, a consultant, and a trainer, I have always operated under a philosophy of "running scared." I know that sounds paranoid, but it works. When you are making deals that could affect you in a dramatic way, you must be slightly paranoid in advance.

You will notice that in each of the examples the people who were hurt relied on the performance of the other individual. They weren't "running scared." They failed to think about what would happen if the other individual would not perform. My running scared philosophy contains a sub-philosophy of, "Most people don't do what they say they're going to do." When you stop to think about it, you know that's true.

If the people in the examples had thought that way, they would have provided themselves with some alternative action. Here are some tactics they could have used:

Situation Number 1 — If you get a huge order, that's nice . . . be excited about it, but do not spend money in anticipation of performance by the other party. It's a matter of staying ahead of the customer. Make sure the customer builds a history of performance before you decide that you can make an investment in his performance track record. In my consulting business, I make sure I get enough of a down payment to cover at least the first one-third of my anticipated activities with the client. If they aren't willing to do this, I'm better off spending my time recruiting other clients or going after other orders. You must do the same thing as a professional salesperson and negotiator.

Situation Number 2 — You can't really know how a new employer is going to perform. Anytime you make an important career change, you must think about a fall back position. Indeed, using the "running scared" philosophy, you must actually anticipate nonperformance by the new employer. In the business world, there is a phrase known as the "Golden Parachute." Now the "Golden Parachute" is a legally binding statement that gives you some guarantees in case your terms of employment are not met exactly the way you had agreed up front. So, how do you approach this matter with a new employer without turning him off? Well, simply say, "I am very anxious to be working with you because I feel that you are the number one organization in this industry. However, suppose you are personally struck by lightning tomorrow. Where would I be without a record of our conversation?" (This actually happened to an executive friend of mine as he was getting off an airplane).

Situation Number 3 — If you have a fee coming or a commission, make sure it's not in verbal form. This applies especially if you are counting on the money in a personal way that's going to affect your immediate or long term future. It's too important to leave to chance. Make sure the terms are recorded, legally, or before you perform your service. Simply tell the other party exactly why you are doing this. It's very important to you that there be no slip ups. My father used to say to me. "There are many a slip between the cup and the lip." And then, of course, he would add not to cry over "spilt milk." Yes, it's all a part of the "running scared" philosophy and a belief that "most people don't do what they say they are going to do."

Situation Number 4 — Anytime you have made a deal that involves delayed payments, installments, etc., never rely on the fact that you can sue the other individual. In business situations, going to court is just not the most practical "fall-back" position. We all depend upon revenues coming in to take care of our business so that we can handle payments due our own suppliers. Depending upon legal recourse in making decisions, will leave you vulnerable in the event the other person fails to perform. Always anticipate nonperformance and avoid committing yourself to the spending of money before you have it at hand. If the business is too costly, from the standpoint of up-front investment, you must pass it up and spend your valuable time and skills acquiring a more favorable deal, elsewhere.

Three Tips for Handling Surprises

Make it a big issue — It doesn't matter if it's really a big issue or not. When your client, customer or other individual springs a surprise on you, you want to make that person "pay the price" every time they act in this way. Slow down the negotiations. Ask as many questions as you can about the surprise. Express how you feel it's an unreasonable position. Jab every time you can. Ask questions like, "Why would you do that?" "What in the world makes you bring that up?" "When did we ever discuss that?" "What makes you think that would even be considered?" "Why would I ever want to do that?"

Hit them with your own surprise — Say something like this, "Well, if you want that, I suppose I am going to have to . . ." You see, you turn it into an exchange of values. Again you are showing if he gets what he wants, he's going to have to pay the price. Now, you have to be very careful that you're not appearing to say, "You're trying to get me so that I'll get you." Simply take a little time to go over the surprise demand and develop a new strategy which asks for something you need as an offset to what he wants.

Increase the value so it's a "big deal" — In some cases, what the customer wants is not really a big deal for you or your company. When this happens, don't immediately say, "Oh, that's easy." You see, if you put it that way, you decrease the value of what he is getting. Pause, think it over, and say something like, "Well, this isn't something we would ordinarily do, but if this will bring us to an agreement, then I suppose it's okay." Be reluctant. Don't jump into it. Be sure your customer feels that he is a **winner**.

Ego attacks and massages — Many buyers will try to work this on you. The purpose of ego tactics by a skilled customer negotiator is to, obviously, gain a concession by way of a non-rational influence. Many salesmen fall prey to this tactic. The counter tactic has to be one that will move the bargaining back into a rational decision making or problem solving situation. So, this would involve the universal counter tactic of **patience**. It would also call for a series of questions that would help you probe and focus on relevant information.

A buyer who is skilled in negotiation will always try, at one time or another, to work on your ego. He will also try various ways of working on that ego. They are not all going to be positive. Often a skilled buyer will use **negative leverage** that is intended to put you on the defensive.

You must always keep in mind that emotional influences will tend to destroy your bargaining position. Focus on the business details. I've met many buyers who are excellent negotiators using the "nasty" approach to attack ego. They get away with it because they are dealing with unskilled negotiators. Really, when you think about, this is one of the easiest tactics to overcome.

The more subtle ego pressures, both stroking and attacking, require self-discipline. Avoid giving away your previous concessions. The "nice guy" negotiating customer is after the same thing as the nasty one . . . maximum concessions from you to benefit himself and his company. Discipline means you must stick to your preplanned call and use all of the negotiating tactics that you had previously decided would work with this customer. Of course, as you discipline yourself, you must also be patient as your customer keeps pressing through stroking or negative leverage.

Let's take a little closer look at this **negative leverage**. A salesman walks into the customer's office prepared to talk about a new job. He's greeted with this comment, "John, the products we got from you last week didn't meet the performance requirements that I told you I needed. I think your company should pay me for all the losses on this job!" In this situation, the contractor never said anything about using the product in a situation for which it was never designed. And that, of course, is the reason it didn't perform the way he wanted it to.

So, in this case, the counter tactic should be set on a **high objective**. The high objective should be something like **no reimbursement**. And, of course, you would clearly state your position at the beginning. Remember, "start high." Eventually, to save the account, a salesperson may have to very slowly and diplomatically concede a bit. However, it's absolutely necessary to start high so as not to lose entirely. The customer knows he's wrong, but he just isn't going to admit it.

The customer must be convinced in this situation that any adjustment is going to be a **real favor** to him since he misused the product in his application.

Too many salespeople fail to learn that when a customer gets himself trapped into this kind of situation, he is going to try all sorts of "mind blowing" claims and tactics to get that salesperson to negotiate with him. Actually, the customer's got himself in a jam and really needs the salesperson to help him get out of it. At the same time, he needs to save face. So, calmly, gently and with a lot of patience, investigate the situation, maintain your discipline and help the customer without extraordinary cost to your own company.

You cannot let the customer fool you into making expensive concessions.

Test the tough guys — Sales negotiation is an art and a process in which you must participate to come out ahead. This is always true when the negotiation results in a win/win situation for both your company and the customer. Customers like to use intimidation tactics. Many of them will take the "tough guy" approach. Why do they do this? Simply because they've learned over the years that by using that tactic, they can get everything they want from inexperienced, unskilled salesperson negotiators.

In the situation where the customer is being a "tough guy", you should **always** negotiate. Again, you should use patience, some facts, ego boosters, and as many counter tactics as you can think about until you discover the right combination to bring a "tough guy" around. The idea is to not give in to intimidation. In fact, if you are going to have repeated contact with a customer who uses intimidation, he will gain respect for you and change his tactics. He won't change his tactics with everyone, but he'll change them with you. On the other hand, if you give in to intimidation, he will increase the use of that tactic and make your relationship with that customer, eventually, unbearable.

Counter tactics can and should be planned. For the most part, however, they must be learned and practiced so that when situations come up in a sales negotiation, they can be smoothly used. As a sales negotiator, you must learn to anticipate what customers are going to say and develop a response to every situation that will change that situation from a problem in to an opportunity for you to close the deal.

— Tactic # 145 —

Gaining Commitment Through Negotiation

Many salespeople do a great job of preparation and they make nice smooth sales presentations. However, some of them just can't seem to close a sale. The same thing seems to be applying to selling negotiations, but unfortunately, it is a more subtle and oftentimes more costly situation.

The purpose of a sales negotiator is to gain "a highly desirable" commitment from both sides . . . not just to gain a **commitment**. The real difficulty is that most salespeople who have authority are not the people with negotiating skills. They gain commitment, much to the satisfaction of the buyer, but not necessarily to that of their own company.

Let's look at a situation and see how well this salesman does.

Salesman: "Okay, Jack, we agree on the price . . . you said the dating terms were fine and our deliveries will meet your schedule. It looks like the only thing we have left now is to talk about the warranty period.

Customer: "Yeah, and this is where the problem comes in. We have to have two years on this instead of the one year your factory gives. One year never has been, and is not, now, acceptable."

Salesman: "I appreciate what you're saying, Jack, and if you were using the units indoors, we wouldn't have that much exposure. We could go along with your two year warranty on parts. But, I just can't sell a two year warranty to my management for a year round outdoor installation of that condensing unit. You are going to subject it to salt air, high winds and a lot of moisture. No company would expect their equipment to perform under those conditions as if it was inside and protected from the elements."

Customer: "You know, I only see you once a month and I was hoping that we could wrap this up on this visit. Looks like we're not going to be able to do it because I know my boss won't go with a one year warranty."

Salesman: "Jack, you said our price is competitive. The three point payment schedule is acceptable to us. In turn, you agreed to spreading the deliveries over six weeks. Now, with all of that, we've got a deal that's good for both of us. You know that no other manufacturer is going to give you two years. Why let that warranty issue block the rest of this agreement?"

Customer: "I agree with you. Why don't we compromise and just write it for 18 months?"

Salesman: "Jack, you've negotiated probably the best agreement I've offered any customer in many years. Again, the price is right, the terms are right, the delivery schedule is right, and I'm offering all that to you because we trust you and we know that your company will make the payments on schedule and, of course, you'll treat us right within the warranty conditions. Extending that warranty, though, is something I can't bend on because of your installation conditions. That's something you decided upon yourself."

Customer: "Would you really leave here without the order?"

Salesman: "I certainly don't want to do that. However, I just can't give on that . . . it's absolutely impossible."

Customer: "Okay, you're right, nobody else will give us the two year warranty. We're just going to have to live with it."

Salesman: "Hey, that's great. Let's go ahead and okay the agreement."

Customer: "Oh, incidentally, could you throw in a set of those manifold gauges?"

Salesman: "You bet we can . . . we'll pack them in with the first shipment. Here's a copy of the price list for those, along with a set of instructions."

This is not idealized fiction. It actually happened. The salesman won his point by being patient and persistent. You will also notice that he was disciplined when he kept reminding the customer of all of the concessions he was getting. It was impossible for him to give in on the warranty.

Please notice that at the end, the customer tried to get a free set of manifold gauges, and the salesman said he would certainly put them in the next shipment. Then he gave the customer a price list. He answered the negotiating tactic with a counter tactic.

Here are some key points to remember in gaining commitment during negotiation.

Decide if you really want to reach the agreement. You should assess what you learn from a negotiation based on whether or not the payoff for your company is going to be marginal. You must decide whether or not your company has the capability to deliver **profitably** everything that has been negotiated. If you find you have been negotiated or bargained into an unacceptable level of projected net profit or cash flow buying,

reassess your position. If you don't feel your position is acceptable, you should back out before the final handshake. There's nothing wrong with you saying to the customer. "You know, when I think about this whole thing, this is really not a good deal for my company. We would have to buy an inventory $50,000 worth of products that you're going to take over ten months. Our cost of handling far outweighs any profit we would make. I think we have to look at you taking more of the inventory and paying for it in advance."

Avoid splitting the difference. Many customers use this in a very clever way. They will try to suggest that in order to wrap things up, why not just split the difference. **Never**, I repeat, **never** immediately agree to split a difference. Neither is it a good deal to simply strike some kind of an average. When a customer wants to split the difference, he is already mentally past the point of purchase and he is simply trying to get a little extra. Remember, an offer to split the difference is **always** an opportunity to negotiate . . . it is not a time to **give**.

Summarize benefits. I suppose we are back to basic salesmanship. Summarizing benefits is always good salesmanship at the close of a sale. So, why not do it at the close of a negotiation? Of course, you must not jeopardize getting commitment by spending a lot of time on summarizing the benefits. The right amount of time, with the right amount of conversation, is appropriate.

Summarizing benefits helps to put a customer in a positive mood. It might just be enough to push him over the hump in a negotiation. It is also good psychology. The harder the bargain being driven, the wiser it is to make the customer feel satisfaction.

Summarizing benefits the customer is going to get from a transaction is extremely important to customer ego satisfaction. If you have gained a price level which is in your favor, you must stress the value the customer is receiving and make him feel that he is the overall winner. If you receive a short-term advantage in the negotiation, you must remind the customer of the long-term benefits to his company and point out what a smart decision he has made.

Ask for commitment. This seems to be another tough one for salespeople. It's almost as if they fear, after being through a negotiation, they don't want to tempt fate by asking for a conclusion. They hesitate, pushing for closure. Twenty percent of the time, after negotiation, the customer will initiate action. Twenty percent of the time, the salesman initiates action. Sixty percent of the time, nobody does and the negotiation is left hanging.

Often the customer will simply decide to buy from someone else and will do so at the negotiated level. In that case, you will have done the work and another company will have gotten the advantage. So, how can you ask for a commitment? Just ask for it . . . of course!

After negotiation, however, you must be careful you don't give in to a final demand by you customer. Again, you must have a counter demand ready just in case.

Closing the negotiation on details. The negotiation basically is over and everyone feels that they have won. Now the order has been signed and your job has been complete. It's simply a matter of the shipping people carrying the ball. Is that right? Not really. In order to get agreement from the customer, there were probably some details that you did not discuss just so you did not delay a successful conclusion in the negotiation.

These details are not a matter of oversight and it's not a matter of side stepping some operation situations. Legitimately, details that don't directly relate to the main agreement are generally not discussed. Still, they need to be attended to in order to make sure the commitments are met.

These details are such things as, "Okay, I'll have the order typed up and sent to you in two copies in tomorrow's mail." Or, "Susan will send you the modified specifications on Friday." In this manner, you see that the successful sales negotiator always makes sure that he ties up loose ends.

— Tactic # 146 —

Getting Back to Price

As we leave this area on negotiation, I think it's important to get back to the basic issue of price and give you at least six more tactics that you can employ.

Remember that before negotiation, you really don't know how high you can make a demand. Unless you're selling a commodity product, you usually don't have the time or the money to test market what your merchandise will bring in a controlled, accurate analysis. So, depending upon what you're selling, you're going to test your market customer by customer, in rather informal ways. This is going to let you know what you can reasonably charge for your product and/or services. Still, you really can't be sure in a given circumstance. Oftentimes a product or a service will bring more money when a customer perceives a greater value.

Finding the right price for your offering, in many cases, amounts to a guessing game. Until you ask the customer, you have no way of knowing. Thomas Edison faced this situation when he sold his telegraph system. He was afraid to ask as much as $5,000 for the invention. When he was asked, he stuttered and hesitated, and finally the buyer said, "Well, how about a hundred thousand dollars?"

Well, we may not be just that fortunate with the type of product or services we have, but the point is not to sell yourself short when negotiating.

Think of timing. Buyers take time to shop around. What about you as a salesperson? Shouldn't you take time to shop around and find customers who are willing to negotiate a higher price with you? The more time you have to shop around for buyers, the greater will be your chance of receiving a higher price. Stating it another way, not being in a big hurry to negotiate can actually pay off. I have mentioned this several times previously when I suggested there's time to close down a negotiation and go out and find another client or prospect.

One good way of getting the most for your merchandise is to have several negotiations going on. When you've got a really great product (and you should believe wholeheartedly in the item that you're selling) you end up in a situation where you actually have customers bidding against each other. Of course, they won't realize that, but you will be keeping track of the negotiations and making decisions on who you are going to sell. This even applies in situations where you are setting up wholesale distributors to handle your product. There are some that are willing to pay more in price and also to offer you more in a valued relationship by the way you do business. You decide which is most beneficial to you. You see, again, you must take the time to wait until you get more than one individual is willing to give you over the other.

Let's face it, even when the price is the same, there are some people you would rather do business with than others. This is **value added** for you, the salesperson.

When we consider timing, we also see that it can influence price increases and decreases. Situations will affect you. For instance, you could have secured the business, on paper, but a competitor comes in and offers it at a lower price. One way or another, you're going to have to adjust . . . negotiate. If you're selling a very expensive item, interest rates may have risen. You have to deal with this. Executives may change in the company you are selling. As the executive moves into his new job, he's going to want to look at anything that requires the use of company money. Buyers may even change their mood.

You see, negotiations are affected on a day-to-day basis. Timing is extremely important. You need time to get the best price for your product, but time can also work against you if you delay too long and have outside circumstances effect the deal. Again, selling is not just a science . . . it is also an art.

As we close out this segment on negotiating, then, here are some tactics that will help you achieve more, relative to price, while you are negotiating:

1. **Get agreement on everything else** — Try to get agreement on everything else before you handle the price issue. At the same time, have some concessions in your back pocket so that price doesn't become the only situation where someone has to be the loser.
2. **Don't worry about price till you've gained other information** — When you look at other agenda items, other than price, you are going to get insight into your customer's mood, his character, his wants, needs and desires. You're also going to find out if he has the ability to pay and the authority to make a decision. It's not necessary to worry about price until all of these things have been covered.
3. **Qualify the buyer** — Actually you are in the process of qualifying the potential buyer to see if he has interest and is capable of coming to an agreement on the issues. Once you have qualified him in regard to everything else on the agenda, you are ready to explain the value of the proposition and get your price.
4. **Don't give up** — Many times your customer is going to insist on a price that is below your minimum. That's not the time to give up. He's probably "just fishing." Instead of giving in, try to give less product for the same price or try to get some add on material at a higher than normal price to make up for your deficiencies. Keep the calculator out.
5. **Talk price first** — Okay, if he insists, take the opposite approach. Sometimes it's easier to climb down from a high price than it is to go up. If he wants to talk price first, say, "Okay, my price is . . ." In this case, you quote him a much higher price than you ever expect to get. Following this, it's the customer's job to beat you down and you let him go just so far.
6. **Let the customer reject the high price** — When the customer rejects your high price, make him drag you down. Now, if you know you could go down ten percent, don't do it all at once. Go down one percentage point at a time. As you drag your feet on the issue, your customer will often get tired. Also, once you have gone down three or four times, he feels as if he has won. Don't be impatient. Generally, using this method, you will end up at a much higher price than you initially expected.

As you become an agent of change and learn to use tactics of persuasion, you will find that you automatically will be a skilled negotiator. Negotiating is a continuous cycle of planning, face-to-face deal making, and then follow-through. During the follow-through stage, you begin planning for the next go around. You will set your strategy for future negotiations. It is through this process that you will become a skilled, effective, successful negotiator.

SECTION III

Features, Benefits, Proof and Value Presentations

I love conducting open forum conferences in which salespeople can ask any question, seek the help they feel they need, and, generally, work to solve problems. During these sessions, one of the most frequently asked questions is, "What is the best way to present my products so that the customer really wants it?"

I don't mean my answer to be short, but I usually start with, "Get them to first Mentally Own your product."

For those of you who have read this book so far, that will come as no surprise. I've repeatedly stated that a customer must first mentally own the product before he will physically take it. This being so, the logical question has to deal with how we get him to do that. The answer has to be simply the proper tactics of presentation. These tactics will involve explaining the features and the benefits of the product and giving the customer some proof that what you say is so. In addition, it involves proper presentation that employs all the customer's senses in such a way that he mentally receives the product at its highest value producing level.

All of the tactics in this chapter, then, are put forth to accomplish those goals. Let's begin with feature and benefit presentation.

— Tactic # 147 —

When You Sell Features, People Think, "So What?"

Imagine this situation. A retail salesman is trying to sell a chair. He says something like this:

"You have certainly come to the right place for a chair. Here's a real beauty. This chair is made of selected hardwood. See these arms . . . they've been sanded real smooth . . . then stained and shellacked. Here! Feel them. That seat is extra-firm, inch-and-a-half, double-ply foam rubber. Notice all this cross-bracing under the seat . . . from one leg to another. Look at the back. It's curved in toward the seat real low."

Well, that's feature selling. I'm going to assume that the salesman covered all the features of the chair. He talked about the kind of material, the arms, the cross-bracing, the seat, the back. However, he didn't tell his customer what those features would do for that customer. He didn't tell any of the **benefits** to him if he bought the chair. He simply told the customer, "Hardwood arms, sanded, stained . . . seat-foam rubber . . . legs-cross-braced . . . back-curved low."

So what?!

Maybe the customer perceives that distressed look pine furniture is what is wanted. Perhaps a lacquered finish means more. Maybe cross-braced doesn't mean a thing. Perhaps the image of a low curved back is negative and not positive. **Features don't sell.**

The customer doesn't really know what the individual features mean in terms of what that customer will get if he purchases the chair.

— Tactic # 148 —

Use Benefits to Get into the Customer's Mind

Let's try it a different way. This time, with the knowledge of the features, we are going to talk to the customer about the benefits that would be received from buying the chair. As a salesman starts to present benefits, he would say something like this, "Mr. Customer, because this chair is made of selected hardwood, it will give you years of service. Unless you or your kids take an ax to it, this chair will last you a lifetime. Here, sit down in it. How about that? Isn't this chair one of the most comfortable chairs you ever sat on? There's a lot of foam rubber there and that means after you've been sitting in it for a long time, you won't feel like you've been riding the range all day. Now, settle back and get real comfortable. How does the back feel? Feels good, doesn't it? Because it has a curved back, it will fit right in the small of your back . . . gives you real good support. You can sit there and be comfortable for hours on end without getting a pain in your back."

"Now, lay your arms along the length of the chair arms. They are comfortable, too, aren't they . . . and they keep your arms at just the right height for perfect relaxation, don't they?"

"Now, rock your body back and forth a little. See that! The chair is rocked firm. It has cross braced legs and that means it's going to be solid for years because the bracing ties it together from every angle. It's steady and firm. It doesn't jiggle. Not only does that make it more comfortable . . . it's another sign that you will make a good investment with this chair."

In this very simplistic example, you are able to see the difference between feature selling described in Tactic 147 and benefit selling described in Tactic 148. When the customer buys the chair, he doesn't buy hardwood, sanded arms, foam rubber and braced legs. He buys years of comfortable, relaxed sitting that will support his back.

Of course, the customers want to know what makes the product tick or what it's made of. But these tend to be supporting elements to benefit selling. The customer wants to know why the product will do the things you claim it will do and that's the reason you give some **proof** elements every time you give a feature and a benefit. We'll talk about proof in the next tactic.

Here's another story that will point out the impact of using the **right benefits** with customers.

When Bendex Corporation brought out the first washer-dryer combination, they got it out to all the dealers and promoted it enthusiastically. Their sales didn't come up to what they expected, so they checked with their dealers to find out what was wrong.

They found out that their sales were very good when a woman came in alone. They were also good when a man came in alone. However, when a man and wife came in together . . . and that happened most of the time . . . sales were poor. It took them a little while to figure out what was happening through observation.

When a women came in alone, they told her how convenient the washer-dryer combination was. They would explain how much of her time it would save and how much lighter her work would be . . . and **she** bought.

When a man came in, they told him how economical the combination was and how much money he would save over buying both units separately . . . and **he** bought.

When they came in together, as a couple, the salespeople would stress the same benefits. They were now asking the woman to buy an easier life for herself . . . **while he was listening**. They were asking him to buy economy . . . **while she was listening**. Do you see what's happening here?

She didn't want her husband to think that she was looking for an easier life and he didn't want her to think that he was looking for a cheap way out. So, they didn't buy.

They were the same benefits. Also, the salespeople were talking to the same people. However, it didn't work because the circumstances had changed.

What would you do in this situation? Well, they solved it this way: When he came in alone, they kept telling him about the economy and they sold him because that's what he wanted. When she came in alone, they kept telling her about convenience and sold her because that's what she wanted. However, when they came in together, they simply switched the appeals. They told **her** it was economical and they told **him** it would save her a lot of work. By doing this, they appealed to what both thought were good motives for the other and they sold them like hot cakes.

You see, he was still getting the economy because that's what he wanted. When she came in alone, they kept telling her about convenience she wanted because she heard them tell him about it.

Those weren't the deciding benefits, however. You see, they were both getting something else. She was saving **him** money and he was making **her** life easier.

Now the moral to this entire scenario is that if you are going to talk benefits, make sure you are talking the **right** benefit. Don't stress economy to someone who wants convenience. Don't stress convenience to someone who wants speed. Don't stress speed to someone who wants safety. Be sure you figure out what benefit will get them "mentally past the point of purchase" (thinking about using the product), talk that benefit and then **prove** what you say.

— Tactic # 149 —

Use Proof to Support Your Feature and Benefit Statements

It's true . . . one of the hazards of our profession is that some people think we would say anything to make a sale. Even if that "anything" is not the truth. For this reason, a salesperson must not expect a customer to accept his benefit presentation at face value. It is necessary to say something that gets the customer to **agree** to the benefit statement. This is done by giving **proof**.

So, what we are developing is the F-B-P system of getting into the customer's mind and getting him mentally past the point of purchase. This is the **feature-benefit-proof** method.

— Tactic # 150 —

Change a Feature to a Benefit with "That Means"

Let's take the first part of the F-B-P process . . . that is, changing a feature into a benefit. Think of the feature of any product. Then say to yourself, "that means" and state a benefit for the customer. It's just that simple. You can take any of your products and list all of the features, then along side of the features, put what it means to the customer. In that way, you have come up with the benefits. Here's an example: A water heater has foam insulation instead of fiberglass. Now, as a student of your product, you know that foam has a higher heat resistance factor than fiberglass. Foam has an R factor of 16 and fiberglass has an R factor of 12. To get that point across, you would say this, "This water heater has foam insulation, and that means you will save on your energy bills." You see, stated that way, the feature of foam suddenly has meaning to the customer. The customer sees what he **will get**.

This feature is a physical part of the product and a benefit is what the customer gets out of it.

— Tactic # 151 —

Show Proof by Using the Word "Because"

It's very simple to get agreement by using the word "because". Let's take the same example of the water heater. This water heater has foam insulation and **that means** you will save on your energy bills **because** foam has a heat resistant factor of 16 while fiberglass is only 12.

— Tactic # 152 —

Put It All Together for Convincing F-B-P Presentation

The most highly successful salespeople, today, choose their presentation points very carefully. By doing so, they "deliver" what the customer wants to buy.

This is done my matching customer wants, needs and desires with the benefits of your "available" products. If you listen carefully to your customers comments and responses during presentation, you'll have several good points to use in the feature/benefit/proof presentation.

You are attempting to establish value and increase the desire of ownership by using the feature-benefit-proof method of describing your product and service. The system really involves translating all of your product's features into reasons for the customer to buy (benefits). The "proof" encourages the customer to agree that the benefit is something desirable and worth paying money for (value). **Remember, people don't buy what it has, they buy what it does.**

In the above examples, you'll notice that I have spoken plainly and simplistically so that everybody understands what is being said. You must do the same thing when you are talking with your customers . Often, salespeople want to impress customers with their knowledge and will simply confuse them by using industry jargon in their presentations. Most customers are embarrassed about asking salespeople to explain further. Industry jargon really developed out of the need for people working within an industry to be able to communicate quickly and easily. It should not be used to try and impress customers with your vast knowledge. Remember, your words in your feature-benefit-proof presentations should be used to **express** not **impress**.

Let's look at an example of an F-B-P on an item you would not be selling to understand how a feature-benefit-proof is constructed.

Item:

The **item** is always referred to in its simplest form. For example "stop sign."

Feature:

For **each** F-B-P, choose **one** feature. Remember, a feature is something that stands out or is important about the item. For example, "Bright red color."

Benefit:

The **benefit** gives reasons to buy by telling **what the feature will do for the customer**. For example, "More likely to see it and avoid an accident." The benefit can establish value.

Proof:

The **proof** prompts the customers to agree that the **benefit** is valuable to them. Simply, **restate the benefit as a question to gain their agreement**. For example, "It's always better to avoid an accident whenever possible, isn't it?" Or, as in previous examples, use the word "because" and give a logical reason why they receive a benefit.

Now let's look at the complete F-B-P based upon the above example of a stop sign:

"I'd like to show you this particular stop sign. One of the nice things about it is the bright red color that has a very high visibility. That way, you're more likely to see it and avoid an accident. It's always better to avoid accidents whenever possible, isn't it?"

You will notice that it was not necessary to verbalize "that means" and "because." However, the feature-benefit-proof element was in the example. Using transitional phrases "that means" and "because" is intended as a **study element**. In other words, you line up your features, benefits and proof on tablet paper and merely think the transitional phrases. When you are an actual presentation, just make sure you get all elements in . . . get the customer mentally past the point of purchase, thinking about using the benefits you have presented.

— Tactic # 153 —

Use Motivational Words

The words you choose when you're constructing your F-B-P's have a bearing on their effectiveness. A study was conducted and the following words were determined to be the most persuasive in the English language.

EASY	FREE	SAVE	NEW	LOVE
MONEY	HEALTH	RESULTS	YOU, YOUR	
PROVEN	SAFETY	DISCOVERY	GUARANTEE	

Let me put these words into an example paragraph for you:

These **proven** words are **free** for you to use. You will be communicating with words people **love** to hear. And, when **you** do, you'll make an important **discovery**. You'll be making more **money**, **save** more time, and even improve your **health**. These words will **guarantee** you **new results** by helping you be **easy** to buy from.

Do you see what's happening? By using this system and carefully choosing your words, you are letting the customer, in every case, know what's in it for him. That's the W.I.I.F.M. principle . . . it's what the customer's always asking . . . "What's in it for me?" When you answer that question, you get the customer mentally past the point of purchase (M.P.T.P.O.P.!).

—— Tactic # 154 ——

Consider Price Against Value

Occasionally, while you are presenting features, benefits and proof statements, you will find yourself asked to compare one product with another. Most often the customer will want you to make a price comparison between product A and product B. Try not to let yourself get maneuvered into having to do this. Remember this rule:

Sell Everything on its Own Merit. Never Compare.

Let's assume that product A costs $4,500 and product B costs $3,000. If you begin to compare the two by saying, "product A is **better** than product B . . .," you will simply be killing the possible sale of product B when he decides he is willing or able to spend the $3,000. He won't buy product B . . . at least not from you. He may buy a similar product from somebody else. So what do you do? Well, always talk about products based on their own merit. Never compare! If you find yourself in a presentation showing two similar, yet quite differently priced products, say this, "Product B is good because . . .." This way, if the customer decides that his or her budget can only handle product B and not the more expensive product A, there isn't a problem. In fact, when you present the lowest priced product, tell the customer that at this price it is a "good buy."

If the customer should ask you why there is such a difference in price between the products, don't worry. Simply explain that the features found in the higher priced product are more expensive to produce and therefore, the finished product is more costly. Workmanship, materials used, ornamentation, even designer names are all features that affect the price. This is very logical and customers will understand.

Become your customer for a few seconds.

As you are presenting features-benefits-proof to your customer, temporarily (for a few seconds) take his part in the conversation. Be aware that your customer has to make some major decisions before he will buy a product. Those decisions are:

- Do I have a need?
- Does this salesman's product fill that need?
- Is this product the best possible way of fulfilling that need?
- Is it worth the cost?

When you are able to answer those questions on behalf of your customer, you will be talking customer benefits and not just general benefits of the product. So, I am suggesting that you have a special benefit story for every customer and with every product that you present.

You may ask, "How can this be accomplished with hundreds of different products that I have the opportunity to present to literally dozens of customers?"

Well, just as it is true that about 55% of sales come from 15% of customers and prospects . . . it is true that the **bulk of your volume and profits can come from some very important products**. Just think about that for a moment. There are certain products that lend themselves well to strong benefits presentation with **most** of your prospects and customers.

Even with salespeople who have dozens or thousands of products, the major products that could and should be presented are generally a handful. It's these major products that offer you the greatest return for your time investment in a face-to-face selling situation.

Many salespeople complain that they don't have enough time to learn their products thoroughly. This could be true if it was all done outside the normal working day. However, in practical application, and with the use of a modern learning tool . . . the information is absorbed in detail and almost effortlessly.

Here's how you can accomplish the mission:

You probably average four to five hours a day traveling in your automobile. Most of that time is spent listening to the automobile radio and the usual "air pollution" that comes out of it. In some cases, that travel time is spent with the salesman's brain in neutral.

I don't intend to be harshly critical . . . just to encourage you to mentally assess what you do during driving time and with a moment's self-appraisal, you should realize that most of that time is wasted. Get yourself a tape recorder . . . use your driving time as learning time.

You can use your driving time to acquire a tremendous amount of product knowledge . . . organized on a feature-benefit-proof basis.

First, dictate the information that you would learn into your tape recorder, using your company's literature. Once you have programmed this information, it simply becomes a matter of listening.

There is a residual benefit to you when you become highly knowledgeable and benefit oriented. You will gain a tremendous amount of confidence and will become aggressively competent which further builds confidence.

— Tactic # 155 —

Learn to Use Minus Benefits

In the process of listing benefits that are meaningful to your customer, you must know that there are two types of benefits . . . there are **plus benefits** and there are **minus benefits**.

The plus benefits are those your prospect **gains** through buying your products. The minus benefits are the risks or the losses he or she **avoids** by buying that product from you. For example: If your customer buys an automobile with an air bag safety device, he gets the benefit of safety. That's a plus benefit. At the same time . . . he avoids the danger of injury or death in a possible crash. **That's a minus benefit**.

When you can build both plus and minus benefits into your conversation, you will create interest immediately. Now, you want to use benefit conversation to **create desire**.

— Tactic # 156 —

Build Confidence and Desire

A customer will seldom agree to your proposition unless he has a high degree of confidence in what you are talking about and he feels more than just a want or a need . . . he now has a **desire**. In order to get to desire, however, you must first build confidence in yourself, your company, your service and, of course, in your product.

The winning of your customer's confidence is a vital part of your presentation because most people have been taught, perhaps by their own experience, that you can't believe everything you hear, especially when you hear it from someone who seems to be trying to sell something. Frankly, when you are doing benefit selling to industrial accounts, the better your offer sounds, the more skeptical some of them will become.

In order to win their **confidence**, you have to be mindful of two things:

First, the winning of your customer's confidence is of no value unless he has been made to **want your product or service** first.

Your prospect must be convinced that your product is the finest of its kind . . . but he still might not buy until he has been made to see the need for the product and **want it . . . desire it**. Again, this is getting the customer mentally past the point of purchase.

It is the **want** that makes people buy.

For instance. . .a building contractor may need the extra volume and profit he can get from selling upgraded kitchen products and yet may not want to sell those kitchen products because he doesn't know what those products will actually do to build his business. This has to be explained to him very carefully so that he finally **wants** to increase his business by installing and selling the upscale products.

The contractor will not buy until he wants the profit that he can get, even though the need may have existed for some time. On the other hand, how often have you watched people buy something **they do not actually need just because they wanted it**?

Your job is to arouse a sense of want and desire before you spend too much time in gaining confidence.

Spend only as much time as is needed to win the customer's confidence. Too many facts, figures, charts and proofs of various kinds could bore a busy prospect and a bored prospect begins losing interest. Essentially, the best way to convince a buyer is to **make it his idea**. You do this by making your benefit statements so strong that the customer wants your product and your proposition. This applies with both positive and negative benefits.

— Tactic # 157 —

Generate Ideas to Help the Buyer

Any sales presentation, loaded with feature-benefit-proof elements is an exercise in creativity. It is a tailor made type of conversation put together to meet the specific needs of an individual customer. It must contain these five elements:

- A total knowledge of your product and service offering.
- A complete understanding of the individual customer's needs, wants, and desires.
- If possible, a personalized visual aid that can be used to help the customer "see" the benefits he will get.
- Communication skills in making the presentation that will help the customer mentally own the product.
- The ability to fulfill the customer needs to his total satisfaction based on your company's capabilities.

—— Tactic # 158 ——

Set up for Success

Here are some specific how to's that will enable you to get ready for presentation success:

- Choose the prospect you are most eager to sell. When you think about it, that prospect will probably be the one that has the greatest potential. After you have selected that prospect, list your second one as the one with the second greatest potential and so on until you have pretty well covered your entire territory. Do this with every product. Once you have covered your territory in this manner, select another product, thoroughly analyze it on the feature-benefit-proof basis and start again.
- Survey all of your prospect's needs. Always be prepared for the next call. Once you have sold the customer a product, start asking about his needs relative to the next item you intend to present. Sometimes you will uncover a need and will be able to sell that next product immediately.
- Get as much information as possible about your customer's purchasing procedures, policies and customs. Find out if he is buying from a competitor, what he is buying and why. Find out how much he is buying, on what terms, and how often. Once you have done that, develop a plan that would help him save money, reduce his "hassle factor" or, in general, improve his situation.
- Prepare a comparison sheet of your product with your competitors. Point out the advantages that your product has. Show where you meet the competitor head on and then list five or

six benefits that the competitor does not have. What if you have disadvantages? See if the additional benefits offset those disadvantages and show the comparative increased value. If your product has a higher price tag (that could be a disadvantage), it is probably a superior item, therefore you will sell those superior features, relating them into benefits and you must give elements of proof .

- Be sure you give ample attention to the people who **help** make the buying decision. If you are calling on a factory purchasing agent, make sure you talk to the floor supervisors, machine operators and engineers who are responsible for maintenance. The people who are actually going to use your products will influence the purchasing agent. In this way, it is not a matter of "price only" buying on the part of that purchasing agent.

—— Tactic # 159 ——

Get Immediate Attention

Many buyers are bored by selling presentations. They have been carefully taught to be bored and disinterested . . . by salespeople.

Your first seconds with the customer are extremely important. You must be able to focus your customer's attention on yourself and what you have to say. Remember, whether the customer says it or not, he's always asking, "What's in it for me?" For this reason, the very beginning of your sales talk must hit the target. It must talk about what he actually wants: greater profits, reduced "hassle factor", more customers, the growth of his business . . . anything that will **benefit** him. Here are some examples of opening statements that will get attention:

"Mr. Customer, were you aware that over 50% of the companies in our industry are now using our units for their maintenance department?"

"Mr. Customer, would you like to know how you can increase your productivity by 10% and at the same time, cut costs by 5%?"

"Mr. Customer, I have been thinking about you and I've developed a plan that has been used with other companies in your situation to increase their volume of business by 20% and their profits by 2%. Would you give me an opportunity to discuss this with you?"

With the above tactic, you will have gained some attention. This does not necessarily mean that you have a great deal of interest. You at least have an opportunity to make your customer want to hear more about your proposition. Please remember that your customer's concerned only with himself and how he is going to benefit with his relationship with you. More specifically, he's concerned how he is going to benefit from the immediate conversation.

The next step, then, is to change his attention into interest. Now is the time to hit him with some benefits that he will gain when he orders your product or contracts for your services.

Before we go on, I want you to bring this home a little bit. Think of yourself whenever you buy something. If you are going to buy a suit, you probably won't be concentrating on thread, buttons, or just the material from which it is made. Of course, all of these are important so that you eventually receive the benefits that you want. You want quality, the self-confidence that you feel when you put on the suit, prestige and overall improved appearance. Well, that's what your customer/prospect is going to buy.

All of this simply means that you have to immediately talk about benefits that are most likely to appeal to a particular customer. Here is where you must take into consideration **plus** and **minus** benefits. Remember the plus benefits are the things that we get out of the proposition. Beyond the scope of business benefits, there are such plus benefits as emotional enhancement, physical, mental, financial and social additions to our lives. **Minus** benefits are the risks that we want to avoid. They are certainly the opposite of the plus benefits, such as financial loss, loss of prestige, destruction of self-image, loss of health and so forth.

So, with the basic business benefits, you must also know the customer well enough to decide which plus and minus benefits should be mentioned in order to arouse his interest. Here is a five step method for accomplishing this:

- Do some research to analyze **why** they do what they do in an effort to get **what** they most want.
- Look at your products and services so that you can match what you are selling to those desires and wants.
- Construct a list of benefits that your product would offer the customer.
- Practice. Take the list out and practice on all types of prospects. Make sure that you concentrate on the benefits that are exclusive with your product and service and make the competition look weak by comparison.

- Once you have practiced, select the benefits that get the greatest response from typical customers. Use these benefits on your prime prospects.

— Tactic # 160 —

Now It's Time to Create Desire

Once you have properly matched the benefits of your product and service to the customer's wants and desires, he will be thinking of himself and how he is going to gain from the proposition.

You are likely to hear him say such things as, "That sounds pretty good, but how do I know what you say is really true?" (There's that old "credibility gap" that requires proof). Obviously, your objective at this point is to convince the customer that everything you say is the absolute truth and that he is going to gain the benefits that you have promised. The best way to do that is to give him **facts**. This is actually one of the easiest parts of the presentation if you are well prepared. There are four methods of getting this accomplished:

- **Use expert evidence** — To build your credibility with the customer, you'll want to use reports of various authorities that he might respect. Also, use the results of tests on your products . . . the more recognized the name of the authority, the more believable will be the proof that you offer.
- **Testimonial Information** — The experiences of other users of your product and service are powerful convincers. If possible, use testimonial information in previous user's own words. This means you should solicit testimonial letters or accumulate a series of testimonial comments.
- **Specifications** — These are the hard facts. This information has to do with the design, workmanship, materials . . . all of the physical aspects of your product. When you are selling a service, it means having an outline of exactly what the customer might expect your performance criteria to be. In case of a service, you want to tie the specification in with testimonial information to show that previous clients have achieved results.
- **Guarantee** — People want to feel that they have little or no risk when they do business with you. For this reason, use all of the guarantee information you have available and empha-

size that your company has been in business for a long time, continues to be successful today and will be in business for an even longer time in the future.

—— Tactic # 161 ——

Get Him to Take Action

Don't do what 60% of salespeople do. That's right, 60% of salespeople walk away at this point. They tell the customer to "think it over." Remember, 20% of the time, the customer initiates the action to take the product . . . 20% of the time the salesman closes the sale . . . 60% of the time, no one takes action. Action! The entire purpose of your presentation was to arouse the customer to take action. Without that, there is no satisfaction on the part of either the salesperson or the customer. You don't get an order and he doesn't receive the benefits that you have promised throughout your presentation.

Don't leave it to chance . . . you take the initiative and tell your prospect that you want him to begin enjoying the benefits of your product right away. Actually, this is the most logical conclusion to your conversations. If you gained attention, aroused interest and stimulated some desire for your product, he will be letting you know that, indeed, he would enjoy receiving the benefits that you have described. These comments, of course, are **buying signals**. You must be alert to the signals which are indications that your prospect is ready and willing to come to an agreement.

Here's a brief example of the buying example: Let's suppose you are at the point where you have aroused some interest. Perhaps the customer isn't saying anything, but he is listening intently. He reaches over and picks up the specification sheet or the product sample that you have brought with you. He looks at it and then he asks for more information about some benefit that he might be getting from the product . . . is a buying signal. That is the time to ask him to go ahead with the agreement.

—— Tactic 162 ——

Put it on a Cue Card

In the previous four tactics we covered four areas that will help you change the features of a product into benefits that your customer will want.

Sometimes during a presentation, we forget or skip some of the elements. A good method is to use what many speakers, actors, teachers, preachers, and salespeople use to remind themselves of the elements of a presentation . . . a cue card.

Here's what we've been talking about:

- Get attention by aiming at the prospect's self-interest.
- Arouse interest by describing benefits.
- Stimulate desire by offering proof.
- Motivate him to take action.

The above belongs on a cue card. Keep it on your clipboard or on the inside cover of your briefcase.

—— Tactic # 163 ——

Work from the Customer's Frame of Reference

To be sure that your customer is working "with you" and not "against you" during your presentation, you must learn to look at every presentation from the customer's point of view.

Put aside the natural tendency to look at only your own interest and ask yourself: "What's in it for the customer?"

Undoubtedly, your company has invested a lot of time, effort and money to create goodwill between itself and the customers. All of this must be backed up by the salesperson who calls on the account . . . who is the living representation of the company. This means, simply, you must put yourself in the customer's place . . . hear things as he would hear them, see things as he would see them, and think as he might be expected to intelligently consider your proposition.

Anytime you put your interests ahead of that of your customers, your presentation will come off sounding phony when you try to convince the customer that everything is being presented to his benefit. When you legitimately put your customer's interests first, looking at things from that customer's point of view, giving him ideas that will help improve his situation, solve his problems, and generally reduce his hassle factor, you both will feel that the presentation is designed based on a dedication to help the customer.

When this climate for doing business exists, you will solidify your relationship with your customer and find him more willing to listen to all of your presentations and buy your products in the future.

Don't Fall Victim to Excusitis

Here's a real test of your attitude and how you actually feel regarding the customer's interests. What has been your typical reaction when a customer has complained about a mistake you or your company has made?

If, at those times, you have tried to "weasel" out of problem areas with various excuses and such comments as, "Well it really isn't my fault . . . someone else must have messed up," you immediately lose your customer's respect and eventually his trust and his business. There are many cases when you are not at fault, but that's not the time to pass the buck to someone else within your company. Remember, you are the sum total of all of your company's resources and you are their representative to the customer.

Anytime you make excuses by placing the blame elsewhere, you are removing yourself from the situation, making yourself less valuable to the customer as his problem solver.

Instead of finding fault elsewhere, try this approach:

"I'm sorry this happened and I certainly understand your concern. It won't do any good to find someone to blame . . . let's see how we can fix this situation and then take steps to make sure that it never happens again."

Looking at things from the customer's point of view means that you will frequently make telephone calls to your customers to let them know that you are concerned about their problems and that you want to make sure they remain satisfied with your products and services. So, even when a product does not exist . . . you want to impress your customer with the fact that you truly are looking out for him and have his best interests in mind.

Don't be Challenging

When you are truly working from your customer's frame of reference, you will avoid any kind of an atmosphere that puts up a challenge.

A challenging atmosphere could come about because of the natural state of affairs . . . a difference of opinion between you and your customer based on his frame of reference and the beliefs you have regarding your products, services, and in yourself as a salesperson.

When you are an extremely confident individual, you tend to make very strong and positive claims about your products and services . . . it's almost as if you are presenting a challenge for someone to argue against these strong, wonderful points. You don't mean it, but it comes off that way.

There are many people who love to develop an opposite point of view to any strong statements. Some of these people are your customers. They can't help themselves. It is an automatic psychological response to anyone expressing a strong sentiment.

How do you avoid this? Well, there's a very easy way to make sure that you don't put any of your customers on the defensive, feeling it necessary to rebut a strong statement. Don't make extremely strong, assertive statements about your product . . . **simply ask your customer's opinion on the results he should get while stating the results other people have received through the use of the products and services you offer.**

How to Work With Customers

In order to work from the customer's frame of reference, and in order to avoid creating challenging situations, follow these five simple steps:

1. Always see things through the customer's eyes. Look at every situation from the customer's frame of reference and put his interests up front.
2. Search for a problem your customer might have and suggest ways to solve those problems.
3. Deliberately question your customer regarding what kind of help he would like to get from salespeople that he's not receiving now. This means help over and beyond the benefits your products and services offer.
4. Always follow up on orders to make sure that your customer receives exactly what you promised and then some.
5. Never fall into the trap of excusitis. Don't make excuses or try to place blame on someone else for any mistakes that are made by you, your company, or a third party.

Do In-Field Follow-Up

A sure way to be certain that your customer appreciates that you are working from his frame of reference is to take time for in-field follow-ups.

The follow-up of a sale is always the responsibility of the salesman . . . especially in the world of industrial selling, with established customers and an opportunity for repeat orders. You can check up on an order or a job situation by simply making a telephone call to make sure the product was delivered in a satisfactory way and on time. Beyond that, you could actually visit the end user location to make sure your product is performing exactly as you had promised.

The above suggestions seem like just good common sense, but more than 70% of the salespeople feel they are too busy to engage in this follow-up activity and find themselves simply reacting to problems. When you engage in this follow-up activity and let your customer know that you are working in his best interest, he will consider you above those other salespeople and think of you first when he needs a repeat order of the type of products you sell.

Even with a new customer, you can greatly advantage yourself by making follow-up calls:

1. It will help you see your product in use and build your own confidence regarding the fact that it is performing as you have promised. You can then report back to that new customer, confirming the original confidence he had when he purchased the product. You can make sure that the product is being used properly. You can give your customer instructions and make sure that he does not make mistakes. You can offer technical assistance or, simply, make small adjustments which will help your customer and assure your product will give the satisfaction that he expected.
2. Your new customer and his people who see you make the follow-up call will think well for you because of your interest. You'll have a very pleasant, positive reinforcement call when everything is going well. You will create good will at all levels within your customer's organization.
3. You will be able to find out if anyone in your customer's organization is upset because your customer purchased your product. You will then have an opportunity to help that person appreciate his boss's action and to get him on your side. If an individual within your customer's organization has some kind of resentment, you can take care of it before it becomes a problem. If there is a genuine problem, such as the poor performance of one of your products in the past, you could look into the situation and take care of it with a replacement, a credit, or by making some other adjustment that will remove a potentially dangerous situation. Again, you will establish legitimate goodwill with the customer, showing that you are constantly working with his best interests in mind . . . concerned about looking at his situation from his frame of reference.
4. And, finally, by making follow-up calls, you will be able to gain information that will help you decide what other products in your line you should be presenting to your customer on your

next call. In some cases, you might see a competitor's product being used and develop a presentation to compare your product to your competitor's. Remember, 70% of the salespeople do not make these types of follow-up calls and these are the salespeople that are subject to losing business from the observation of a customer minded professional.

— Tactic # 164 —

Be an Empathetic Salesperson

Look at a successful salesperson who enjoys good relationships with his customers and you will find someone who is extremely sensitive to his customers . . . someone who has a well developed sense of **empathy**.

Empathy is actually a Greek word and it literally means "feeling pain with." That's right. It means that you are sensitive to the conditions experienced or felt by another person. When you keep a customer's feelings in mind, when you see things from his frame of reference, you are empathetic.

When you're empathetic, you have given yourself a tremendous advantage. The advantage is the fact that you can predict what your customer will do . . . you can predict his reactions to situations and can, therefore, be in a better position to serve him well.

As an empathetic salesperson, you must realize that people do not necessarily "act", basically they "react." This means that you must be a true student of a customer's mannerisms, his speech, gestures, postures, facial expressions, manners and his mannerisms . . . in general, perceive how your customer responds to the environment of your presentation.

Develop empathy — In order to develop empathy that will help you become a better presenter, start with **courtesy**. Now, this may seem like a simplistic subject, but upon closer look, it involves several habits that are excellent empathy developers. Here are those habits:

Be on time for appointments — The most precious asset we all have is time. There are so many profitable ways in which you as a salesperson or your customer as a buyer could invest this precious asset of time.

When you keep your customer waiting, you are wasting the time asset and you are giving him the impression of someone who is thoughtless and who has bad work habits. At the same time, when you are late, you create a customer resistance to your presentation before you start.

All top performing professionals make sure that they arrive at an appointment at least five minutes in advance. Then, if it's necessary to wait at the appointment, the professional doesn't exhibit impatience . . . rather he makes good use of the extra time by doing paperwork or reviewing the presentation he is about to make.

Pay attention to your dress — As a salesperson, you must be nice to be near. I believe salespeople should carry, in their automobile, deodorant, breath mints and an electric razor in order to freshen up throughout the day.

A salesperson's appearance really reflects upon the company, the products and the services that are being presented.

All top level performing salespeople have, at one time or another, seen how other successful salespeople and executives dress. In your geographic location, in your particular business environment that is a good guide for dressing appropriately.

Know that your posture will speak for you — Walk into a doctor's waiting room and you'll be able to read what's on the mind of the people seated by their postures. The same situation exists when you walk into the waiting room of a purchasing agent. You see a lot of "sprawlers." Their lazy posture fairly accurately is a prediction of the type of presentation they will make.

As a professional, you will want to make sure that you don't commit such unpardonable errors of posture such as sprawling in front of the customer, leaning or sitting on the customer's desk, or propping your feet on an adjoining chair. And don't sit unless you are invited to do so. When you do sit . . . sit straight and quiet in order to hold the buyer's attention. When you walk, make sure that your posture is straight so that you can project an image of confidence and vitality. All in all, you'll be telling the customer you care enough about his business to be mindful of even the smallest detail.

Watch your language — Many of the tactics of persuasion in this book involves the use of words. Words will reveal to the customer what type of person you are. Words you use will tell your customer a lot about your mental processes, your ability, your personality, and your overall character.

Experts tell us that the average person, in a normal day, will speak an estimated 30,000 words. Salespeople generally speak much more than those 30,000. That means that all day long, a salesperson is revealing exactly who and what he is.

Professional salespeople who want to make a favorable impact on a customer will use a type of "level" language that is used by network and local newscasters. This is a language of an educated person that is simple, not spiced with slang, grammatical, not crude, but a language designed to communicate ideas.

Of course, you will want to avoid swearing or using any kind of filthy language . . . even if the customer uses it. Filthy language simply shows the sewage of an individual's mind.

If you find yourself falling into the trap of using slang, vulgarities, or other inappropriate language, deliberately make an effort for a period of time to eliminate such phrases and words from your vocabulary. Work on it consciously. Be sure you eliminate such language from your personal life as well as your business life or surely one will spill over into the other.

Pay attention to your facial expressions — When you are communicating with another individual, that person will constantly be attempting to read your facial expressions in order to receive the entire content of your message. Your face will convey visible messages.

I've seen many salesman, because of nervousness, develop an annoying habit such as a twitch, a squint, or a particularly disturbing frown. Whenever this happens, the buyer reads a negative message. Of course, the salesperson never intended a negative message but the outward expression of his nervousness is expressed by a salesperson achieving a sort of grimace on his face and keeping it throughout the entire presentation . . . sort of a Jack Palance look.

Regarding facial expressions, while you are listening to a customer, your face should show that you are sympathetically in tune with the customer. You should smile at appropriate times, and show concern at others. Be sure you don't over use a smile but understand that it will, also, never wear out. In fact, when used appropriately, a smile becomes more welcome each and every time.

Be a very good listener — You should learn to listen even better than you talk. Too many salesman are too concerned about the content of their spoken presentation . . . to the exclusion of including listening moments. In fact, I have observed salespeople who obviously considered the customer's remark as some sort of a tedious interruption. It was obvious, to me, that the customer received this impression.

Good listening means more than just hearing the words a customer would utter . . . it means trying to see the problem exactly as your customer is seeing it.

You must listen actively as you mentally put yourself into your customer's situation in order that you might see his point of view and momentarily share it.

When I have interviewed purchasing agents and owner/buyers, I have found out that they are concerned about two bad listening habits of most salespeople who call on them. The first habit is that the salesman tries to reply before the buyer has finished talking. The second habit involves the salesman waiting too long to answer a question or to respond to a comment.

In the second situation, the salesman will generally stare at the buyer or somewhere else in an effort to dig up some kind of response.

There was another problem mentioned that was not brought up as frequently but deserves some exposure here. According to many buyers, too many salespeople ask the buyer to repeat what they said. Now, this certainly is a method of overcoming resistance and handling objections, but when overdone, it becomes irritating.

Be friendly but not familiar — Winston Churchill had a notable response to the phrase, "Familiarity breeds contempt!" When this was stated to him, he replied with, "Ah, ah, yes, But I don't know how you can breed anything without a certain degree of familiarity." So, for the purposes of this brief discussion, we are going to rely on the words "degree" as the most meaningful in Churchill's remarks.

Many salespeople are just a little bit too familiar. They feel that the only way to sell is to become so closely associated (friendly) with a customer that he would feel an obligation to do business only with "his friend," the salesman. Well , that might help in some situations, but the old W.I.I.F.M. is eventually going to get those types of salespeople. Today, as a professional salesperson, you must be a responsible salesman, using the tactics of persuasion that let the customers know you have their best interests in mind. You should talk with your customers by using proper "Mr.", "Mrs.", or "Miss" . . . (I don't know how you express "Ms.") . . . unless you are invited to use their first names. By showing respect, using a formal address, you will not be detracting in any way from a friendly presentation. Still, you will be preserving some advantages of giving deference to your customer.

It is true that most salespeople don't use the customer's name often enough in a presentation. On the other hand, I have heard some salespeople who obviously learned the technique of using the customer's name and then over used it in such a way that these salespeople came across as being overbearing, obsequious, phony, and quite transparent. **Degree! Discretion! Judgment! Balance!.** You must know your customer and apply the meanings of these words in each and every situation.

—— Tactic # 165 ——

Use Good Body Language to Be a Better Presenter

All salespeople should try to brush up on body language, no matter how well they are doing. Body language plays a bigger role in communication and in overall success than many salespeople realize.

A leading expert in body language communication, Dr. Albert Mehrabian, has calculated the importance of three elements of communication. As a result of his studies, he has concluded that the words we use account for only about 7% of our impact of others. Our tone of voice accounts for 38% and our facial expressions, an outstanding **55%**! From the above figures, we can conclude that the nonverbal elements of communication account for 93% of the impact we make on other people. And, of course, that's not taking into account such nonverbal factors as how we use our hands or how we walk across a room.

It should point out to you, the professional salesperson, that just using words to get ideas across or to change the attitude of the customer, or to get an order, is not sufficient. If you want to communicate, make an excellent presentation, effectively use tactics of persuasion, you have to put your entire self into your presentation. You must, as mentioned before, pay attention to your posture, facial expression, body position, and even such things as your movement, gestures, your tone of voice and the underlying attitudes that will be projected to you customer.

Your dealings with individual customers and with buying groups (decision making committees) can be greatly improved if you employ some of these nonverbal signs and signals:

Know when people are too polite to tell you they disapprove — A young salesman was telling a customer about how he overcame a problem by outsmarting another buyer. His customer looked down and began picking lint off his sleeve. That was a clear sign of disapproval.

Many times a customer may not like what you are saying, but they are not going to say so out loud. You can tell that they disapprove, however, if you notice a change in their behavior.

For example, if a customer thinks your comments are off the wall, he may lean back in his chair or have a sudden need to clear his throat, or as in the above example, pick lint off his suit.

These signs should be a cue for you to change your conversation, realize they have a problem, get to the bottom of it, and get on more positive ground.

Watch for visual cues in a group situation that shows others are ganging up on you — If you are making a presentation to a buying committee, you must be aware of any disruptive action by one or several members of the group, particularly, pay attention to signals from any hostile portion of that group. For example:

- Three or four people folding their arms and frowning.
- Two participants exchanging sly smiles.
- A couple of people whispering to one another while you are talking.
- A few people seated next to each other moving their chairs slightly back.

Other negative actions simply mean that several other people in the group are "with" the other dissenters. You can identify a hostile faction within a group by such things as mutual foot tapping, even crossing of legs or placing a finger behind an ear. These are all indicators of premeditated "ganging up". When you finally identify people who are acting in an antagonistic way, you are at least able to develop some sort of strategy to do something about this situation.

Indicators of "votes" from buying committees — Some salespeople have an uncanny knack of getting their proposals accepted. Others seem to have a way of getting their proposals turned down. What would explain the difference between the two?

In many situations, it is simply a matter of knowing when to bring up a subject for discussion. Yes, it's a matter of timing. The more observant salespeople read body language signs that tell them if they are going to be accepted or turned down as they make a proposal.

These empathetic salespeople detect the body language of hostile factions, notice key people are looking away or are frowning and they back off with such comments as, "We probably should take a little bit more time to study this before we make a decision."

The salesman who is constantly losing in these situations, might say something like this, "Well, what do you say? Should we go ahead?"

The winners only ask for decisions when they know that the signs are positive such as nods, relaxed faces and everyone paying attention to what they are saying.

Don't let ego contests destroy your presentation — You can easily detect an ego contest developing between two people of a buying group. They simply start arguing. You don't want it to get this far. See if, through nonverbal communication, you can notice early signs of conflict. Then try to intercede before any real damage is done to your presentation.

Look for exchanges of dominant behavior. For example:

- When individuals look each other in the eye without smiling, and hold this look for a longer than usual period of time.
- When individuals speak, one after the other, even when they have nothing important to say.

- When individuals spend a ridiculous amount of time chewing over a very small point in the presentation.
- When individuals look at each other with hands on hips or thumbs hooked on a belt or in some other confrontational manner.
- When one individual invades another's personal space by pointing a finger or moving into a close face-to-face confrontation.

As soon as you become aware of any of these signs, do whatever is reasonably possible to divert the attention of the individuals. If you can resolve the source of the confrontation, do so. If you don't take some kind of action, the essence of your presentation will be lost and your time will eventually be wasted.

Sometimes, you can use confrontation to your advantage, particularly when it will help clear the air or develop a foundation for respect. You could permit a confrontation to continue when you know you have a resolution that will be satisfactory to both parties. In these situations, everybody wins and your presentation becomes that much stronger.

Change your presentation before the "yawns"— Individuals will show signs of disassociation when they feel that they are alienated for any reason. This applies to the single/customer prospect or to a group buying committee. Signs of disassociation include the following:

- Folded arms.
- Looking downward or away.
- A bored, vacant look on the face.
- Frowning.
- Looking around for someone else to talk to.
- Obviously hunching over at the table or desk.

Hostility or aggression are negative nonverbal indicators and can certainly ruin your presentation. Disassociation can be just as bad for the salesperson who needs the approval of the disassociated individual.

You must recapture interest of the disassociated person. You do this by getting them involved. Simply ask a question or give some information that would make them feel a part of the group. Mention their name when you are making a point.

Simply look at the individual while you are talking. Usually this direct approach will bring them back.

Watch for the "one eye covered" signal — A customer may say to you, "Okay, I understand what you say and I'll think it over." While he says this, he covers and rubs one eye. What does that mean? Does he really understand? Will he really consider placing an order with you when he thinks it over?

According to experts on body language, the covering and/or rubbing of an eye means that there is refusal. It means that what has been seen or heard is inwardly being rejected and the eye gesture is telling you that the individual really does not want to see.

This should be treated like an objection. The aware salesperson will start to talk more with the customer, further explaining the reason that he should buy the product . . . building benefits and try to get a response that does not include the negative eye covering nonverbal refusal.

Now, you must be thinking, the covering and rubbing an eye might mean the person is tired, having trouble with contact lenses or has a headache. That's true. Still, treat it as if it is a subliminal refusal in order to be sure.

Get the truth by watching hands and feet — Many customers and perspective buyers have very carefully learned how to control their words and even their facial expressions. However, they have not paid much attention to how they react or communicate with their hands and feet, which in many cases reveal their inward most feeling about the subject. Pay attention to these nonverbal signs:

- A customer may tell you that he has no reservations about taking on a new line of products, he smiles, but is tapping his foot, revealing anxiety. This customer needs reassured. Do a little bit more "assistant buying" by reviewing all the benefits he is going to receive. Talk about your warranty.
- Your customer tells you that he is not looking at any of your competitors at this time. Most of his body signs support that what he says is the truth, however, the forefinger and the thumb of his left hand are rubbing together nervously. This customer probably is not looking at your competitors, but is planning to do so as soon as you leave. Now is the time to give him a competitive analysis. Show him what all your competitors offer and how your product is superior. Save him the time of looking. Close the order.

There are other nervous movements to look for in hands and feet such as clenched fists, or completely stationary feet in an otherwise relaxed position. Look for "contrary" movements or gestures such as the "lint-picking" or any "brush-off" gesture on the sleeve or the pant's leg when someone says, "We're looking forward to considering, perhaps, doing business with your company."

A customer could give you an okay sign (thumb held to forefinger to form a ring) and really mean it. However, if he gives you the same sign held below his waist, it should be taken with less enthusiasm than if it was held at face level.

Look to the face to find the lie — Your customers will always try to control their facial expressions. Most people try to do this. Most people, however, do not entirely succeed at this type of control. As a perceptive salesman, you should be able to catch most liars by reading facial signs that will telegraph when they are lying.

Paul Eckman is the author of the book, Telling Lies, published by W.W. Norton. In his book, he says there are some key facial clues to look for:

- **A crooked smile** — Phony smiles tend to be a little bit lop-sided. Not a lot . . . just a little bit. Genuine smiles are nearly always symmetrical. Of course, we are talking about knowing the customers normal state and adjusting accordingly.
- **An over long smile, frown, or look of disbelief** — Observe authentic expressions and you will find they last only four to five seconds . . . or less. Anything longer is requiring extraordinary effort and is masking the truth or could be an attempt at manipulation.
- **Forced eye contact** — This usually means the person is trying to fake a sign of truth-telling. Look very closely at his face to see indications of facial tension.
- **Frequent rubbing of the nose** — The person's nose may be itchy. However, combined with other cues, this generally indicates a falsehood.
- **Facial slips** — A facial slip is a fleeting expression, such as a frown, that is quickly replaced by another expression, such as a smile or a serene face. You often see comic actors using an exaggerated form of this to show some sort of comical duplicity.

In a normal situation, however, this nonverbal communication can often be more telling than lie detectors.

Sell with "synchronicity"— Every salesman knows that there are certain people that they are constantly "with". As previously stated, these are the people who make it easy for you to operate from their frame of reference.

You want to get most of your customers in a position where you are "with" them . . . enjoying a high rapport, empathy, unconsciously copying another's body positions, gestures, etc.

You will notice wives begin to emulate husbands and husbands begin to emulate their wives as they start to speak alike, walk alike, sit and stand alike, to some degree. Managers and employees do the same thing. If one person crosses his legs in a meeting, another person will soon do the same.

As a successful sales representative, you must develop the habit of unconsciously emulating the behavior of your prospects. Also try to match the rates of their speech. Some salespeople even go so far as to match the breathing rate of a customer.

All in all, these controlled activities generate rapport even though neither person may actually verbalize the reason for this rapport . . . this empathy.

People in the helping profession, such as psychiatrists, teachers, etc., tend to mirror others. They develop this, do it unconsciously and, therefore, establish rapport very quickly.

When you work on developing your ability to adopt the behavior and the posture of others, you're going to find it much easier for them to accept the elements of your sales presentation.

Be very careful. Excessive intentional mirroring can come across as mimickry. If you overdo it, you could anger the other individual and find it very difficult to reestablish a relationship.

Look for fake body language — Most nonverbal communication is unconscious and is not an intentional display. Some, however, is intentional . . . in fact, it is intended to be manipulative. There are a lot of publications, books, magazine articles, topics of periodicals, newsletters, etc. that supply business people with nonverbal techniques. For this reason, there is a lot of game-playing going on. This simply means that you have to look out for the intentioal body language signal and differentiate that from the natural. Here are some key ways of accomplishing this precautionary analysis:

Observe timing errors — Notice when the person's smile comes a little too soon. This is certainly manipulative. Or, it might be a little too late or linger a bit too long. What about the "eyebrow flash" of greeting and acceptance. Does it last a little bit too long? This type of intentional body language tends to be just a little bit out of step, like a poorly made movie where the actors' lips don't sync with the words that are spoken. You see, the person has to think to accomplish the expression, causing a delay, an exaggeration or have it come too quickly, like jumping the gun at a race.

Look for conflicting signs — Once you have read a natural sign such as crossed arms, signifying hostility, your customer may try to affect an open and accepting pose. You can see him catching himself. You can also see through that deception if you'll notice other signs such as flared nostrils, or when the customer leans forward, tensed arms and chest.

Through experience you will find that very few people can control **all** of their physical signs. In most cases, there will be some minor discrepancy that you will be able to detect as your conversation continues. Is your customer displaying an open palm which means, "I am very accepting"? At the same time, if you notice a slightly tensed brow . . . be very cautious. This customer may be simply trying to get you to give him more information so that he can pass it on to a competitor and later stab you in the back.

Look for signals you're talking too loud or standing too close — Everybody has a personal space. Whenever you invade a customer's personal space, he will tend to back off, recoil, evade or do something to regain that space all to himself. He will do the following:

- Flinch
- Step backward
- Show startle signs such as retracting their head or raising their eyebrows.

You must be very aware of these reactions and respond to them in such a way that you will regain an empathetic situation. Lower your voice or simply allow the other individual more space.

I have noticed some salespeople respond to recoiling by customers by talking louder or, even stepping closer. This is a terrible mistake. It shows insensitivity on the part of the salesperson or the individual committing this personal unempathetic transgression.

Be aware of ethnic difference in spacing — Most Americans, North Americans, and the British, tend to like a lot of space during a normal conversation. They do not often touch when they are talking and they usually stand out of touching range.

People from Mexico, French people, European Jews, Latin Americans, and South American people like to stand close and they often touch one another. The Jewish culture is especially a touching, communicating, tactile group.

This does not mean that you have to adopt different spacing patterns when you meet with people of different ethnic backgrounds. However, be sensitive to the communication-touching needs of other people. Allow space when it is desired and don't be stand-offish if someone comes "too close" to you. As we often say in the profession of selling, "It comes with the territory."

Go easy on ethnic gestures — Our business world is truly international. People of all backgrounds and cultures are meeting as suppliers and users. Communication can often be difficult when the wrong nonverbal signals are used.

Gestures often have clear, ambiguous meaning or significance in one part of the world and, yet, could mean something entirely different in another hemisphere. By way of example, here are several gestures that have gotten business people in trouble:

- **The "A-Okay" sign** — (Thumb held to forefinger to make a ring.) This usually means, in America, "That's great", but in France, Belgium, it means, "You are worth zero." In Greece and Turkey, it's an invitation for sex or it is a vulgar insult.
- **The "thumbs-up" gesture** — You would think that this always meant "good" or "all right." But, in Northern Greece, Sardinia, and in many other places in the world, it means "up yours."
- **Nodding the head up and down** — Of course, this gesture simply means "Yes." And, we Americans assume it means the same thing throughout the world. In Greece or Turkey, it could mean "no" if the head is tilted high or if the head nodding is accompanied by a clicking of the tongue.

The above was part of research done by Wallace V. Frieson of the University of California Medical School in San Francisco. He advises all salespeople who deal in an international market to become students of all gestures in order not to make these errors of nonverbal communication.

As a sales professional, when you are dealing with people of unfamiliar ethnic background, take all of their gestures with a grain of salt. Also, be sure to go very easy on your own gestures, limiting them to slight undramatic hand movements or facial expressions simply intended to emphasize your words.

Don't let your body language study backfire — The reason for discussing body language in this section on presentation is to enable you to make your selling presentations more effective. Body language tactics are certainly a necessary element when you are attempting to persuade a customer to buy your products and services. However, as with all things, to overdo is simply to have the tactical techniques backfire.

Dr. L. R. Birdwhistell, a kenesics expert, advises that there is a "moral looking time." We are told that it's okay to look another person over, but make sure we are quick about it. Whenever it goes beyond a certain few seconds, it becomes offensive, impolite, even considered by some as aggressive and intrusive.

As a student and practitioner of nonverbal communication tactics, you may find yourself leisurely studying someone's hands, face, eyes, feet, or their movements. Then you might find the value of the information you get to be greatly diminished and overshadowed by the anger you cause.

So, all the above means that you must do your observing as if you are actually "photographing" the posture and movements of another individual. That's right, take several small little photographs in your mind's eye while you engage in give and take conversation. Allow these "photographic images" to furnish you with the nonverbal communication information needed and adjust your presentation accordingly. Avoid the stare and avoid nonproductive enmity you might create between yourself and another individual.

Don't be misled by a single gesture — Remember, a finger rubbed on the nose, or under the nose, could signify that your customer's lying. On the other hand,a finger held below the nose, perhaps on the lip, could signal a thinking attitude and accepting demeanor.

So, how can you tell what is really a body language sign, what you should pay attention to as a significant part of your communication with another individual? Simply look for multiple signs that indicate the same attitude. Is the person actually giving a fake smile, or is it a coy type of smile that is trying to communicate he or she understands what you are saying, is in agreement and will accept your proposition? Is he lifting an eyebrow at the same time to further indicate agreement or does a backward movement tell you that it is surprise, nonacceptance and a little bit of humor, showing that he thinks your proposal is ridiculous? Try to look for two or more signs, see if they mesh, and you can be more certain of your interpretation.

Be aware that you will often receive conflicting signs because when people catch themselves giving away their position through body language, they try to take actions to correct this communication. We know these corrections as simple "defenses" that are set up by people who have studied body language, are aware of what they are doing, and are trying to manipulate you. Some of the more obvious corrections are:

- A hand over the mouth to "take back" a quickly spoken word.
- Too quickly smiling to make up for an unintended f rown of disapproval.
- Suddenly crossing the arms to counteract an open gesture such as exposing the palms.

Whenever you become aware of this type of corrective gesture, you must ask yourself some questions that will lead you to what the person's real attitude or feelings might have been. You must find out if the other person's feelings and thoughts are divided, devising questions that will draw out responses.

While we're on the subject, look at your own defenses. How often do you use them? What do they tell you about your presentation and the degree to which you actually have the customer's best interests in mind?

Demonstration and Positive Reinforcement

When some salespeople are told that every sale has a demonstration, they will agree. They will say, "Certainly!" They agree because they know it is academically so. However, they will continue to sell the way they always have . . . never using demonstration, convinced that it does not apply to their type of selling.

These salespeople have a very severe problem. Their problem is the exclusion of two supporting elements that should be part of every sales presentation . . . the demonstration and positive reinforcement. When these two elements are used together, every salesperson has a chance to increase closing power.

Before we go on, let's take a minute to define just what a demonstration might be. To put it very simply, a demonstration is the introduction into a sales presentation of something concrete—three dimensional—something which the prospect can see, hear about and can touch.

So, unless salespeople always dig up prospects without any of the three above mentioned senses, they are passing up one of the sure-fire methods of closing a sale. They are also passing up the opportunity later in their sales presentation to reinforce the positive responses that a customer will give to a selling demonstration. Don't you make the same mistake.

As we look at opportunities to demonstrate, some examples will seem somewhat obvious. An automobile sale will involve specifications for the drive train, the mileage rating, color and style. The sale of heating equipment would involve specification sheets for the products, detailing all of the mechanical workings and the ratings of the material used. Further, in this type of equipment, a demonstration of the energy efficiency would be appropriate.

Demonstrators in these above examples are rather obvious. They are specification sheets, literature, cross sections of products, actual working models, etc. But what about the sale of less tangible items offered by your company? These might include the sale of product quality . . . or the sale of service and product guarantee which is a key reason for your customer to buy from you.

Understand that demonstrating is showing through example and through **proof** how your product or service will benefit your potential customer. A demonstration will oftentimes give your customer the opportunity to sell himself by "experiencing" the benefits or profits he will gain through the ownership of your product or from taking advantage of your service. A demonstration will directly affect your customer's feelings and his thinking as a result of his personal impressions. Your customer will best understand the merits of a product by personal use or observation.

— Tactic # 166 —

Give the Buyer an Opportunity to Experience

Since even the most intangible idea must be demonstrated to get the customer involved, you must try to figure a way where you can introduce a three dimensional item (even if it is literature or a specification sheet) into the selling situation.

To sell some ideas, to give your customer an opportunity to enjoy the benefits of your product, you might submit layout plans or blueprints, charts, diagrams or estimates. These items represent a demonstration because they are three dimensional things . . . things that a prospect can see or touch. Most importantly, they also give your customer an opportunity to make **positive comments** about elements of your sales call that relate to benefits for him. These positive comments are the very responses that we will be discussing when we talk about **reinforcement**.

— Tactic # 167 —

Know When to Demonstrate

Your demonstration should coincide with your verbal presentation. Once you notice that your prospect is beginning to recognize his need for your product, a demonstration will show him how your product can satisfy that need. Don't rush your customer into a demonstration in the opening stages of your sales presentation. In fact, if possible, reserve your demonstration as a climax . . . a proof element. Save the demonstration to show your prospect that you really have the things you claim to have. But, this doesn't mean to use it as a "last-resort." Use it as proof, but make sure it fits into the presentation at the proper time . . . just after you have gotten agreement on several features and benefits.

Your demonstration should not be a separate part of your presentation. For example, you should not stop your verbal presentation and say, "Now

I'm going to demonstrate the product." You see, if you did that, you would separate and formalize your demonstration making it an unnatural part of the presentation.

— Tactic # 168 —

Never Ask the Buyer Permission to Do a Demonstration

Never ask your buyer, "Would you like me to give you a demonstration?" When you do that, you are going to invite refusal. Most times the buyer will simply state that he is familiar with the product or that he doesn't have time, right now, or will use some other stalling tactic. Your demonstration should be smoothly coincidental with the feature and benefit description of your product and service.

— Tactic # 169 —

Prepare the Equipment You Are Going to Demonstrate

I've seen it many times . . . and I have experienced it personally. Demonstrations that come apart, product that will not work, "show and tell" that actually convinces the buyer he won't buy under any circumstances. When there is a breakdown, the entire presentation is wasted. Make sure that all of the devices that you are going to use are thoroughly inspected in advance and that they are in good working order. By carefully checking over the equipment and practicing, you will not only save embarrassment but, most likely, you will save lost orders.

Also, make sure everything you are going to show is polished, freshly painted, thoroughly cleaned and otherwise prepared to make the most favorable impression possible on your prospective customer.

If you are going to be demonstrating several parts, make sure the parts are packed in the order you are going to show them. In this way, you will avoid delay and confusion . . . you will be assured of a smooth and professional demonstration/presentation.

Of course, you will want to be completely familiar with the operation of the product or the devices that you are going to show to your customer. In this way, you will be able to demonstrate efficiently and avoid any awkward fumbling that would actually weaken your presentation. If you demonstrate that you are not sure about the product you're demonstrating, your customer's confidence will lessen with each passing moment.

Thoroughly prepare your demonstration sales talk.

This is not too much different from an actor in a play, a teacher preparing a lesson plan or a doctor getting ready for surgery. Every step in a planned demonstration requires that you also plan your verbal explanation. Every feature that you are going to point out with a demonstrator must be discussed in relation to the specific need of the customer who will be receiving your demonstration/presentation. That's right! **A verbal presentation must be prepared for every step in your demonstration.** Now, this does not mean that you are going to have a "canned" presentation. Most of it, of course, will be memorized for use in demonstration. However, it can be adapted to the individual needs of each and every customer.

— Tactic # 170 —

Make Separate Appointments for Demonstrations

Oftentimes products are too large or bulky to carry on regular sales calls. When this is the case, you will want to make a separate appointment for a convenient time and place so that you can favorably demonstrate your product to your prospect. By doing this, you place special emphasis on the upcoming call and you will help yourself by avoiding waiting time . . . further, you will make sure that you have adequate time to make a completely effective demonstration/presentation.

— Tactic # 171 —

Prepare Your Customer for Your Demonstration

Create some anticipation in the mind of your customer. Arouse interest in a customer's mind regarding the pending event of a demonstration by showing a piece of the equipment you are going to demonstrate, or stimulate your customer's curiosity by saying something like this: "In a few minutes, I'm going to be able to show you how you can save 15% on your annual operating costs with this little item."

Heavy equipment salespeople will often build anticipation by having a prospective buyer walk around the piece of heavy equipment, viewing it from all sides, while the salesman points out the mechanical features. Then, he will have him sit in the operator's cabin and point out all of the features relative to the operation of the equipment. Finally, the salesman will actually demontrate the equipment. In this process, he will have built anticipation, getting his customer **ready for the demonstration**.

Your customers can be prepared for a demonstration simply by telling a testimonial story about other people who have used the product and report great results. Or, you could simply ask a question that would a-rouse your customer's curiosity such as , "Have you ever seen an alarm system that works without wires?" asked by salespeople of radio and infrared operating security systems.

— Tactic # 172 —

Carefully Select the Features of Your Product or Service to Demonstrate

Most of your customers will have little interest, time or patience in seeing a demonstration of all of your product features. Make sure when you prepare a demonstration that you don't end up boring the customer with a long list of mechanical advantages, facts and figures that he really is not interested in. Remember, he is interested in W.I.I.F.M. (what's in it for me). When your demonstration goes on and on with the buyer simply a listener and not a participant, it will degenerate into a monologue while the customer becomes an uninterested "Zomboid."

Carefully select one or two features that you know are outstanding and are likely appealed to your customer's needs and his motives for buying. Concentrate on those. When you do this, you are going to be sure to get the customer's attention and interest and keep it throughout the demonstration. As your demonstration relates to your customer's needs, sales resistance will be reduced.

Remember, when you opened your interview with your customer and went through some probing questions, you were able to determine these needs and motives. Without having done this, your demonstration will lose much of its effectiveness. Again, that is the reason I suggest the demonstration be saved for the latter part of your presentation . . . so it can appropriately relate to what the customer wants.

—— Tactic # 173 ——

Get Your Customer to Participate

Remember that you are trying to get your customer to believe what you have said about your product. You want that customer to experience and prove for himself that he is going to get satisfaction from owning the product. You want him, now, while you demonstrate, to get mentally past the point of purchase. When you get the customer to participate in the demonstration, you will create, in his mind, a sense of ownership.

You want your customer's full attention. The best way of doing that is getting him to take part in your demonstration. When he is taking part, he will begin to forget his objections and he will start to investigate what your product will do for him. He will actually convince himself that your product meets his needs as he visualizes himself using it.

Make sure you place your product within easy reach of your customer so that he can operate the features, control the knobs, switch on the current, or do anything that you can show him how to do in the demonstration.

—— Tactic # 174 ——

Ask Committing Questions

As you speak with your customer or prospect, you will notice that he will indicate acceptance of some of your ideas and will want to discuss others. He will want to give his point of view. As he explains his position, he will be looking for positive reassurance from you about his ideas and his feelings. This seeking reinforcement on his part is something that is worth special attention. It is particularly effective to use a system of reinforcement during your entire demonstration.

Suppose that your demonstration is being accepted by your customer. Your presentation is well practiced and is being done smoothly. Your customer is involved. You have established a two way conversation, and you are appealing to all of your customer's senses. You feel that your customer's

participating with you. He is experiencing your demonstration and is a part of your selling message. When this is the situation, your customer's responses to you will be very strong and very positive. They will also be somewhat frequent. You will notice that these positive responses will be more noticeable during good demonstrations. It would be very logical, then that the demonstration phase of your selling conversation gives you the greatest opportunity to reinforce what is on your customer's mind.

Make sure, that you don't reinforce the customer's responses in such a way that it seems you're rushing him. Try to get some commitment, but don't seem to be "pushing" the customer to a conclusion.

For example: A salesman talking about a new car could reinforce the customer by asking a question such as this, "You mentioned you were interested in safety . . . doesn't the new braking system prove that this car is safer than most?" Or the representative selling a stainless steel kitchen sink could say, "Isn't this stainless steel sink easy to keep clean . . . it's especially good if you want to just biff-bam, clean the pan and get out of the kitchen!?" By asking these test questions, you can find out whether or not your customer or prospect is in agreement on the point and you also reinforce the comments that have been made during the demonstration.

Be sure, however, that you always reinforce the customer's positive comments. Then, ask some committing questions relative to those positive comments.

— Tactic # 175 —

Listen Carefully for Customer Commitments

Some customers will actually commit themselves. When your customer indicates that he's pretty well convinced by your demonstration, you should go on to another feature that relates to another need and continue your demonstration. Simply reinforce the customer's comment . . . tell him he's right . . . then move on.

Sometimes the customer might just give a one word clue such as "interesting." In that case, you'll want to consider the word, but you will want to be able to feel how it was stated. There are many common phrases such as "Oh really," "Uh-huh," "Is that so?" These all represent positive responses and they really have more meaning than would appear on the surface. Most times, they are commitments on the part of the customer. Recognize them, positively reinforce them and move on.

Remember your body language . . . read the customer's face. Some positive responses could seem negative to you. They could be put in the form of a question and seem as if the customer was raising an objection. For example, let's say you are in the bathroom and kitchen remodeling business and that you are selling a bathroom vanity. During your demonstration, the prospect might suddenly ask about price. You respond, but you quickly attempt to get back into your demonstration to point out the **benefits**, thereby attempting to raise the value of the product higher than the price. Remember, when the customer is asking about the price, he is "mentally past the point of purchase." He has bought the product and now he has to pay the invoice.

Suppose, however, before you have a chance to continue your benefit story, the customer responds sarcastically by saying, "Does that price include the accessories or are the accessories extra?" This, too, can be a positive response, even though the customer is trying to disguise his positive feelings with a sarcastic remark. He is really indicating that he finds it hard to believe that the price would include all of the accessories. If you are not able to recognize this as a positive response, you might just simply answer him in the affirmative and continue your benefit story.

When you recognize this as a positive response, however, you will reinforce it by saying something to this effect, "Yes, Mr. Prospect, that price does include all of the drawer package you see here and the accessory packs. Most people don't know that these items are extras with other lines of vanities. It is pretty obvious that you know what you are buying."

You see, the customer is actually committing himself to the fact that he wants these extras. If you listen carefully, then, you know that you simply must reinforce that commitment. When you have reinforced the customer adequately, he is well on his way to buying your product.

Occasionally, you are going to run into a prospect who does not commit himself at all. He will not give any positive responses during your selling demonstration. This is the type of person who just does not want to make any commitment. That doesn't mean that he is not willing to buy. This type of customer very often needs considerable encouragement to give any positive response. When this is the case, be sure to pause in your demonstration to simply ask for a positive response. You may want to say something as simplistic as, "Don't you agree, Mr. Prospect, that this **demonstrates** exactly what you are looking for?" You are trying to get a commitment.

It doesn't matter how he responds, whatever his response, you have something to work with. It will give you an idea as to his thinking and will give you an opportunity to reinforce the positive aspects of his reply.

— Tactic # 176 —

Use the Four Steps of Demonstration

A successful demonstration is merely the sum total of many small parts that focus on four basic steps. These steps are:

- You say something.
- You do something.
- You get the prospect into the act.
- You ask leading questions.

— Tactic # 177 —

You Say Something . . . Verbalize

How you talk to the customer during the demonstration can make it successful or have it fall flat. Here are some simple hints that may seem all too obvious, but are often forgotten, or in some cases, have never been learned by salespeople:

Be enthusiastic — Think about your own experiences when you have gone into a retail store. What about the salespeople who don't know anything and, further, don't care. They are less than lukewarm about helping you . . . they probably don't like their job and are totally unenthusiastic. How did you feel? What about another salesperson who was courteous, gave you close attention, asked about your needs, listened to your questions and gave sufficient answers and made an overall effort to help you get what you want? Assume the same product, just a different approach. The answer is self evident. Be enthusiastic about your product when you are presenting and, as long as you are going to be face-to-face with the customer, be enthusiastic for how he will benefit when he finally owns that product.

Use conversation, not "pitch" — Talk to your customer as if he was a friend. Don't make a speech. Draw your customer into the conversation with questions and positively reinforce what he says favorably about your product. Discuss the product as if you were his "assistant buyer", helping him to investigate all of the advantages he is going to gain by owning it. Again, use a conversational tone . . . don't pitch.

Speak slowly — You are familiar with your product, but if you start to speak very rapidly and just snow your customer with words, you will find that your conversation will outdistance his understanding. He may not say so, but he will tell you, "Well, I'll think about it." Talk slowly so that he can understand.

Tell first, and then show — Get your customer's mind going, first. Tell him what you are going to show him. Then, use the product as the proof. For years, we have been taught to "show and tell." That's the wrong approach. You must tell . . . verbally . . . getting his mind thinking about the product, and then **show**.

SECTION IV

Getting Ready to Sell — Planning

So far, we have been into the nitty-gritty of closing sales, negotiating, and overcoming objections. We have also discussed some details of proper presentation. These are good tools to make you effective on the sales call. At this point, we must back up and look at the get ready part of selling. The planning. The techniques and tactics by which you imagine the desired result and build a tactical plan to have it happen.

It's an absolute fact that salespeople who plan their presentations in advance are tremendously more successful than people who just rely on pure inspiration whenever they are face-to-face with their potential buyer. Many successful salespeople have told me that the results they achieve are basically because of 90 percent preparation and 10 percent presentation.

Before we go on, however, we have to understand that when I'm talking about planning, I'm not talking about "canned" sales talks. This is a mistake many salespeople make. They think a planned sales talk is something that is memorized and presented word for word. No wonder they resist planning if this is their mental concept of the activity. Planning your sales call, even in retail situations, has many advantages.

The unplanned presentation will cause you as the salesperson to lack the total confidence needed to help the buyer finally make a decision. It'll cause you to substitute verbosity or personality for good logical statements . . . it'll cause you to exaggerate, ramble, leave out important feature-benefit-proof sales points and, in general, waste your time.

Think of other professionals. Think of a lawyer. Before he faces a jury, that lawyer is going to spend many hours preparing the case. Why does he do this? Simply because he knows that the better prepared his presentation, the more likely he is to have a success convincing the jury of the plea he is going to make on behalf of his client. As salespeople, we should be applying these same techniques. As salespeople, we must always acquaint ourselves with the needs of our customers and prospects and assemble ideas, demonstrators and all the logical facts that will convince the prospect that we are able to meet those needs. When I say assemble, I mean arrange them in such a way that they will be effective when they are presented.

You see, you must anticipate any objections that your prospect might have and be ready for the answers. The lawyer does that. So should you.

Think of your competition. Slowly, but surely, competitive salespeople are realizing the benefits of planned presentations. If you don't do the same, you are not going to keep up .

Think of the buyers. They are demanding that salespeople be better informed today and be better able to render superior service.

To be the complete professional, then, you must plan what you will say, plan what you will do, and plan alternatives.

— Tactic # 178 —

Learn the Types of Planned Sales Presentations

You must be a student of the four types of sales presentations that are being used by successful salespeople all over the world. We will discuss each one, individually, showing how each of the four systems has its own value, depending upon the type of product you sell, or the type of customer that might be involved. Also, you will probably be making some mental selection of the type of planned sales presentation best for you based on your experience. Further, you might select a particular type of presentation based on the objective of the sales conversation.

The four types of planned presentations are:

- The standard presentation.
- The outlined presentation.
- The survey program presentation.
- The work-sheet presentation.

Don't be misled into thinking that these presentations are only used by beginning salespeople. They are used **all the time** by experienced salespeople who know that an organized approach will make their jobs much easier. These are **tactics** to make you more successful. These methods of presentation will prevent you from wasting time; will stop you from becoming involved in irrelevant conversations with buyers, and will help you from digressing. All of this will result in more interesting sales interviews and will create a more logical order in which you can present significant facts of interest to your prospect.

— Tactic # 179 —

Use the Standard Sales Presentation

This is the one that people call a "canned" sales talk. Remember, however, it's not that. It is, however, the most common type of sales conversation because it's one that has been completely written out in advance . . . many times by management. It is more or less memorized and it is repeated in that memorized format to the buyer.

Many of these presentations are formulated based on management's understanding of what their prospective buyers want. Sometimes the company will give you, the salesperson, a written, or even a recorded sample, of the most effective presentation. This is good if used as a tool. However, I don't believe you should adapt the speech patterns of another individual. I don't think you should memorize something word for word and use it each and every time.

The up side of the standard presentation, however, is that you should be memorizing the sales arguments and presenting them in a logical order that will lead to a conclusion. You should realize that the management of your company has done research and they are giving you one of the best ways to make the presentation to increase your closes. You will not have to necessarily **adopt** the presentation in total, but, certainly, **adapt** the presentation to your style.

More than 75 years ago, John Patterson, then president of the National Cash Register Company, created the standard sales presentation. He visited 50 sales agencies in 50 days and had his secretary record some of the best sales points of his most successful salespeople. From those notes, Mr. Patterson then prepared a presentation that he felt would work for most of his salespeople in most selling situations. The presentation included the proper approach and a demonstration. All of his salespeople were required to memorize the presentation to sell his cash registers. Of course it worked. It was the basis for the building of that great company.

Your standard sales presentation will cover all of the features of your product and service, make sure you get the benefits in and will certainly include elements of proof that will get your customer to start nodding his head. What should you include as part of the presentation? Well, I will take the original outline from John Patterson . . . he included:

- **An opening** — This is done to get the attention and arouse the interest of a buyer in a specific need for your product or service.
- **Description of need satisfaction** — A statement of how your product solves the customer problem or meets the need that you know he has.
- **Proof** — This is a statement that gives evidence of how the product has satisfied the needs of other people that are similar to the customer or prospect involved in the interview. You would use facts in the form of statistics, testimonial information, laboratory tests, statements of guarantee, etc.
- **A conclusion** — This would be a statement or several statements that are intended to move the buyer to action. They are statements that get the buyer to say yes through special inducements or through the use of "fear of loss."

If we were to look at mechanical types of products which are sold by many manufacturers, wholesalers, trade retailers and others, we could include a procedure of demonstration that would follow these four steps:

Step # 1: Arouse the interest of the buyer while demonstrating several features of the product.

Step # 2: Show him the W.I.I.F.M. (What's in it for me?) by demonstrating how the product meets the buyer's needs, using the features as reinforcement.

Step # 3: Get the prospective buyer involved in the process. Have your potential customer take part in the demonstration. Give him the product. Have him operate it.

Step # 4: Simply ask for an order.

There's another great advantage about your using a standard presentation that you have thoroughly worked out. It will help you avoid making any exaggerated statements or claims for your product. it will also help you use better speech patterns and remind you to emphasize the sales points that have been successful in the past. It'll assure that you always have something worthwhile to say, and by using the standard presentation, you will be sure to tell a complete story and do it in a shorter period of time.

You may be asking what the weakness of the standard presentation might be. As you read this, I'm sure that they are somewhat obvious. The standard presentation is more difficult to adapt to the wants and needs of an individual prospect. It also might not suit your personality. And here's another . . . when you are interrupted or you digress because of a buyer's question, you might lose track of where you were and not be able to go back to the standard presentation. There is still another drawback to the standard presentation . . . it doesn't give you much of an opportunity to probe the customer to find out his basic interests and his motives for buying. It assumes that this prospect is very similar or the same as all other prospects and the motives are the same. In a high percentage of cases, that is true, but it doesn't work every time. Of course, the primary objection by most salespeople to the standard presentation (memorized sales talk) is that it seems to be unnatural. Too many salespeople start to speed up their conversation, since the presentation is memorized, and go rapid-fire through the entire presentation. The prospect loses track of the concept being presented. So, what do you do about these problem areas of the standard presentation?

To overcome the problems of the standard presentation, I believe you ought to accept it and then rewrite it in your own words. In this way, you will be able to deliver it naturally. You will also be much more effective. Also, you will tend to slow down and present your words in a convincing way and not just run over them because they are somebody elses. You will have a lot more confidence in the presentation and be able to find your spot if you happen to be interrupted.

Give yourself a chance. Try the standard presentation and you're going to find that throughout the process of preparation, you will acquire a lot of knowledge about the principle sales points that you need to present your product. You are also going to anticipate answers to some common objections that you have heard in the past, but never really totally solved. In the process, you will gain more confidence because you will know that you have a mental storehouse of reasons why your customer should buy your product.

Use your standard presentation in sales situations of this type:

With new products — When you are unfamiliar with a product or service, formulate a standard presentation that you can use for a period of time.

Consumer sales of inexpensive products — Vacuum cleaners, some appliances, books, cosmetics, and other products that are from medium to inexpensive, sold directly to consumers, should be presented in a standard presentation that quickly gets the benefits over to the customer.

Selling intangibles — Salespeople who sell life insurance or investments or a single need item such as cemetary plots, retirement programs, an educational program, or other items of this nature, should be using a standard presentation in order to get most of the selling points across. In the process of using the standard presentation, these types of selling activities enable the salesperson to find the actual needs of a prospect. So if you are working in this area , the standard presentation should be a valuable tool.

Now, let's get more specific. We are going to look at how you are going to put together your presentation and we are going to put them into the tactical format of this book. So, the next four tactical items involve putting together your standard presentation.

— Tactic # 180 —

Always Adapt to the Needs of Your Prospect

All standard presentations start out by being constructed based on the general need for your product or service. Make sure that everyone that you talk with actually has a need. My observation has shown that many times, salespeople present a standard presentation to people who actually don't have any need for the product. This should be established in advance. Simply ask the prospect if he has a need for this type of product.

If there are several types of needs for your product, you will want to have a standard presentation that explains each **individual** need to each **individual** buyer. Here's an example out of the insurance industry. A salesman who is talking with a father who is planning to send his children to college would want to use a planned presentation that explains how his insurance package is actually an "educational fund." In the case of a school teacher, without dependents, the insurance program becomes a "retirement income." Two separate standard presentations would be more logical than to have one that tried to cover both these types of prospects.

— Tactic # 181 —

Use a Natural Delivery

Don't fall into the trap of sounding like a tape recording. If you are unable to deliver your standard presentation naturally, you shouldn't use it. Go to one of the other forms that follow in this chapter. If you speak too rapidly and have an artificial delivery, or if it seems very mechanical, your presentation will actually turn off the prospective buyer. Nobody wants to feel as if they are part of a "mechanical" situation. Every once in a while, purposely digress. Tell a story. Ask a question. Be sure to know where you left your planned presentation and get back. This will help to make it more natural. If your company gives you a planned presentation, rewrite it in your own words. Add example stories or anything else that makes it a part of you.

—— Tactic # 182 ——

Invite the Buyer to Participate in the Planned Presentation

A standard planned presentation must never be delivered in some kind of a monologue form. Monologues will tend to bore your prospects. People want to participate. They want to have an opportunity to express their feelings, explain their own wants and needs about the offering under discussion. So, from time-to-time, you will want to pause and allow your prospective buyer to ask questions, or, even, raise objections. That's right . . . raise objections. You have already learned how to handle them and this should present no problem. Give consideration to your prospect Is opinions. Discuss them. Overall, avoid the impression of any high-pressure tactics.

—— Tactic # 183 ——

Get Action

Your standard planned presentation is intended to get some action from your buyer. You want a signed order or, in industrial selling, you may simply be trying to set up an appointment for a returned call. Whatever your objective, however, make sure that you plan it as part of your standard presentation.

So, basically, that is the standard planned presentation. Now, we are going to discuss the **outlined sales presentation**.

— Tactic # 184 —

Use the Outlined Sales Presentation

The outlined sales presentation is still a **planned presentation**. It is very similar to the standard presentation, since it involves listing the most significant points that you are going to cover. However, instead of having it written out word for word, the outlined sales presentation is one that enables you to memorize each **heading** in an outline in the order in which it is to be presented. The supporting material, then, is spoken in an extemporaneous manner, being adjusted according to the situation.

Your sales presentation outline could also be developed by management from observation of presentations done by other successful salespeople. Most often, however, salespeople prepare their own outlines going from one logical step to another all the way from the opening to the close of the anticipated sales call. These outlines are adjusted, from time to time, based on the responses of prospects.

There are many advantages to an outlined sales presentation. Advantages that favorably compare with the standard sales talk. First, you are free to change your presentation according to the motives, wants, needs, and desires of your prospect. Once you are interrupted, or you digress based on a customer injecting an opinion, you are more easily able to return to your outline. It promotes a more natural conversation which tends to make the entire sales interview much more interesting for the prospect (and for the salesperson) therefore, making it more convincing. Most customers feel.that there is less domination on the part of the salesperson. When less domination is felt, there is less tension or buyer resistance.

Whenever you use an outlined presentation, you're going to find that your points are more coherent. You will avoid extraneous ideas that suddenly pop into your mind. You will emphasize the most important sales points and will save time.

What about the down side? Many salespeople, who lack knowledge about their own product or service, find that they cannot develop a sufficient outline to convince their customers. Of course, if this problem exists, it's one that will be discovered when the outline is attempted. In those cases, it's time to go back to square one and do diagnostic homework. Remember, most people are **down on** the things they are not **up on** . . . and this is the case of the salesman who cannot come up with an outline for his product.

Outlined presentations can be extremely effective for people who want to sell up-scale products or services that tend to satisfy many wants, needs and desires of prospective customers. Also, outlined presentations help salespeople who want to appeal to diverse buying motives on the part of their various customers. The up-scale or higher priced industrial products and consumer specialty items are often sold with well developed outlined sales presentations.

You must be experienced and thoroughly familiar with all of the features, benefits, and proof elements of your products, however, before you can use an outlined sales presentation. Also, you must be able to express yourself adequately, adjusting to each customer, in terms that the individual customer will understand and appreciate.

—— Tactic # 185 ——

Use Outlines Based on Product Points

Probably one of the easiest forms of an outlined sales presentation is the principle selling point process. This will help you present the advantages of your product feature by feature, and benefit by benefit.

A carpeting manufacturer prepared sales points outlines for every product they had in their line. The outlines are then memorized by all of their retail outlet salespeople so that the features are recalled every time the product is discussed with a potential buyer. You see, when the carpet salespeople have memorized the product point outline, all of the major features immediately come to mind. They are also arranged in a logical order that will help the dealer carpet salesperson make a demonstration that illustrates all the advantages of each carpet product.

You can do this same thing. Simply list the features, benefits, and proof statements of the products you want to present and then memorize these lists by memorizing the features. The benefits and proof elements will be contained in your subconscious mind and they will follow easily and naturally while you present.

— Tactic # 186 —

Use This Procedure to Construct an Outlined Presentation

Stick to the presentation outline — Your presentation will be effective because it is a logical arrangement of the most convincing sales arguments based on your past experience. For that reason, make sure you don't get off the subject matter, for too long a period of time. Present each step in the same logical order as you prepared it in the outline.Your outline should contain only enough points that are easily memorized so that you can closely follow them in your presentation. By adhering to your full outline, you are going to take full advantage of the affect that every point will have on your prospect.

Fully explain each point in your outline — Remember that the outline is just that . . . **an outline**. They are "trigger points" in your mind. They are there to keep you on track. As you present, then, you must amplify each of the points that are in your outline. This means you have to be thoroughly familiar with everything around each outlined point. It means you have to be familiar with the needs of your customer regarding each point, and the features and benefits of your products as they relate to those needs. If necessary, you should prepare information around each point regarding raw materials, your superior process of manufacturing, style, design, alternatives, etc. In other words, don't just have an outline . . . know your stuff!

Involve your buyer — Don't forget that you are going to try to create a conversation with your outlined presentation. In other words, you are going to establish a dialogue with your prospective buyer. Actually program some questions into your outline that will encourage your prospect to participate. The outline is a guide for discussion, then, in which you will get your prospect involved. In this way, you are going to more quickly get your prospect mentally past the point of purchase . . . mentally owning your product so that he will eventually buy.

Move your prospect to action — Get an order. That's why you are in business. That's why you have prepared an outline. Make sure that you have listed several good points in your outline that will lead you to a logical close. When you have made those points, ask for the order.

So, we have discussed the standard presentation which is a fully written presentation, memorized and given practically word for word. We have just discussed the outlined presentation which will give you much more flexibility and enable you to more greatly involve your prospect. Now, let's consider the **survey** or **program** presentation which will enable you to present your features and benefits based on an analysis of your buyer's needs.

— Tactic # 187 —

Use the Survey Presentation

This type of presentation requires that you take a survey or do an analysis of your customer's needs. It also involves determining if a customer has the ability to buy your product or service. Once this is done, you will prepare a written or verbal sales presentation that is especially prepared for a particular buyer.

The process of constructing a survey presentation has been compared to the steps used in photography . . . you would take a picture, and then, prepare the photographic print. You would do the same thing in a survey presentation as you get a clear impression (or picture) of your prospect's requirements and then prepare a proposal which would show how your product or service can take care of those wants, needs, and desires.

— Tactic # 188 —

Sell the Survey

There are basically five steps in a survey presentation. They include:

- Selling the survey.
- Getting the facts.
- Diagnosing the facts.
- Building a proposal.
- Selling the proposal.

Under this tactic, we will discuss selling the survey to a potential customer. That is the first step that you must take. It is possible that you may want to set up one or two appointments to devote to this single purpose. Your idea would be to sell your potential customer on allowing you to conduct a survey . . . at the same time, you would be reducing sales resistence and would be making the potential buyer aware of his needs for your products and service. To properly sell your survey, you would want to be able to show your potential customer samples of surveys you have conducted with other buyers and, further, show testimonials from satisfied customers who have taken your recommendations to use your products and services.

—— Tactic # 189 ——

Get The Facts

Once you have gotten a prospect to agree to a survey, you will initiate the second step in the process; that of uncovering all facts relevant to a customer's problem. This can be done in the very first interview with the customer, or, in the case of complex situations, be accomplished through several interviews. You may find that you need the assistance of other individuals in your company such as engineers, financial analysts, technicians, or other specialists that could assist you in the process of diagnosing your customer's situation and then recommending the proper product or service to remedy his problems.

You should probably have some sort of prepared questionnaire that will help you get at the facts . . . discovering your buyer's needs. Get as much information as you can. The more information you get, the better you will be able to prepare your survey presentation which is to be offered as an acceptable solution to your potential customer's problems.

—— Tactic # 190 ——

Diagnose the Facts

Now it is time to go through a process of diagnosing all of the facts in order to begin preparing your survey presentation. Please notice that I keep using terminology that would normally be applied to a doctor. Well, the situation is exactly the same. Your doctor makes a physical examination, considers all of the facts that his examination has revealed, and will determine the significance of these facts. When you make a diagnosis of your potential customer's situation, you will follow this same procedure.

Your ability to diagnose the customer's problem and recommend a solution will depend, to a great extent, on your knowledge of your product and service and, of course, on the applications that your products and services will have to your potential customers situation.

—— Tactic # 191 ——

Build Your Survey Proposal

Now you need to put together a written description of your potential customer's current situation, present your own recommendations for a solution, including the investment the customer is required to make.

This type of proposal should be typewritten, could contain some illustrations, charts, specification sheets or other material that would graphically explain your proposal in detail. Every buyer situation will be different, therefore, every proposal will, eventually, be a "custom made" presentation.

—— Tactic # 192 ——

Sell The Proposal

The final and most important step in the survey proposal system is to actually **sell the proposal**. You should make an appointment at a time when your prospective customer can give careful consideration to your proposal. There are actually five steps you will want to follow to make sure you have a successful presentation. These steps are:

- Thank the buyer for the opportunity.
- Exercise control.
- Encourage participation by the buyer.
- Get a commitment from the buyer.
- Get the buyer's consent or establish a compromise position.

Let's look at these one at a time:

Thank the buyer for the opportunity — In order to have gotten this far, your potential customer will have generously given of his time and may even have been put to some inconvenience to help you. It is absolutely necessary that you let the customer know you are aware of his sacrifices. Tell him that you appreciate his help and his cooperation. This will prepare the way for you to get on with your proposal.

Exercise control — Be sure that you control the use of all of the typewritten material, your charts, your graphs, and backup support items. If you hand everything over to your buyer at once, he cannot possibly absorb the material in a convincing way. Every page of the proposal and each support item must be injected into the presentation separately, and thoroughly discussed before you go on to another segment of your proposal.

Try to position yourself so that you are at the side of your prospect instead of across a desk. You will be better able to point out significant items in the written proposal or fully explain the backup material. **Don't read the material verbatum**. Develop your own comments, testimonial stories, additional information and other support elements that will help you get your point across.

Encourage participation by the buyer — Don't conduct a monologue with the customer as an audience of one person. Give your customer an opportunity to ask questions . . . raise objections or, in general, make comments on your recommendations. Unless you are able to get the customer into the conversation, you will never be able to assess his attitude concerning your proposal. Further, you won't be able to uncover any objections and overcome them so that you can convince him of the value of your proposal. How do you do this? While you are presenting, stop every so often and simply ask, "Does this make sense?" Ask him, "What do you think of this idea?" Or, "Does this seem reasonable to you?"

Get a commitment from the buyer — You want the customer to eventually agree to the proposal and, therefore, buy your product and service. To assure this, it will be necessary for you to test your buyer's interest by getting small commitments along the way. As you make major points, ask your customer if he agrees. Try to get the customer to agree to at least six points and then prepare to close the sale.

Get the buyer's consent or establish a compromise position — When you have gotten approximately six commitments from the customer, you can be fairly sure that he is ready to buy. Now is the time to use any of the closing methods discussed in Section I. Ask him a question that relates to something that would happen once he has accepted the proposal. For instance, ask him if he would be ready to start within a week or would he prepare to wait until next month? This gives him an either/or choice and assumes that he has accepted the proposal.

If the customer doesn't agree with your proposal, try a compromise. Have an alternative solution prepared, holding it in reserve, bringing it up at a time when the customer indicates that he is not sold on the original idea. Be sure that you do not discuss the alternate proposal during your original presentation. **Only introduce the alternate proposal when the customer has declined the original.**

— Tactic # 193 —

Use the Worksheet Presentation

A very simplistic type of presentation is the worksheet presentation which involves the preparation of a chart that shows the customer situation, his needs, and the sales points that will meet the needs of the customer. A prepared worksheet, then, becomes a guide for making the actual sales presentation.

To prepare such a worksheet, merely put the following columns across the top of a sheet of tablet paper and fill in information below each subject:

Name of Buyer	**Buyer Description**	**Needs**	**Proposal**

In the first column, you would simply put down the name of a prospect that you believe needs your product or service. In the second column, you would write all of the available information about your prospective buyer. You would put down such information as his age, personal likes and dislikes, buying habits, and other information that would be helpful when relating to the customer.

In the third column, under "Needs", you will list the various reasons why the buyer should buy your product or service.

Finally, the fourth column would contain all of the selling points that you would bring up in the presentation.

The worksheet is designed to force you into obtaining as much information as possible about your prospective buyer before you make an approach. By doing this, you will save yourself and your prospect's time. You will know what sales points you are going to present and you will relate them to the specific needs of the prospect.

Most experienced salespeople use the worksheet method as a short cut, but thorough tool of preparation. Beginners also find this method an excellent way of preparing for a sales call.

To use the worksheet method, it is absolutely essential that you know your products and services well and that you are able to fully explain their applications as they relate to the needs of your customers.

Pre-approach Tactics

Planning a sales call means that you will want to give a lot of consideration to anything involving pre-approach activities. This means you will want to find out all you can about your prospect, how your product relates to his needs, and how you can best present your presentation points.

An important part of being able to win in the game of selling is to use successful pre-approach. You will be able to find out about your prospect before the actual call, and you will increase your chances of being successful.

— Tactic # 194 —

Find Out All You Can About Your Prospect

If you want to make a great presentation and feel confident during your call on your prospect, you simply have to be well prepared. So what should you know about the prospect? The following seven points should be well covered during your pre-approach analysis:

- What his company does.
- Vital statistics such as the net worth of the company, the number of employees, the overall size relative to the industry, and the **reach** of the company (regional or national).
- What the company needs relative to your line of services . . . what volume of products and what types.
- How the company is financed. What is its capitalization and its credit rating?
- Is the company stagnant or is it growing? Is it involved in a growing industry or an industry in decline?
- Who are the buying influences? Who is the number one person to see?
- All the specific information you might need to make a presentation that shows a customer's needs and how your products will fulfill those needs.

Many salespeople will look at this seven point criteria and say they can get this information at the opening of their sales interview. To do that would be to defeat the purpose of pre-approach tactics. Remember, your sales interview is for **selling**, not for doing research.

— Tactic # 195 —

Know Your Market

It is absolutely necessary that you know all about the business conducted by your prospect. When you do, you will be able to imagine how your prospective customer can use your product. Essentially, you will be relating your products to your customer's needs.

When you study your prospect's business and his market, you will acquire some of the "lingo" used by the trade in which he is involved. It will help you to talk to your customer on his level, in his language.

Read trade publications — Find out what magazines your prospect reads. Get several current copies of these magazines, and read them cover to cover. You cannot fail to get good information that will help you on a future call.

If you are in doubt as to how to find the name of the trade publications, call any large company (even the prospect's company) involved in the industry and ask the name of the magazine that is most read. Another way is to send for a copy of the *Encyclopedia of American Associations*, published by Gale Research Company, Book Tower, Detroit, Michigan 48205 .

Ask other salespeople — Ask your sales manager or other salespeople in your organization about information relative to the industry in which your prospect is involved. You'll undoubtedly find that much information is contained within your own company.

— Tactic # 196 —

Use Your Company Material

Your company undoubtedly has advertising material, demonstration samples, specification information, and other printed items that are available to help you do your best in a sales interview. The use of the material depends entirely upon you. So, as you plan your pre-approach, consider the following:

- Find out exactly what your company has available in the area of advertising, technical information, sales literature, and special mailings.
- Carefully select the material that you feel would be best for each and every customer. Plan to send this material to the customer, through the mail, prior to your sales call.
- Prepare specialized mailers, based on the material you plan to use on your sales interview. This material will be reinforced, later, in person, when you make your presentation to your prospect.
- When you are conducting a personal interview with your prospect, be sure you mention the mailed material and reinforce the intent of each item. Plan to mention the mailed material in your opening remarks. Have extra copies of the material with you so that you can use it during the interview.

— Tactic # 197 —

Think Big in Order to Sell Big

You are valued by your company according to the amount of business you **create**, more so than the business you **secure**. For example, an industrial salesman could go out and sell three truckloads of plastic pipe and pile up a decent **volume** , however, this would not be profitable business. Another salesman working for the same company might sell a much smaller volume of fittings, but the items would show a higher **profit**.

The second salesman would be of greater value to his company. The second salesman realizes that he is a businessman and he is thinking bigger than just making a sale . . . he is thinking about the return on investment of his time which comes from his ability to make a profit on every sale. That's thinking beyond the normal, usual day-to-day activity of **securing** business. Thinking **bigger** means thinking **creatively**.

Use your imagination. Think about how you can create more dollars for yourself and your company. Imagination can be one of your most powerful weapons. It will help you control your habits of **securing** business and will enable you to **create** both business and profits.

Of imagination, Albert Einstein said, "Imagination is more important than knowledge."

According to Napoleon, "Imagination rules the world."

A salesperson without imagination is like a golfer without a club, a tennis player without a racket, or a bowler with an underweight ball. Here are eight simple guidelines that will help you use your imagination, think big, and increase your sales profits:

- Make your sales presentations unique.
- Get an insider (in your customer's company) on your side.
- Plan to get your prospect in a relaxed and receptive mood.
- Use an unusual approach to illustrate solutions for unusual problems.
- Start out with the "something for nothing" approach.
- Multiply your selling effectiveness by getting several people within the customer's organization recommending your product to the decision maker.
- Look for non-routine lead sources and follow up.
- Look for the best salesman in your industry, find out how he does it, and follow his techniques.

—— Tactic # 198 ——

Develop More Leads

No matter how well you service your existing customers, you are going to suffer some losses. Attrition will occur each and every year. This means you must develop new leads to keep ahead of the game.

Probably your company will provide some leads for you, however, how well you screen these leads and then track them down is your total responsibility. Here are some pointers that will help you be more successful with the lead handling and will also help you build new business in the face of attrition.

- Remember your best source of leads is probably the customers you already have. Be sure you ask for their help. Ask each customer if they can think of two people you should be calling on.
- Don't overlook leads that are given to you by people who service your customers such as repairmen, vending machine people, public utility employees, etc.
- If you are involved in consumer sales, the best lead service is a satisfied user of your product. If Mr. Jones was happy with

the installation of the new alarm system, for example, ask him if he could recommend any friends or neighbors that he thinks would be interested. In many cases, salespeople will offer cash incentives for leads that eventually become sales.

- Think of customer complaints as potential leads. If the complaint was a result of a piece of equipment that has outlived its usefulness, you have a good candidate for replacement of the item.
- Read your trade publications and check newspapers to see if you can find changes in company projects, executive personnel, or company relocations.
- Get to know all of the important people in your local chamber of commerce, Elks, Kiwannis, Rotary, or other associations that contain business people.

—— Tactic # 199 ——

Use the "Japanese Style" of Lead Follow Up

Japanese salespeople are taught that they have to make at **least** 12 courtesy calls on a prospective buyer before they should expect that prospect to give permission for the salesman to even show his product.

Beyond those 12 calls, the closing of the deal might involve 20 or 30 more calls.

The primary reason for so many calls is that most Japanese companies do their buying only twice a year. **The dates on which they do the buying is kept top secret**. Since salespeople are never told the purchasing date, they can only keep making calls to be sure that they are considered.

Now, it isn't expected that you are going to take that approach 100% into your tactical programming. In fact, you just don't have enough days in the year to cover all of your potential in that manner. However, learn from the Japanese style that you must **persist** once you have made an initial call, in order to finally have the opportunity to make a sale.

— Tactic # 200 —

Check Your Selling Habits

You may not know it, but you probably get on some people's nerves. I've been told I do. And, I know many others that get on my nerves. There could be a particular mannerism, a behavior pattern, any little thing that could seem perfectly natural to you, yet, it might drive others crazy. Before you go out to sell, check yourself:

- **Check your handshake** — A handshake can make a bad first impression. You want to endeavor to have a dry, firm handshake that exhibits self-confidence and . . . don't be a pumper. Keep the handshake brief but confident.
- **Don't talk too fast** — If you talk too fast, you are going to detract from the content of your own message. You can be sure your listener will miss some of the facts.
- **Watch out for faltering speech** — This means you must practice what you are going to say. Also, try not to use the common, "You know" and "Uh" or "Er". . . it's all just bad speech.
- **Watch out if you are a smoker** — Don't even ask permission to smoke. Smoke after you have left the customer. Even if there's an ashtray on your buyer's desk, he may detest the habit. If he lights up first . . . well, that's a different situation.
- **Watch your joke telling** — It's true that a lot of men enjoy jokes . . . in fact they look forward to hearing something new from salespeople. But you must be careful. Find out if this guy's a deacon in his church, or if he resents his time being taken up with joke telling.
- **Don't be a "fussy fixer"**— This is a bad habit of mine and I've seen other salespeople fall into this same compulsive activity. Don't straighten papers up on the customer's desk, or flick lint off his jacket, or pick ravelling off his sleeve. Don't even draw his attention to it. It's insulting. I know, I've been told.
- **Don't be a "sly looker"**— Sometimes your customer will leave the room. While he's away, do you take a "peak" at his papers? Don't do this, not even openly or secretly. He may have left just to see if you are going to do that and have a vantage point to observe.
- **Don't be a pointer** — A lot of salespeople use their forefinger to emphasize every point. They do this by poking at the

customer's chest. If you develop this habit, you're going to find that your customers are busy dodging your finger instead of listening to you. This is very offensive. If you are one of these . . . stop it now!

- **Don't be rude** — Now that would seem rather obvious, wouldn't it? However, just listen to salespeople. Listen to how often they interrupt other people. They cut off their customer in mid sentence. What about you? Are you too flamboyant, loud, or overbearing? How about subtle things such as sitting down without an invitation? This type of behavior can lose the sale before you have an opportunity to begin.
- **Don't be, "I remeber when"**— This one gets me, personally. I really don't care about the good old days. The good old days are gone . . . let them be. If you are constantly reminiscing, you are going to be wasting your time and your prospect's. Most people really don't care to hear about your old war stories.

—— Tactic # 201 ——

Avoid Indifference

A Canadian marketing study showed that out of every 100 customers lost, 80% take their business elsewhere because the company they stopped doing business with simply did not care. They were indifferent to the decrease in business. You can take advantage of this situation by following a couple of suggestions made in the study.

- If a customer's angry, don't give him excuses. If you are wrong, admit it and offer a solution to the problem. If the customer is wrong, tell him, but don't be condescending.
- If there's been a misunderstanding, let him know that you enjoy doing business with him, and that you very much regret the problem that was created. You are better off handling it this way than to simply win an argument through some sort of logic and then lose the customer.

Just don't be indifferent. Remember,customers care what you know, but even more, they want to know that you care.

—— Tactic # 202 ——

Practice the Art of Accepting Criticism

Many salespeople develop an attitude of indifference because of criticism given them by customers. Don't react this way. When a customer complains, you can follow eight steps that will help you get back into his good graces:

- Start out by saying to the customer, "I may be wrong, let's examine the facts together." Then sit back quietly while hearing your customer's complaint. Make it very clear that **you are listening**.
- Look directly at the person who is speaking so that he will know that you are concerned.
- Don't indicate that you're finding any fault with the person who is complaining. Don't do it with a lifted eyebrow or a gesture or a word. Don't let him feel that his complaint, in your mind, is unjustified, or that you think that he is at fault.
- Be sure you don't reduce your customer's complaint to a joke. If you try to make a joke out of it, he could think that you are showing contempt.
- Don't look crestfallen. Don't give your customer the impression that he is crushing you or killing your spirit.
- Don't exaggerate the complaint by your customer. If you try to make it more important than it is (as a method of appeasing him), you make it more difficult to overcome the problem.
- Don't try to change the subject. Help your customer express his complaint as clearly as possible and as honestly as possible and let him know that you understand it.
- Don't imply that you think he has some kind of ulterior motive. This will simply anger him because it will seem as if you're questioning his honesty.

Once you have followed these rules and have a good focus on the complaint, ask him to work with you for a solution. The art of accepting criticism can help you hold business while you prospect and build new business through lead follow-up. Also, of course, how you handle complaints and criticism is all a part of the good word-of-mouth recognition that you will get in your industry.

— Tactic # 203 —

Plan to Sell Big Ticket Items

You can probably identify many products in your offering that seem to sell themselves. Many of your customers realize the benefits of the product and they want to make the purchase. This is a matter of simply making a presentation and getting a signed order. However, selling big ticket items will take an entirely different approach. You must have a system that works to get into the mind of the customer and gets him thinking of the benefits as he would a smaller item.

Choose your prospects selectively — In order to sell big ticket items, you must be absolutely accurate from the very start of your presentation. Your proposal will probably go before a board of directors and they are going to want to see exactly what they are going to get right down to the bottom line figures.

All of this means that you want to make sure you are presenting to the right prospect. Discuss the company needs with as many people as possible within your prospect's organization. Find out if your product really meets the needs of the company before you decide to go ahead. Be very conservative. Make your proposal based on the specific needs of the companies you have selected as potential prospects.

Follow up closely — Follow up to make sure your proposal is being considered. Follow up to find out if there is additional information needed. Follow up to see if any changes have been made that change the prospect's needs. Then, simply follow up to "see how things are going." All during that time, give your prospect as much additional information as you can.

Use satisfied customers as salespeople — Customer testimonials are always great selling tools. When you can, put your prospect in touch with a current user of your product. Let them know that other people responsible for buying the product are happy with it. Many of your current customers will become excellent salespeople for you.

Understand it's a tough job — With big ticket items, it often takes a long time to get an order. It is always an up hill climb. Be patient. Remember that selling the big ticket item is an art. Success at this level is only achieved by a result of investing many hours and staying constantly aware of your prospect's thinking. The rewards, however, are worth the effort.

Rise above the field of mediocrity . . . don't just sell the products with the obvious benefits . . . be a "big ticket" sales professional.

—— Tactic # 204 ——

Plan to Outsell the Low Bidder

In this book, we have already covered handling the price objection. However, as you preplan your calls, you should have a tactic that is going to help you outsell the low bidder. This really is one of the most difficult problems for salespeople to solve. Here are several steps that you can take . . . several strategies that you can apply that will help you outsell the low bidder:

Start by knowing the cost of your products and services thoroughly. When you understand the margin you need to conduct business profitably, you will be able to negotiate an increase in quantity for a lower overall price per piece.

Be sure the buyer is not just putting up a smoke screen when he is talking about price. Effectively use the "smoke out" process contained under **Handling Objections** portion of this book. Be sure he's not bringing up price because he's trying to conceal some other objection he might have.

Learn how to sell quality. Prove to your buyer that when he purchases your product, it will cost him less over the lifetime of the product.

Make sure your buyer understands the total value of your product. Bring his attention to all of the extra features, the benefits, the back-up your company offers, services, and the expertise of your staff. Be sure he understands that this is all a part of the product that he is buying.

Ask yourself this very legitimate question, "Is this prospect ethical?" You see, you have to be thinking that when he mentioned the lower price of a competitor, he may just be trying to undercut the fair profit that you should be getting. You must assess the situation to determine if he is just trying to put the squeeze on you or, if indeed, he does have a lower price.

Know your market. Is it a buyer's market or a seller's market? Does the prospect really need what you are selling him? How available is the item? It might be true that he has a lower price, but perhaps your competitor can't deliver.

Always expect you are going to get price resistance. Always be ready for it when it comes. Always have your answers set. Never let any buyer take you by surprise.

Don't ever become a soft touch. You should develop a reputation as a professional who offers the best quality at the best price the first time. Don't be the person who can be easily cut down in price.

Let the customer know that he is going to have some risks when he buys the lower price. Not just the quality. Explain to him that you have been his regular supplier and that when products are short, preferences will be given to customers who have remained loyal to you. A part of the price, then, is a continuation of service into the future.

—— Tactic # 205 ——

Plan to Get Your Prospects to Agree with You

You know your price is right. You know that your products and services are exactly what your customers need. You know that the benefits he is going to receive will solve his problems.

Just because you know all of this, however, does not necessarily mean that your prospects have this information solidly in their minds. It is up to you to get the message across . . . to get them believing you and to get them to **agree** with all of those selling points. If you can't get them to agree, continued talking and firing of great sales ammunition is going to result in shooting blanks.

Here are some procedures you can use to get your customer agreeing with you:

- **Explain why you are there** — Don't start right off by presenting your product. Let the customer know why you are there and how your product is going to help him. You see, if your prospect doesn't know where you are trying to lead him with your presentation, he might be afraid that he is going to be captured about a subject or product that is of no interest to him. You must make your prospect a **partner in your thinking** . . . he must not feel that he is an adversary or that he's trapped.
- **Pause while you present** — As you are emphasizing your product features and benefits, pause and wait for your customer to say **something**. Or, ask a question that will help you find out what is on your prospect's mind. The questioning will help to activate the customer's thinking process in the direction of your call objective.

- **Get focus** — You must get your prospect to focus on what you're talking about. If you don't, his mind will wander. To get his attention, let him know that you are going to be asking some questions. When your prospect knows that he is going to have to react, he will pay attention.
- **Use empathy** — Whenever your prospect opposes what you say, tell him that you understand. Of course, when you do this, rephrase your point of view and then present the reasons why what you have said is correct. Compare your view with those of your prospect's. This will keep him actively involved.
- **Present one idea at a time** — No one can entertain many ideas at one time. Also, you should keep in mind that when too many ideas are given too quickly, your prospect will lose his train of thought, and, of course, interest in what you have to present. Get agreement on every point before you go on to another one.

—— Tactic # 206 ——

Plan to Use Testimonials

Watch television for an hour and you will eventually see a testimonial given by a celebrity to endorse a product.

For you, an effective testimonial would be from a former customer who is satisfied with your product and service. Someone within your own territory is much more effective than the "Big Names", and they are extremely easy for you to acquire. Follow these simple steps for gaining and using testimonials and you will be far better prepared for your next series of sales calls.

- When one of your customers says something positive, or is highly enthusiastic about a product, ask him for written testimonial. Most of your customers will be flattered that you want the endorsement and will give it to you willingly.
- When a buyer is pleased with products he has bought from you, find out the names of friends in the same type of business. If he's close to these people, his testimonial will help you get new business.
- Try to get pictures. If a customer is making good use of one of your products, ask him if you can take a picture to show

other people. Oftentimes, a picture has the effect of being more positive proof than a written testimonial to many prospects.

- Have one of your satisfied customers call a prospect for you. Or, ask your customer if you could call the prospect from your office and have him speak with your prospect.
- Keep your testimonials on file. Index them alphabetically by name and also by territory.
- Go over your list of satisfied users immediately before making a call on a prospect. In this way, you will be sure you have the right names at the right time.
- Try to get many testimonials that have a variety of comments with special emphasis on the benefits that you want to present.
- Make sure all of your testimonials are believable. If they sound too enthusiastic, some people will think that the testimonials were written by you. Try to get testimonials that have pertinent facts and not vague generalities.

—— Tactic # 207 ——

Plan to Tear Your Competition Down

Many times you've heard that you should not "knock your competition." You're going to have to do this, however, if you truly feel your product is better.

When you are trying to sell somebody something that they are already getting . . . from somebody else, a very touchy point always comes up when you have to finally say, "Ours is better."

You have to be careful when you put down your competition because you will actually be put in a position of putting down your customer's judgment. When you put down his judgment, he is likely to become defensive.

That means you must build up the competition to a point before tearing that competitor down. Ask questions about what it is the competition offers. Treat the answers very seriously. Express your appreciation for some of the features and benefits. Let the customer know that you think he's made a good decision and that he got a good deal.

While the customer is enjoying your opinion of his good business sense, show how your product will do everything as well as the competitor's, and then some. Explain that products and services evolve. Let him know that he made a good decision then, and he would certainly be making a good one now as you stress the advantages of what you have. Don't dwell on the drawbacks of the competitor's product, but subtlely tear it down as you show the increased value of your offering.

— Tactic # 208 —

Plan to Handle the Difficult Buyer

Throughout your selling career, you are going to find that most of the people you deal with are friendly, polite, and are sincerely interested in the services and products you offer. There are, unfortunately, some who are a little warped. They gain a great deal of pleasure out of turning the thumb screws on salespeople. At the very least, dealing with these people is unpleasant. Other times, it's extremely difficult, and often, it's actually impossible.

The fact of selling life, however, is that you are going to meet these people. Be prepared. Have a plan. Don't let them get the best of you. Follow these suggestions and you will come out the winner every time.

Don't submit — Decide in advance that the bully or tyrant is not going to get to you. Don't run at the first sign of a rough, gruff, buyer. One of the reasons this buyer is exhibiting this behavior is because he has been successful. Other salespeople haven't done anything to break the cycle or change the buyer's behavior. For this reason, he continues to be abusive. When salespeople start standing up to this individual, he will back down. You owe it to your self respect, and to your company and to every salesperson who follows you, to make sure that you politely respond to whatever this character can dish out. That does not mean, however, that you also get abusive.

Don't return insult for insult — You will feel that you want to return to the abusive buyer, the same kind of baloney that he's giving you. Don't do it. That tactic is too risky for future business. You might momentarily silence the guy, but you will never make a sale. You see, this type of buyer may easily insult salespeople, but he won't accept the same treatment. Use the good selling techniques you have discovered in this book to overcome his abusive statements, comments, objections and questions. Very calmly and with self-confidence, use the smoke out method, the boomerang method, the offset method, the Columbo method, and the "is it" method. Use all of them! He cannot continue in the face of that type of professionalism.

Don't threaten him — Think about this . . . if a buyer is scaring away salespeople with his obnoxious behavior, his company can't possibly be getting value for what they're paying. That buyer just isn't doing the job that he or she is hired to do. The buyer's job is to help his company get the best possible product and service at the best possible prices. If fewer and fewer salespeople are willing to make a presentation to the buyer, his choices are going to be limited.

You might think that you can take the case to the buyer's boss and explain that the company isn't getting value because the buyer is so abusive. However, even though that might stir things up a bit in the company, it probably will not work to your advantage. The buyer may modify his approach, but he still won't buy from you.

So, what do you do? Well, once again, stick to the basic principles. Maintain your professionalism. Use the tactics.

Be at your professional best — Overall, the best way to handle the abusive buyer is to use all of the tactics you have learned regarding the handling of objections and keep your discussion on a business level. When a buyer finds out that he cannot intimidate you, and that you are not interested in trading insults with him, he will probably begin to listen to your proposition. He has little other choice. And, of course, you have allowed him to air what insults or negatives he wanted and he will probably, therefore, be in a receptive mood.

If, while you're presenting, he still starts to say negative things about your product or company, tell him how proud you are of that product and of your company, and of your profession and yourself as a salesperson . . . let him know that you are a cut above anybody else he's talked with. Don't lose your cool. Stay calm and be dignified. He has to buy something, eventually, and you will be sure, using these tactics, that he will end up buying from you.

Manage Your Time and Territory

"Wow! Now I see where I was just a little bit wrong, but with a whole lot of people."

This was theenthused comment of an industrial salesman after he developed a method of time and territory planning. Like many good salespeople, he had worked to perfect his presentations, he knew his product well, could effectively handle objections, and was a good closer. He worked hard and put in long hours, as most salespeople will. Still, he knew he was not reaching his full potential, but couldn't figure out why. One brief lesson during a seminar gave him the methods that now enable him to continually get more and more from two basic resources . . . his time and the territory assigned to him.

When you learn to get the most out of one (time), you will automatically be able to get more out of the other. **Both** resources will become great assets. Before we get into the specific tactics, I think it is important that you know something about the development of the methods I am going to describe.

During classroom sessions, salespeople have been asked to list their daily activities and to assign the amount of time devoted to each.

After some humorous comments on the various activities described, a sobering conclusion was drawn. Every classroom analysis, across the country, indicated that salespeople spend less than three hours a day in face-to-face "real" **selling** situations. In some cases, it worked out to be as low as one hour a day.

Even the most knowledgeable salesperson, who is an excellent presenter of products, is going to find it is a matter of playing "quota catch-up" in this situation.

Mismanaged time is the cause of great frustration for many salespeople. They work longer hours to make more calls and end up in a condition of exhausted futility. Not knowing what to do about it, some salespeople simply quit their job. Others continue to plod along, doing the best that is possible without a method for planning their activities. The tactics that follow add up to a method that is responsible for the enthusiastic comment of the industrial salesman. Using his own customer list, his sales figures and a road map of his territory, he changed from, a meandoring salesman to a **territory sales manager** in a matter of hours.

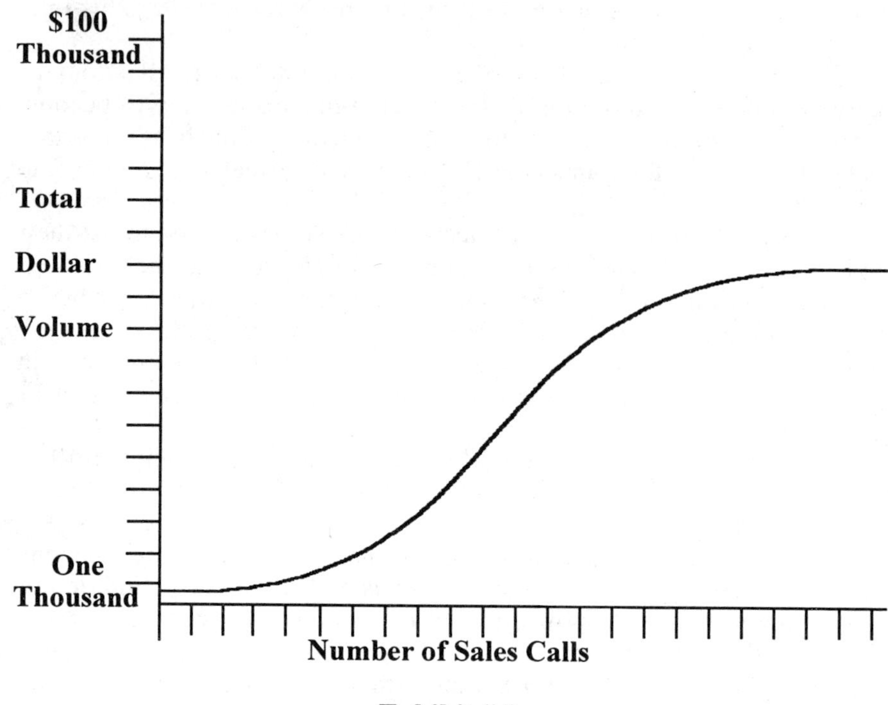

Exhibit # 1

— Tactic # 209 —

More Calls Mean More Dollar Volume

Think of any customer and refer to Exhibit #1. On the vertical, graph his volume, and on the horizontal, indicate the number of calls that would be made on this customer on a one year period.

For this customer, let's assume the salesperson made one or two calls. The result would be as shown . . . little or no sales volume. In industrial selling, where it is necessary to service an account frequently, more attention is needed. It is rarely, if ever, a one-shot deal. Now assume that the salesperson continues to call, using good presentation techniques, preplanning the sales message along the way, and acquainting the customer with the entire offering. We can expect sales to increase as shown. This would happen until we reach the point where this particular customer is incapable of buying more. This is the point of diminishing returns. Theoretically, the salesperson has scheduled calls throughout the year for a frequency that will extract the greatest amount of business possible. Additional calls, throughout this year's calling period, will create little or no additional sales volume from this customer. A greater number of calls will actually decrease the salesperson's efficiency. Keep in mind, this is the number of calls allocated over a year's time. The important point to be derived from this graph is simply that calls beyond the point of diminishing returns are wasted calls!

— Tactic # 210 —

Consider the Average Return on Call Investment

Now, look at Exhibit #2. This graph will show the **average return** on call investment. How much volume can be generated per call, **on average**? Exhibit #2 is similar to Exhibit #1, except the vertical line represents **average return per call**.

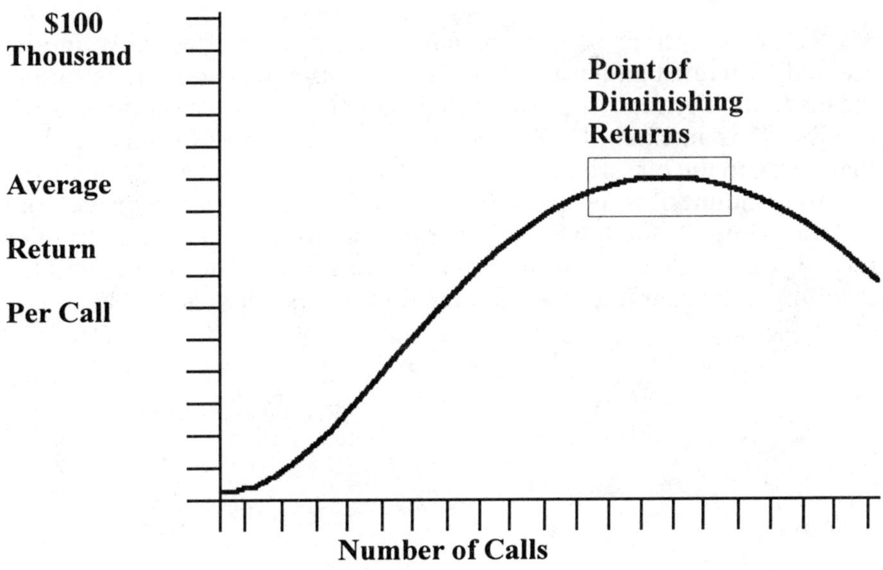

Exhibit # 2

If the salesperson makes one or two calls, there will be the same effect as in Exhibit #1. As more calls are made and the dollar volume increases, the average return increases. By dividing the number of calls into the year-to-date volume, the salesman can track the average return for this customer. When we reach the point of diminishing returns, the average return per call now starts to decline as more calls are added. Here, the salesperson is actually working against self-interest because the greater the call frequency with this customer, the less efficient the salesperson will become. Ideally, it would be necessary to adjust the call frequency so that the customer is contacted at the point of diminishing returns. This is where the salesperson would maximize time investment.

Of course, the above examples are for one customer or prospect. Every customer has such a curve and each curve is different.

So, how can the salesperson determine the proper time investment for each customer without spending a great deal of time and effort on preparation? It is done by using a time survey and a monthly summary.

— Tactic # 211 —

Develop Your Own Time Survey

Before a system of time management can be effectively implemented, you must gather facts on which to base decisions. This simply means that daily reports are essential. The time survey report shown in Exhibit #3 is an example. This gathers the same type of information as that given in the classroom example. It shows the number of daily calls and the amount of time spent on each call, which **includes travel and waiting time**. In the lower right corner, the first line is the daily sales record. Below that is the running total for the month-to-date, and the last line is the running total of sales for the current year-to-date.

Exhibit # 3

Time Survey For ____________________________

Day ____________________ **Date** ____________________

Do Not Try to Account for Every Minute —
Do Not Spend Over 5 Minutes on This Report

Name Address	Person Interviewed	Time	Results of Interview	Amount Sold

Comments

Total Sales Today
Total Sales This Month
Total Sales This Year

The form can be printed using N. C. R. paper so that a copy can be pulled for your sales manager at the end of each day. You are to carry the copy in your briefcase, or keep it in your car, and fill it out immediately after you leave a customer. **This form should not take more than five minutes a day**.

The information you obtain will allow you and your manager to analyze calls after a full month of reporting. You might want to enlist the aid of a secretary or office clerk to compile all of the facts needed to properly analyze your activities.

—— Tactic # 212 ——

Construct a Monthly Summary

Now, it will be necessary to get a list of each customer you called on during the month. Then, take a total of the number of calls made on these customers as well as a total of hours spent on each account. (See Exhibit #4.) With these facts, you can determine how many hours you spend with each account for what dollar volume of business.

Salesman's Monthly Summary

Salesman:

Account	**Visits**	**Number of Hrs.**	**Amt. Sold**
ABC Plumbing	6	9	$ 100
Wright Mfg.	4	4	2,600
Consolidated P.H.C.	2	3	——
Inland P.H.C.	3	3	2,400
General Baths	5	11	5,000
Border Builders	4	8	22,500
Refrigerated, Inc.	2	2	600
Watson P.H.C.	3	1½	——
Quiet Heat	3	3	——
Acme Engineering	8	16	10,700
Sullivan & Company	2	2	——
Johnson Plumbing Co.	6	9	5,000
Agway #1	5	3	——
Scott P.H.C.	2	1	500
Agway #2	1	½	——
Quick & Easy Plumbing	1	½	——
Watergy, Inc.	2	1	2,300
Fixzit Man, Inc.	1	½	——
Precision P.H.C.	10	5	12,000
Austin Home Improvement	4	2	2,500
Brewster P.H.C.	2	4	5,200
Crescent Plumbing	1	1	600
The Boutique	1	7	——
I.D.T. Builders	2	2	1,500
Totals	80	90	$74,000

Average Sales per Call ($74,000/ 80 Calls) = $925 per Call

Exhibit # 4

In our specific example, you can see that the salesperson spent 9 hours with ABC Plumbing for $100 of business. Was it worth it? Should this be a regular practice? What is this customer's potential? Is this amount of time justified?

You will have to make some of the same judgments. You will see by looking at the summary that you can divide the number of calls into your sales dollars and get your average sales per call. You can then compare your average with other salespeople in your company. You can determine whether or not you have to increase your average and you can identify those accounts that fall below your average. Once having done this, you can make decisions as to which accounts are important and which are not.

— Tactic # 213 —

Work Based on the Principle of "Important Few and Unimportant Many"

You will see, very quickly, how necessary it is to make decisions based on the principle of which accounts are very important to you and which are not. This is operating under the principle of "the important few and the unimportant many."As you complete your monthly summary, you will see that out of all of the prospects available to you, in your territory, only a few really can and do make a major contribution to your sales total. Generally, 65% of your volume will come from 15% of your customers. Another 20% in sales will come from about 20% of customers, while a small 15% will come from a large group of 65%. This is called the Girand principle which covers many things in sales and marketing. It generally holds true. Of course, this will vary from salesperson to salesperson, depending upon the type of business. The situation of important few/unimportant many, can be expressed as shown in Exhibit #5.

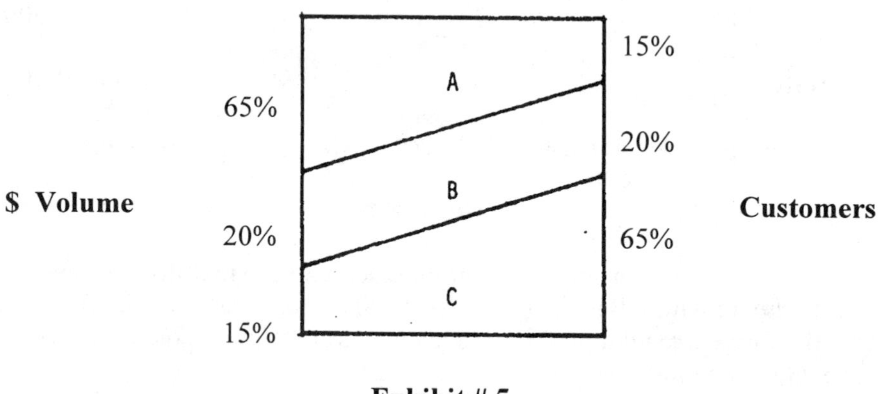

Exhibit # 5

The customers shown in the area marked A become the "important few", while those in area C are the "unimportant many."

— Tactic # 214 —

Now You Must Classify Your Accounts

In my 30 years of experience, I have found that most salespeople make an average of five to six calls a day. That means about 30 calls a week must be divided among a field of possible 100 to 200 customers and prospects . . . all of which would like to be called on once a week. You can see how very important it is that the scarce asset of time be properly allocated.

To do this, you must classify your accounts from the standpoint of time allocation . . . how much time should be spent for maximum return on your time investment?

Use your time surveys and your monthly summaries to classify accounts into A, B, and C groups. With this data, you can easily determine which accounts should be called on more frequently and which less often.

— Tactic # 215 —

Establish Your Call Frequency

It was at this point that the industrial salesman stated that now he saw, "I was a little bit wrong, but with a whole lot of people."

You see, he had two good sales tactics going for him: **quality calls** and **number of calls**. They did produce dollars as shown in the formula: Q x N = $, with "Q" for quality and "N" for number of calls. He needed the third item that relieved his work frustrations, made him a manager and gave him new horizons. Added to the formula, this third item of **allocation** (Q x N x **A** = $), enables all salespeople to produce more. It is the one element that makes the salesperson a manager.

So, how should your calls be allocated? Once your accounts have been classified into the A, B, & C classifications, a rule of thumb can be applied that says, "A" customers should be called on every call cycle, "B" customers, one-half as much, and "C" customers, one-fourth as much. A call cycle is the time it takes you to cover your entire territory. Your cycle could consist of many loops and circles that, daily, take you in and out of your home area and may extend a week to a couple of weeks, or even an entire month. It's important to remember that your call cycle will cover your territory in a specific period of time.

As an example of call frequency, suppose you have 60 customers and you have a weekly call cycle. Your A, B, C classifications would break down as follows:

A —	15% of	60	=	9 (Call on Each Cycle)	=	9
B —	20% of	60	=	12 (Call on ½ Each Cycle)	=	6
C —	65% of	60	=	39 (Call on ¼ Each Cycle)	=	10
Total				60 Customers		25 Calls

This system does several things for you. It properly identifies your prime accounts . . . the ones you are (or should be) "married" to. You would call on all nine each time you fully cover your territory on your normal one-week call cycle. Half of your B accounts would be covered each call cycle. That means it will take you two weeks to cover all of your B accounts. You will pick up one-fourth of your C accounts each call cycle. You, therefore, will cover all the C accounts in four weeks.

With this schedule, you will cover 60 selected accounts in a month, giving each the time properly allocated that will give you the greatest return on your sales call investment.

—— Tactic # 216 ——

Route Yourself for More Calls

Once you have worked out an efficient account classification, and you have established your call frequency, your next step is to manage in such a way that you are able to make more sales calls. No doubt, you are already putting in as many hours as you should. Adding working hours is not the solution. How do you get more time? You must look at your non-selling chores, particularly your travel time. The obvious solution is to do a better job of routing.

The best tool you can use is a road map of your own territory. Using different colored pens, mark the location of every "A" customer, every "B" customer, and every "C" customer. Do your routing based on the location of your "A" customers. Your routes can be loops, sectors, cloverleafs, in and out lines, or any configuration, but they must cover every "A" customer within your established call cycle. You, then, will pick up half of your "B's" and a quarter of your "C's" each time you cycle. (See Exhibit #6)

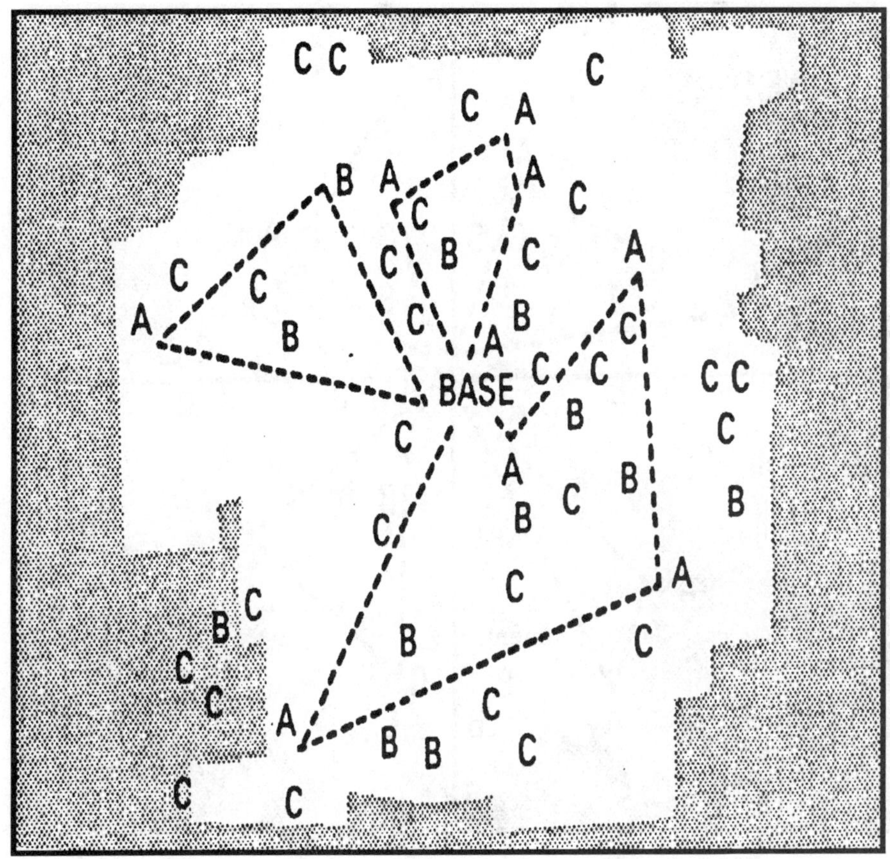

Exhibit # 6

The map in Exhibit #6 shows a simplified version of this routing. As you will become more efficient through routing, you will gain time for more calls. An incidental plus will be reduction in your travel expenses.

Another method of routing, particularly advantageous for very large territories, is to divide the geography into four zones. Starting at your base, draw a horizontal line that will divide your territory into north and south. Then, do the same with a vertical line, dividing your territory into east and west. (See Exhibit #7).

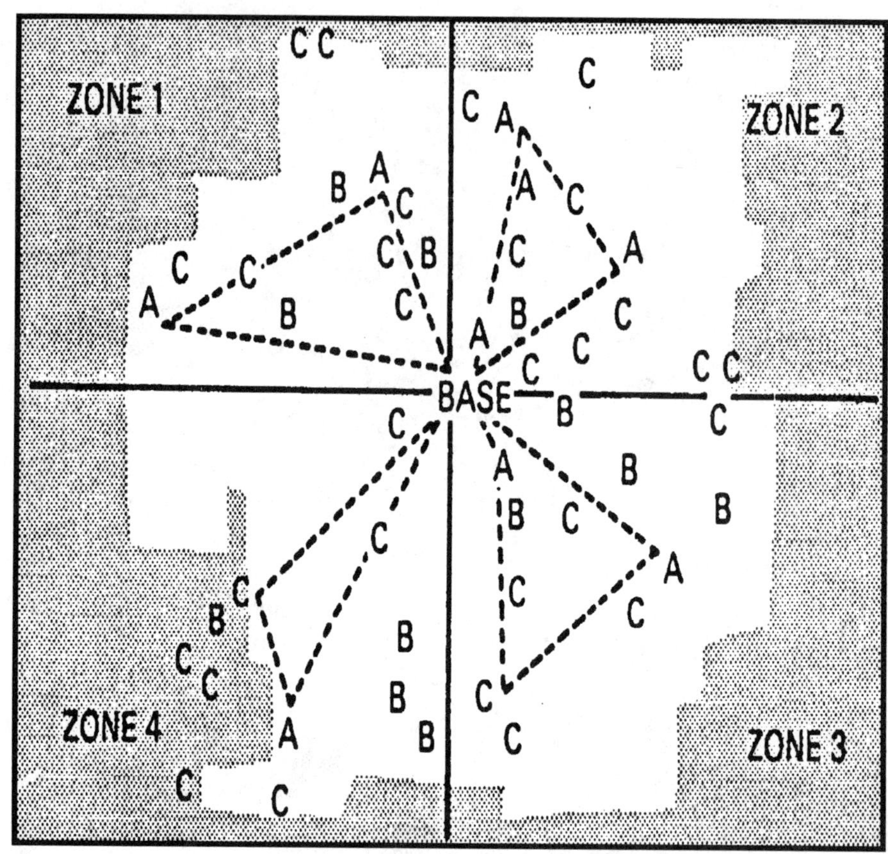

Exhibit #7

This produces four quadrants, which we'll call zones. This is the most efficient way of handling large sales territories. Routing will still be done on the classification of accounts, determined by the A, B, C system. Depending upon the size of your territory, a separate call cycle for each zone might be required. Suppose you wanted to maintain your one week call cycle, however. You could make calls as follows: On the first, second, and third days, you would work zones 1, 2 and 3. On the fourth day, zone 4, and on the fifth day, you would allow time for prospecting and emergency calls.

You must determine which system is best for you after you have placed your classified accounts on a road map and you begin your route planning.

SECTION V

Advertising, Sales Promotion, Trade Shows and Showmanship

There is more to professional selling than simply making the calls and doing all of the right things once you are face-to-face with your customer. Top professionals involve themselves in many of the marketing aspects of the selling profession. For this reason, we are going to close this book with many tactics you can use to augment your personal selling efforts. We will begin with a discussion of advertising techniques you can use, enlisting the help of your company advertising department. We will expand those tactics to include sales promotion techniques, we'll then discuss your function at trade shows and finish up with personal showmanship techniques. Let's begin with advertising and sales promotion.

— Tactic # 217 —

Support Field Selling Effort with Advertising

"Advertising and sales promotion is hard to evaluate. I don't know if I'm getting returns on the money I'm spending. I'd rather put my money into hiring new salespeople."

This is oftentimes what the sales manager of a company might be heard saying when it comes to dividing up budget dollars. Many salespeople feel the same way. However, those that use advertising effectively encourage their managers to develop an aggressive program that helps catapult them to success beyond their competitors. It's this type of aggressive program we are going to discuss here.

First, establish the products that you most want to sell. Determine what items you have to sell, what you **should** have to sell, and what goals you want to set with these products. Be open minded as you develop this part of your program. It's important to get facts from both inside your company and outside. Ask for a brainstorming session with many of your company people, stating that the purpose of the meeting is to help find ways of promoting and selling more products. Get the help of your sales manager to announce the intention of the meeting in a memo which asks company people to come prepared with ideas and suggestions for new items and examples of successes and failures.

When reaching outside your company for information, pay close attention to the feedback from other salespeople. Develop a list of questions relative to specific products, features and benefits, customer objections, etc. Discuss this information at your meeting.

Develop a questionnaire to send to your customers. Don't make it long . . . keep it simple. Your customers and prospects won't spend the time to answer questions that go on and on. They will feel resentment at having been put in a position of having to refuse to help. A single sheet of 10 to 15 questions should do it.

— Tactic # 218 —

Spell Out Product and Personal Benefits

Once you have firmly established your product offering, based on what your customers most want, your company's marketing team must list all of the benefits offered by these products . . . that match your customer's wants, needs, and desires. Write these down.

At the same time, list all of the benefits your customers receive as a result of doing business with **you** and your company. Figure out what you offer that is superior to, or makes you different from your competitors. Is it product knowledge? Technical assistance? Ability to serve? Creative merchandising ideas? Ability to communicate or business information services? These personal "you" benefits are the proprietary, priceless elements that create the basis for your selling message. Once you've listed these product and personal benefits, organize them in a **written story form** as if you were sitting across from a prospect and were charged with the task of convincing him of the advantages of doing business with you. You will have generated a document that is your own unique selling message. This is the message that you want to communicate to your buying audience . . . what you **must** communicate!

While completing this exercise, you have done other things:

- You have isolated promotable items, making it possible to evaluate your advertising.
- You can point to the returns you get as a result of your efforts in the form of new orders, total volume increase and profits.
- You have given direction to yourself which will enable you to increase your effort on the promotion of your market offering message, making you much more effective.
- You will have isolated several lines and products that are important to you and through your commitment, will increase your overall leverage with your company management.

By making your offering more attractive, you'll end up with more sales and a reduced percentage of selling cost to volume. Your next step is to design and implement your program plan.

—— Tactic # 219 ——

The Program Plan

Personal calls will certainly get your message across to your existing customer list. Of course, your calls will be more effective once you are totally sold on your offering. The above analysis will help you become sold. All of this is great, however, you will still be spending most of your time with your existing accounts. Such a great offering should be made to prospects.The best way to do that, initially, is through a good advertising program.

You may be skilled and dedicated, but it's impossible for you to be everywhere at once. By the time you cover all the bases, your situation could change and your market offering could be different. It takes months or years to reach all of your potential accounts. Your advertising program, on the other hand, will:

- Find interested prospects.
- Generate leads that will encourage you to call on these prospects.
- Stimulate existing customers and prospects to buy your products because you have publicized your sales points.
- Permit you to say why your existing, satisfied customers do business with you without looking as if you are bragging.You would use testimonials.
- Allow you, in very precise word, to state exactly all of your selling benefits.
- Give you the opportunity to repeat those benefits over and over where you could not do so in person.
- Enable you to maintain contact with many key people in a company on a frequent basis.
- Keep people sold on your company by reaching those you would not normally see.

You'll want to consider various ways of reaching your customers and prospects with your message. The first contact would logically be made with a **capabilities brochure**.

—— Tactic # 220 ——

Develop a Capabilities Brochure

Your capabilities brochure would explain your offering as previously discussed, but would be professionally done with a suitable cover photo or sketch of your company's physical facility. It would contain information about staff support, trucking, warehouse size and inventories, merchandising programs, and exclusive benefits enjoyed by doing business with your company. This brochure would be mailed to every existing customer and every prospect in your trading area.

—— Tactic # 221 ——

Use Mailings

A series of mailings would follow the capabilities brochure. These mailings would isolate special portions of your offering beginning with detailed information about the personal benefits of doing business with your company. The second mailing would begin a series of pieces designed to sell your special products. Use literature with a cover letter from you, written to highlight the special benefits of these products. Each letter in the series would talk **only** about the product shown in the literature. You would have as many mailings as you have featured products. Every piece would have a mail-back lead card with a return postage permit. You might even consider a one time, product sample purchase offer. When your prospect replies (providing the item is small enough) you could make delivery and have a perfect icebreaker for your first call on that customer.

I know a manufacturing company who has used this mail-sample offer program to continually add new accounts. It is an on-going process. Prospects who don't respond to as many as five or six mailings, eventually are approached at the right time with the right idea or item. Their first response is well worth the cost of all the mailings that have preceded it.

While your mailings are in effect and continuous contact is being made, it is time to add the impact of having customer/prospect meetings.

—— Tactic # 222 ——

Conduct a Capabilities/Product Meeting

There is no better way to convince a prospect of your message than to show him. After the fourth or fifth mailing, arrange a dinner meeting where you will introduce all your new products. Make it a selling meeting by promoting "specials" to be ordered for that night only. Theme the meeting so that it will carry your market offering message throughout. Don't "can" it but have a script outline for your company people who will make the presentation. As the territorial salesperson, you should be the first speaker. **You** set the tone. Keep your message brief, and try to cover no more than three points:

1. Tell them what you stand for as it relates to benefiting them . . . hold up your capabilities brochure explaining they will receive one later.
2. Talk about all of your company people and explain that their purpose is to function to benefit your customers. (Be sure all of your company key people are at the meeting to hear this message.)
3. Talk about your product offering, explaining how it was put together after much consideration to furnish the best items at affordable prices.

Finally, tell them you appreciate them coming and turn the program over to your sales manager, marketing vice president, or other senior executive.

The senior executive would now elaborate on the three areas you mentioned, detailing the message and the capabilities brochure. He would introduce key people and lead into a product review which could be handled by a merchandise manager and/or various product line managers. Keep the product presentation brief and hold all questions until **after** the formal presentation.

Close with an order sheet for "tonight's special offer" on your products.

Another good close is to arrange a plant tour of your manufacturing or distribution facilities. Have as many customers as possible sign up for the tour.

—— Tactic # 223 ——

Conduct a Plant Tour

Plant tours are an excellent way to cement relationships with existing customers and tie down prospects, turning them into new, high volume and **loyal** customers. But do it right. Make it a V.I.P. trip all the way!

— Tactic # 224 —

Develop a Good Newsletter

Consider a newsletter. Your mailings will take care of product information, but there's much more to your organization. Current industry items, advance notice of new products, announcements of the new services and other **non-gossipy** information will be well received by customers and prospects. This newsletter even rides free when put in the same envelope with one of your product pieces. Get your customers and prospects in the habit of reading it. You'll want to start using this communication tool right away if none of your competitors are doing so currently.

— Tactic # 225 —

Develop a Recognizable Logo

Your newsletter and all your communication (even invoices and preprinted order forms) must carry a logo that speaks of who you are and what you stand for. This is not something that a territorial salesman generally creates. However, if you feel your company is in need of a good logo, youcould get the program started by making the suggestion.

Once your company logo is developed, it should be given maximum exposure. As a result of your mailings, meetings, personal contacts and daily track record, the buying influences in your territory will form a mental image of you and your company. Every time they see you logo, that image will play back in their minds. It's like pushing a button on a computer. The logo will key thoughts and services to deliver your message again and again.

Your company should put your logo on **everything**, including trucks, pens, scratch pads; even as labels to put on product cartons. If you have a trade journal that reaches your buying audience, be sure your logo is in every issue, with or without an accompanying ad.

— Tactic # 226 —

Make Good Use of Your Trade Journals

Your trade journal, no matter how modest or elaborate, is read. Perhaps it's just a leaf through situation, but impressions are made. Use it. Keep your ad simple, however. Show a picture and use a single line of copy in healine style to say what you want to get across. Then sign off with your logo, address and telephone number. Keep your ads running. The exposure is excellent and your support of associations who publish these magazines will be appreciated. When it comes time to participate in convention programming, you will deserve some prime consideration.

— Tactic # 227 —

Be a Participant at Conventions

At conventions, maintain a high profile. Bring together all of the things you are doing. If possible, have a mini meeting with your customers. Sponsor an affair with entertainment. Assist the auxiliary in their programming and take a part, if possible. Offer a door prize to the auxiliary. You, personally, should give the door prize to the winner, taking the opportunity of thanking the ladies for their support.

Is this all . . . not really, it's just a start. Later, you might want to recommend that your company improve their printed catalog. If appropriate, use billboards, showroom sales, point of purchase displays, a co-op program with your dealers advertising to consumers using ad slicks, a complete novelty identification program with your logo, a summer "carnival of sales", incentive trips, golf outings, Sunday supplement inserts, radio and television spots, etc. And what about you, the salesperson? You should be a part of all of this. Don't be average. Rise above the field of mediocrity. Use these advertising/promotion **advanced** Tactics of Persuasion.

Use Trade Shows To Sell

Costs of selling are rising every day. Yet, the same old inefficiencies are built into every sales call . . . endless time consuming driving, fantastic gasoline prices, waiting for customers to see you, and all kinds of buying resistance.

As a salesperson, you must, at all times, try to meet non-selling chores with ways to make yourself more selling efficient. Trade shows and home shows are a way of doing just that! Here's how to sell more at these shows:

—— Tactic # 228 ——

Take Advantage of Numbers

You have a great advantage in having a large number of prospects available to you during a very short period of time. They are coming to you in an environment that is especially designd to promote products, and they are prepared to listen to the product story that you have to tell. Of course, you have much immediate competition; but, as always, your selling skills will keep you apart from the field of mediocrity that exists in other booths.

By sheer number of prospects available to you, you are in an advantageous position over day-to-day calling, and by the application of your skill, you are ahead of your competition. Now, operate like a pro.

—— Tactic# 229 ——

Maximize Your Time and Effort

Be sure that you are in your booth every moment possible during show hours. Rarely does a trade show offer hours that are so long that it would be impossible for you to give it full time. The few moments that you are gone can be the very time that you miss your best opportunity. Make a commitment to be there, "all the time," scheduling normal, regular short breaks; but letting everyone else know you will be back at a specified time. Then, return as promised. Be available!

— Tactic # 230 —

Take Advantage of Face-To-Face Demonstrator Selling

Rarely do you have such an opportunity to use your ability to demonstrate as you sell. Your products are actually at your fingertips! You have an unusual number of buyers willing to listen, and you are in control of the selling situation at all times. Beyond all of this, you will probably, also, have your management and service people with you for immediate decisions and answers. Take advantage of all of this.

Sure, plan to use your display as a "Show and Tell," but also structure your message so that you are **selling**. Plan to ask probing questions that will qualify prospects as buyers and go right on with your demonstration with a close intended to get the order.

In the case of a trade show to dealers, have an order pad in your hand as you talk. Write the name of the product down as you describe it. Fill in the prospect's name as you meet him. With action—body language and words—let your prospect know you are there to help him buy.

At home shows, where the homeowner-consumer is the primary audience, use the same note-taking method. Demonstrate your product and ask questions as you go along. As they reply, jot down their answers. During the demonstration and question taking, fill out **when** they need the item, **where** they will need it delivered, etc. As you close, say, "Look, I have all the information. Why don't I write up the order and help you get it right away?"

Because of the numbers of people who will see your demonstration, you will close sales.

— Tactic # 231 —

Get Leads for Opening New Accounts

You are not going to sell everyone, of course. Still, people go to shows because they have the potential to buy and are interested in investigating the product opportunities presented there. At that time, or in the future, they mean more business for you.

A trade show can be very successful for you, even if you sell nothing from the floor, as long as you lineup new customers. This means you use the show primarily as a lead gathering service and make your calls immediately after the show closes. While demonstrating, tell your trade prospect that you would like to call on him when you both can relax and talk about his business. As he agrees, take up a packet of appointment cards, write one for him, and one for yourself, showing the agreed upon appointment. At the bottom of the card, indicate the reason for the call. The card will be a reminder for him and will focus his attention on the subject you want to discuss. It is also one of the few concrete items that he will take out of the trade show and keep. If appropriate, staple the appointment card to a piece of literature that shows the item under discussion or attach it to one of your company's capabilities brochures. Also, give this customer a novelty gift as he walks away. This is a good reinforcer.

—— Tactic # 232 ——

Novelties

Everybody likes to receive gifts. You can use this psychological fact to an advantage but there is a right way and a wrong way to pass out novelties at shows.

If you are just wanting to identify yourself by making a quick impression, advertising specialities, such as key chains, pens, etc., can be used. However, the overall cost of such handouts is generally not worth the questionable benefit for yourself and your company.

The best type of handout is an item that is a sample of one of the products that you are selling. Of course, not all of your products will lend themselves to sampling. However, with the wide range of items handled by a wholesaler, you should be able to ideally find a product or products that will enable you to pass out samples which will show product features and will be a constant reminder to your prospects. Just remember, that the difference between product samples and novelties is that the novelty generally does not relate to the product. Novelties do not do any harm, but usually they do not do any good.

— Tactic # 233 —

How to Put Together an Effective Booth

At some point, in your selling career, you will probably be called upon to assist in the design and set-up of a trade show booth. This could be at a local home show or at an industry show designed to present products to your customers. When this happens, you will want to be able to participate in such a way that you can help design a booth that will get you the very best results at the show. That means, your booth should be put together so that you are able to tell your product story completely to as many of the attendees as possible. Further, you will want to be able to reach the most qualified prospective buyers and have an opportunity of closing a sale with them. Here are eight points that will serve as a guideline:

1. Make it a show —Your booth is not an advertisement for your company. It is a show. Naturally, the booth signing gives identification, but all of the activity should be designed to show your products in action. Be sure to have your booth set-up so that your visitors become involved immediately with the products that you want to demonstrate. Prospective buyers must be able to have a personal experience by being able to see your product, touch it, handle it, and thoroughly investigate it. Your "show and tell" will be more effective with every one of the five senses you employ. For example, if you are going to display a new vent damper, you will want to have a demonstrator that actually operates and also have several other units that the customer can hold in his hand while he is looking at the operating demonstrator. But, do not expect your booth visitor to participate without encouragement. He will not pick up the materials and perform the "show and tell" himself. You must actively work to get him involved. Just remember, your booth is not a mere advertisement, **it is a show**!

2. Make your product the star — We have all attended trade shows where many companies seem more interested in producing a "gimmicky", grandiose or otherwise flashy display, than they were in presenting their products. This is the wrong approach. This type of display might be flashy, but in the hub-bub of a show, this type of image producing booth becomes boring. Worse yet, people who admire these booths, do so from a distance. If you feel it is necessary to build your company's image, you are better off doing it through direct mail and advertisements in your state journals. At trade shows, keep the attention on your products and use your products to bring your visitors into the booth.

3. Be simplistic — Even with the best products, you are going to have some difficulty competing with all of the surrounding activity. Often this activity does not just come from competitive booths, but from the overall show atmosphere, which can range anywhere from carnival to social gathering. Your visitors, therefore, tend to act like very busy people. When they do stop by, they want facts immediately and in a convenient way. Whenever a booth is cluttered, disorganized or over-crowded, visitors will shy away from that environment, in favor of areas that look more appealing. Your booth must appear to be orderly and the products must appear to be displayed in a logical sequence that is easily understood. A visitor must be able to take one glance at your area and immediately understand what you are presenting. This means that your products should be well identified. You can even use signing with descriptions of the characteristics, specifications, and applications of your products.

Naturally, your booth should always be neat and clean. You would think it would be unnecessary to mention this fact, but you have only to observe the next trade shows you attend to look at the overflowing ashtrays, messy floors, filled up wastebaskets, and the overall poor housekeeping that usually predominates.

Many of your visitors will be seeing your products for the first time. Treat each presentation as if it was a first time demonstration with everyone. Be very basic and precise in your explanations, assuming nothing. Do everything possible to make your booth and your presentation easily understood.

4. Show lots of stuff — When you decide on how you are going to display, you will be tempted to want to focus your attention on one or two items. This is okay for a manufacturer who has the luxury of such concentration, but visitors who come into your booth want to know the breadth of your company's product offering. You will want to carefully select a representative sampling of products from the major lines that give you 80 percent of your volume. Having done that, you will want to display these products in a logical sequence, practically departmentalizing them as to booth area. It is okay to have a catalog of all of your products, but remember that you are at a show and pictures are something that a prospective buyer can see at his shop. He is at the show to see the real thing. Use all of your booth. **You cannot show too many products.**

5. Use action to get attention — A display that just sits there is boring. Visitors will go immediately to booths where displays involve products in action. Now this is fairly easy to do when you are demonstrating machinery, or a product with a lot of moving parts. When you decide upon the products to be displayed, be sure you have at least one of this type product available.

Do not give up on other products, however. You can find a way to dramatically and effectively demonstrate everything that will be on display. For instance, a manufacturer of sealing putty, merely placed an open can on the table with a sign that said, "Try me."A company who was demonstrating a new soldering flux kept a live demonstration going where copper joints were actually soldered. The visitors, of course, were invited to participate in the demonstration. You will want to think of ways to show how light a product is, or how heavy, or how strong, or tough, or durable. A durable, tough product can be simply demonstrated with the use of a hammer and a little bit of showmanship.

Other products can be demonstrated by showing how they are made. Cutaway sections can be used. Photographic blowups are always effective when demonstrating smaller items with intricate parts. As, you demonstrate dramatically, you are also doing something else—you are convincing your visitor that your product is everything that you claim it is. You are building proof into every selling demonstration.

6. Put your product to practical use — You want to tie all of your demonstrators together in such a way that you are showing the field use or practical application of your products. Sometimes this is not possible because the products must be installed before they can actually be used. You can, however, use case histories of installations where area contractors are giving testimony to the superiority of your product. Some salesmen will actually take pictures of the product after it is installed and build a portfolio.

You see, your visitors are all asking an unspoken question. They want to know, "What will that product do for me?" By showing them what the product has done for others in your geography, they are able to visualize what it will do for them. This type of practical use demonstration is often all you need to close a sale in your booth.

7. Get audience participation — You will be working hard to prove that your product is exactly what you say it is. You will be doing demonstration after demonstration. You will become frustrated to notice that while you work hard at this demonstration, many of your visitors will only half listen. Many of them might walk away in the middle of your demonstration.

One sure way of holding a visitor's attention is to get him involved in your demonstration. Instead of proving your product to the visitor, let him prove it to himself. Even if your demonstration is just a simple piece of equipment, let the visitor operate it. Be careful to ensure that the visitor cannot be injured or jam the equipment. If the product is one that can be easily jammed by unskilled use, your visitor will become embarrassed and the overall result of the demonstration will be negative. At a recent trade show, an excellent audience participation item was an electric drill. The booth was always busy, because the tradesmen wanted to operate the hand-held tool. In each product area, try to devise a way where you are putting something into your visitor's hands that requires him to be an active part of proving the value of the product.

8. Hand out hard hitting technical information — The next time you are at a trade show, look at the wastebaskets. Every wastebasket is filled with literature that someone picked up at a booth and immediately threw away. This is a big waste of money. If your literature just blows smoke, do not use it. The people who come to a show want very specific information about the products they see. They want very factual material, not advertising cliches. They want dimensional information, material specifications, product finishes, drawings, cross sections, and anything else that will help them better understand the product. This means, give out literature with solid information or do not give out any literature at all.

— Tactic # 234 —

Use Attention Gaining Show Stoppers

Everything that has been discussed so far relates to the practical, basic demonstration of products in your booth. That is the real nuts and bolts selling part of your show activity. Once you have all of that worked out, concentrate on what you can do to attract more people to your area. Studies show that the average visitor to a trade show passes by a booth in approximately ten seconds. In that period of time, you must be able to communicate with that visitor so that he, understands what you are showing and why it is important for him to stop to take a closer look. That information has to be given to him quickly so that he has a chance to mentally process it before he passes you by. There are many ways of attracting this kind of attention, and they have been used successfully at trade shows for years. You will want to select a method that best suits your company and the type of audience you want to attract. Here are a few:

1. Demonstrations are number one. We have already mentioned the impact of demonstrations. This is an absolute must. But not any old demonstration, performed any old way, will do. Your demonstration has to be done right to be effective.

First, you must locate the demonstration in your booth so that it is easily visible to anyone passing by. At the same time, it must be out of the aisle way and far enough into your booth so that you are not blocking traffic.

The demonstration, itself, will attract people. However, you want it to do more. Organize your demonstration so that it is an educational process as well as a selling process. Even go so far as to have a technician conduct the demonstration or give a talk about what is happening. You may even want to play the part of a technician during your time in the booth, combining your selling skills with your technical knowledge, to produce a series of mini training sessions. You would do this at regular intervals, using a sign to announce the time of your next presentation.

Give yourself every benefit possible when demonstrating. Use lots of small signs with short captions, mounted on cards, that are placed under products or areas of the equipment that you are demonstrating. This way, when you talk about a feature or a mechanical part, your visitor will be able to see as well as listen. You are employing two senses instead of one. If at the same time, he can touch, you employ three senses and make an even greater impact. You are actually using showmanship to enhance your sales message instead of competing with it. Whereas a flashy booth competes, your demonstrating salesmanship compliments your effort. For example, if you want to demonstrate that a sheet of acrylic is practically shatterproof, you can have your visitors hit it with a hammer or try to crack it by throwing baseballs. Instead of just saying something, **you are showing.**

Of course, you can use some very dramatic, specialized way to demonstrate your product by using magical illusions, such as a talking head, or one of the new talking robots. These methods are generally very expensive, however, and not something that you would employ in the usual trade show. Much depends upon the methods used by your competition. If a lot of specialized entertainment is being used, you may be forced to do the same.

Still, specialized techniques are not necessary when you are trying to isolate qualified prospects for a particular line of products. These people, who are seeking the merchandise you sell, will relate readily to a well structured booth with a good technical demonstration, followed by testimonial information and well constructed factual literature.

2. Magicians or celebrities — It is true that people of all ages are attracted by a magic show and by the appearance of a celebrity. Both techniques are used in larger trade shows all over the country. At a smaller show, in which you are likely to participate, a celebrity would be too expensive. A magician, however, would be available. There is a caution in using either of these methods, however. Although both methods attract people, neither of them provide a direct connection to what you are trying to sell. Of course, a good magician will try to work your key points into his presentation, but this generally is artificial and tedious, at best.

A well known personality has his own style or he would not be known. For this reason, it is difficult, if not impossible, to train him to present your product. Unless you have a special theme where a particular celebrity would promote a concept, you are better off not using this type of attention getter.

3. Girls! Girls! Girls! — Trade shows are usually attended by men. Girls are always used to attract these men to a booth. If properly done, a girl can be an asset. You know that a pretty girl can ask a visitor to step into a booth and get a positive response where as you, as a salesman, would not. Or, she can be used to have visitors sign-up for a raffle and to collect leads. Also, if you hire a local model for the duration of your show, she can perform many tasks in the booth that would need to be done and relieve you, as well as other salesmen, from activities that do not directly relate to selling. Sometimes, a model can give a product demonstration. This must be very carefully controlled, well scripted, and someone must be available at all times to answer questions from your visitors.

Be very cautious in the use of models at a trade show. It is in very poor taste to use a girl in a sexually provocative way. The only time a girl should be exhibited in skimpy costume is when you are trying to sell a skimpy costume. To use a model in this way is merely to draw attention to her and away from your products. It also makes many serious minded businessmen uncomfortable and they will tend to stay away from the booth, favoring your competitor who is likewise serious minded about the presentation of his products.

4. Give something away free — This is a very simplistic, but effective, method of attracting a lot of people to your booth. You can set up a soft drink bar or a shoe shine chair and have someone pass out a flyer advertising the free service at your booth.

One wholesaler used his booth as the message center for the entire floor. He simply put up a bulletin board where notes could be left and picked up and handed out a flyer announcing the message center.

5. Using audio visuals — Audio visuals can be effective most anywhere. However, it is becoming very difficult to produce the type of audio visual presentation that will bring people in from the aisles. Today, everybody is so oriented to "the tube" that an A/V presentation at a trade show has little or no impact. Your audio visual presentation should really be a part of your overall demonstration. It can be a very brief segment where a slide film would show some of the technical aspects of your product that could not otherwise be shown at the show.

Be very careful when projecting material onto a screen at a trade show. You will find that the ambient light tends to wash out even the best of A/V screens. Test this thoroughly before the opening of the show.

You can also use what is called random access equipment, such as video players in your booth. In this way, when a prospect wants to know more about a product, he merely pushes the button and listens to the story. Today is the day of home video tape. This equipment is easily obtained either through purchase or on a rental basis. You could bring this equipment into your booth and use it as an attention getter, where your visitors see themselves on television, and at the same time have several video tapes of various products that you might want to discuss.

6. Drawings and raffles — If you want to develop a mailing list and generate leads for after show follow-up, you will probably want to consider a raffle. This is simply a method where visitors are asked to fill in an entry blank or drop their business card in a box. The winners are picked at random and there is really no way to qualify prospects for the winning of a prize.

This method does not give you the opportunity to concentrate on the best prospects, but you can, after the show, separate the chaff from the wheat and call on those prospects who are the most likely potential buyers.

7. Playing games — Another way to create action in the booth, is to combine action with the giveaway of a prize and get maximum participation of visitors, by organizing some sort of game.

Here you will have to use your imagination to figure out some sort of a game that involves your product features or the sales points that you are trying to put across. You may want to pass out questionnaires at the beginning of the demonstration and tell your audience that at the end of the demonstration they are to be quizzed and whoever fills out the questionnaire 100 percent correctly will win a prize. Of course, you will be extremely lenient and you will help them fill in the answers as you go through your demonstration. This will hold the attention of your entire audience and they will learn.

Having a game just for the sake of a game, such as guessing the number of pennies in a mason jar is not at all effective. Be sure you tie your game playing to your product.

8. Interesting little tricks — There are literally hundreds of ways to get attention at a trade show. Along with everything else you are going to do, there are several little techniques that you can throw in to add extra punch.

- **Photography** — Prior to coming to the show, contact a photographic house that specializes in doing blowups. You can take pictures of special features of anything you want to talk about and have blowups hanging from the ceiling of your booth or actually form the walls of your booth. You will be able to get these blowups in black and white and have the photographer tint them to add attractive color.

- **Polaroid cameras and artists** — A local artist could paint a humorous backdrop to be used in producing photographs of your visitors. You could either cut out a portion where their head would appear or based on the scene, take pictures of them in front of the artwork. If an artist is good at doing character pictures, you can be assured of building a crowd. This is especially good at small shows where most of the audience knows one another. As soon as you get a half dozen of these character pictures out, virtually everyone will be coming to your booth to have it done.
- **Stage artwork** — For years, local playhouses have been using what is called scrim, which is a method of producing stage art by painting on black netting. You can produce very unusual, attractive effects by painting on the front surface and using the back surface to project various pictures. For example, you could have the picture of one of your products painted on the front surface, and then have the background change to show the product in various installations. This is particularly effective when you use a 35mm slide projector and take slides of your customer's installations.
- **Billboard art** — A local company who produces billboards can produce a huge sign for your show. It will generally cost you about $350, plus approximately $125 for the initial art work. This is a matter of having your board produced and taking it up above your booth or using it as a back wall. You will probably be the first to try this in your trade show, but once you have used it, several other people will adapt the technique. For that reason, plan carefully to make sure you get mileage out of the first introduction of this technique. A big bold message will attract people to your booth from all over the hall.
- **Two-way mirror and light effects** — You can use a two-way mirror to attract attention. You can easily construct what is called an infinity sequential lighting display by placing lights behind a two-way mirror, and further set an ordinary mirror behind the lights. Also, by proper lighting, you can have products appear in the mirror box as you demonstrate.

You are a salesman. Trade shows represent an unusual opportunity for you to use all of your selling skills. The next time your company participates in a trade show, take charge and show them how to sell more.

Selling Showmanship Can Make You a Super Salesperson

There's no doubt about the need for a selling edge when you're selling similar products, backed up with like services. The right selling edge will help you open new accounts and beat the competition with long-standing customers. The selling edge is **showmanship**!

There is an appealing and nearly magical quality in the use of showmanship that can help you sell much more throughout your wholesale selling career. Time that you spend developing this showmanship will be an investment which will give you immediate returns and will keep on earning for you, everyday you sell.

— Tactic # 235 —

Understand Selling Showmanship

Don't be confused. Showmanship is not some sort of trick or deceitful approach to your customers and prospects. Cheap tricks and gimmicks are rarely effective for the short term and **never** long-range.

Selling showmanship is an attractive method of communicating your sales message. It's a presentation that stands out—an approach that is so different from that of all the other salespeople in your territory that you alone are remembered. It's a bright, fresh way of communicating to your customers that makes it impossible to forget what you said and, further, makes it improbable that your customer will compare you to other salespeople that call on him.

— Tactic # 236 —

Investigate Many "Selling Showmanship" Techniques

Sometimes the showmanship part of selling is not a product demonstration. Often it is a part of you that is so different that it deserves to be highlighted on every call.

A salesman enjoyed being an amateur magician and had hundreds of "pocket magic" effects that he used when he called on his customers. Each time, it was something new. His customers were delighted to see him and rarely kept him waiting. Whenever possible, he worked his magical effects into his message.

When demonstrating the storage capability of a vanity cabinet, he painted a magical production box to look like a miniature of the product. He then, in typical magician's fashion, showed an empty cabinet and then began producing small items, such as a brochure on the product, a cutaway wood sample, hinge parts, door pulls, etc. **That's selling showmanship!**

Again, let's emphasize that selling showmanship is not trickery or deceit. Neither was our amateur magician/salesman's approach. Selling showmanship is a positive, interesting, and attractive way of getting your story across to your prospect.

— Tactic # 237 —

Use Ordinary Props to Inject Selling Showmanship

Here's another example: A salesman carried a hair dryer in his belt and called on customers with it in full view at the front of his trousers. Of course, it was the first thing that was noticed. After the usual joking about his carrying a hair dryer, he told them, "I've armed myself to show you how to make more money on gas furnace service calls." He then got permission to plug in the dryer and turn it on. From his briefcase, he produced a bi-metal operating vent damper and used the dryer to show his customer how the hot air caused the vents to open. He closed his selling message by showing his customer how to sell the homeowner on having these energy saving devices installed at the time of servicing.

Another salesman wanted to demonstrate the plus values of overhead radiant heating as opposed to forced hot air. He used a sun lamp purchased at a drug store, and demonstrated how objects and people were heated, not the air around. In this way, he convinced his prospects that they would have less heat loss through open doors in warehouses, in assembly line operations, and would be able to more efficiently heat large bay office areas. In most cases, he was given an opportunity to figure heating replacement jobs where he showed a fuel savings of up to 60 percent. He increased his sales by 300 percent!

— Tactic # 238 —

Develop an Identity

A salesman in the state of Maine is known as the "Peanut Man." Maybe this isn't glamourous, but it works for him. Whenever he makes a call, he leaves a package of peanuts with his customer or prospect. This became so popular, he recently had his name imprinted on the bags. He is welcome everywhere. Someday, he might consider putting his picture on the package and even use a direct mail campaign.

— Tactic # 239 —

Conduct Group Presentations

Another salesman is good at making group salesman presentations. Because of this ability, he conducts two "product training sessions" a month, inviting current customers and prospects. He is the leading new account in his company.

— Tactic # 240 —

Rotate Products as "Try Its"

Still another salesman has a system of rotating "try-it" tools that he lends to his customer for two weeks at a time. He uses five different tools and moves them from one customer to another as he makes his regular calls. His car is never full of these demonstrators because they are always out doing a self-selling job for him. Did his company provide him with the tools? Not at all. As a professional salesman, he made an investment in his selling aids. Is he successful? You bet! He's the top tool salesman in his company of 12 salesmen.

— Tactic # 241 —

Look at Yourself

You have unique talents that can be turned into selling showmanship. Look at your products—they present unlimited opportunities to use creative selling showmanship. Start now to build a brighter career and assure your increased earnings for your future. For more sales power—use selling showmanship!

Afterword

The tactics contained in this book have been used by thousands of successful sales people over the past 20 years. They have been modified to reflect the sophistication of the present day buyer and I am sure they will be even more effective when adjusted to your own style of presentation.

The importance of "personalization" is that you make a believable presentation designed to show your customer you have the best interests in mind. Take the TACTICS OF PERSUASION tools presented here and help your customer realize that what you have to offer will benefit him.

I welcome suggestions regarding this collection of tactics. If you feel changes should be made or if you desire to suggest additional tactics for subsequent printings they would be most appreciated. Write me at:

Dr. William H. Stiles
Bill Stiles Associates
202 E. Maitland Lane
New Castle, PA 16105

Other books by Dr. William H. Stiles:

How To Be A Champion Wholesale Salesman........$19.95 +$3.50 p&h
This book is written for the individual that wants to make a career in the field of industrial distribution. It is particularly focused on the building trades industry. Not just selling theory, it has many real situation examples that will give the reader a head start over his competition. Paperback, 203 pages.

Mind Power To Success..$19.95 +$3.50 p&h
How to use the power of your mind to achieve goals. This book gives the personal testimony of Dr. Stiles and others who have succeeded against odds and have accomplished in the face of many obstacles. It goes beyond positive mental attitude and gives a step by step surefire method of achieving your personal best. Easy to read, as is all of Dr. Stiles books, and taken from real life experiences. The "how to" portions make sense and can be applied immediately. According to Dr. Stiles, "A million dollars worth of information for a very small investment." Paperback, 163 pages.

How Hypnotherapy Can Help You.......................$19.95 +$3.50 p&h
Dr. Stiles has been a hypnotherapist and advocate of the "Tactics Of Persuasion" for over 28 years. This book is written for those individuals that want to use the full potential of their subconscious mind. Although it includes methods of internal motivation, it also addresses such subjects as Stop Smoking, Weight Control, Reducing Stress, Solving Sexual Problems, Curing Insomnia, Improving Your Golf Game, Improving Physical Skills, Slowing Down The Aging Process, and other situations where hypnosis will greatly aid the individual to achieving maximum potential. Paperback, 208 pages.

Hypno-Selling.............$19.95 +$2.50 p&h, available in November 1994
Hailed by many selling professionals as the one truly unique, modern and absolutely 100% effective way to get the client to appreciate your product and service benefits. This easy to understand book is a step by step method of getting your customer and prospect to become "fascinated" over your proposal. Dr. Stiles combines his knowledge of selling with his lifelong practice of Hypnosis and gives you the secrets that only the top salespeople in the world have known and used. Easy to read, but you must devote a lot of practice to the techniques. Once learned and used with skill you will be able to dramatically improve your closing rate. Paperback, 207 pages.

To order these books, write to Dr. Stiles at the address on the preceding page.